DAT

MARXISM AND RELIGION IN EASTERN EUROPE

SOVIETICA

PUBLICATIONS AND MONOGRAPHS

OF THE INSTITUTE OF EAST-EUROPEAN STUDIES AT THE

UNIVERSITY OF FRIBOURG/SWITZERLAND AND

THE CENTER FOR EAST EUROPE, RUSSIA AND ASIA

AT BOSTON COLLEGE AND THE SEMINAR

FOR POLITICAL THEORY AND PHILOSOPHY

AT THE UNIVERSITY OF MUNICH

Founded by J. M. BOCHEŃSKI (Fribourg)

Edited by T. J. BLAKELEY (Boston), GUIDO KÜNG (Fribourg)
and NIKOLAUS LOBKOWICZ (Munich)

Editorial Board

VOLUME 36

MARXISM AND RELIGION
IN EASTERN EUROPE

Papers Presented at the Banff International Slavic Conference,
September 4–7, 1974

Edited by

RICHARD T. DE GEORGE AND JAMES P. SCANLAN

D. REIDEL PUBLISHING COMPANY

DORDRECHT-HOLLAND / BOSTON-U.S.A.

Library of Congress Cataloging in Publication Data

International Slavic Conference, 1st, Banff, Alta., 1974.
    Marxism and religion in Eastern Europe.

    (Sovietica ; v. 36)
    Includes bibliographical references and index.
    1. Dialectical materialism—Congresses. 2. Philosophy—
History—Europe, Eastern—Congresses. 3. Religion and state—
Russia—Congresses. 4. Church and state in Poland—Congresses.
5. Catholics in Russia—Congresses. I. De George, Richard T.
II. Scanlan, James Patrick, 1927–   III. Title. IV. Series.
B809.8.I63 1974   146'.3   75-33051
ISBN 90–277–0636–0

Published by D. Reidel Publishing Company,
P.O. Box 17, Dordrecht, Holland

Sold and distributed in the U.S.A., Canada, and Mexico
by D. Reidel Publishing Company, Inc.
Lincoln Building, 160 Old Derby Street, Hingham,
Mass. 02043, U.S.A.

Printed in The Netherlands by D. Reidel, Dordrecht

TABLE OF CONTENTS

INTRODUCTION

Since the Bolshevik revolution of 1917, two of the most significant but at the same time least understood areas of that revolution's cultural impact have been philosophy and religion. The impact has of course been massive, not only in the Soviet Union but, after the second World War, in Soviet-dominated Eastern Europe as well. Yet the consequences of Communism for philosophy and religion throughout the Soviet orbit are far from having the simplicity suggested by the stereotypes of a single, monolithic 'Marxism' and a consistent, crushing assault on the Church and on religious faith.

Unquestionably Marxism is the ruling philosophy throughout Eastern Europe. In the Soviet Union, 'Marxism-Leninism' or 'dialectical materialism' is the official and the only tolerated philosophy, and most of the other countries of Eastern Europe follow the Soviet lead in philosophy as in other fields. But in the latter countries Marxism was imposed only after World War II, and its development has not always copied the Soviet model. Original thinkers in Yugoslavia, Czechoslovakia, Poland, and Hungary have thought their own way through the writings of Marx and his followers, and have arrived at Marxist positions which are considerably at variance with the Soviet interpretations – and often with each other. Moreover in recent years the Soviet philosophers themselves have been unable to ignore the theoretical questions raised by the other East European Marxists and by representatives of Marxism in the West. By taking positions on these issues within the family of Marxism, the Soviets have only underscored the modern transformation of 'monolithic' Marxism into a surprisingly capacious range of theoretical possibilities.

As for religion, the simple image of 'Godless Communism' may seem amply grounded in Marx's notorious view that religion is both false (a set of self-projective dreams) and socially and humanly damaging ('the opiate of the people') – a view that one might expect to require the literal extirpation of the Church in a Communist regime. And indeed religion, both ecclesiastical and non-ecclesiastical, has been the target of continual attack in Communist-dominated Eastern Europe. The fact that religion is still under attack, however, shows also that it still exists – that the Communist societies of Eastern Europe have not yet been rendered God-less. Examination of the causes and circumstances of the survival of re-ligion in different countries and regions presents a complex picture of the limitations to State power which can be posed by the inertial force of pre-Communist institutions, by the intricacies of European and world politics, and above all by the power of ethnic nationalism. In a multiplicity of forms, religion has endured in Eastern Europe as the only, however grudgingly, tolerated set of alternative institutions and ideas in a Marxist society.

If the stereotypes of Marxism-Leninism and irreligion in Communist Eastern Europe have always been misleading, they have never been more so than in the present day, when alternative forms of Marxist philosophy have become not only thoroughly recognized but in some countries po-litically active, and when the continuing vitality of religion has been dis-played dramatically in the Soviet Union in the form of a broad and vocal dissent movement. It was to illuminate and analyze some of the more significant features of this multifaceted cultural situation in Eastern Europe that the papers included in this volume were prepared for the International Slavic Conference held in Banff, Alberta, Canada on September 4–7, 1974.

The Conference, sponsored jointly by the American Association for the Advancement of Slavic Studies, the British National Association for Soviet and Eastern European Studies, the British Universities Association of Slavists, and the Canadian Association of Slavists, brought together scholars from many countries for a cooperative survey of current work in Slavic studies in all the major academic disciplines. The first four papers below were presented at a session entitled 'Contemporary Marxism', chaired by James P. Scanlan. The remaining five papers are drawn from the three sessions at the conference devoted to religion: 'Church-State Relations in Eastern Europe, 1918–1945', chaired by Vasyl Markus; 'The Catholic Communities of the Soviet Union', chaired by Bohdan R. Bo-ciurkiw; and 'Religious Dissent: Bridge to the Intellectuals?' chaired by William C. Fletcher. Together these nine papers are presented here not as exhausting or even as systematically surveying the present status of philosophy and religion in Eastern Europe, but as investigating in some depth a few symptomatic and informative aspects of the subject.

1. Marxism

The paper by Richard T. De George begins the volume with an overview of the contemporary status of Marxist theory concerning the nature of Communist society. De George finds three basic approaches among Marxist theorists, distinguishable geographically as well as philosophically. The first, which enjoys an ideological monopoly in the U.S.S.R., is that of the 'scientific' Marxist-Leninists who are concerned with discovering the social laws of the development of socialism into Communism, and who emphasize the necessity of building a suitable economic base for Communism. The second approach is that of the 'open' or creative Marxists of Eastern Europe outside the U.S.S.R., who are attempting to provide the theoretical basis for achieving a humanistic type of society, and who therefore reject the Soviet model. The third approach predominates not in Eastern Europe but in the West: it is that of the critical Marxists, including some members of the New Left and the Frankfurt School. Critical Marxism concentrates primarily on the critique of capitalism as it has developed in the West; it makes freedom the chief ingredient of the desired future society, which it does little to characterize further. Each of the three positions, De George argues, continues an aspect of Marx's work. But under the strain of practice what was unified in Marx's doctrine of Communism has been fragmented, and none of the three contemporary versions enjoys the apparent coherence and synoptic attractiveness of the original.

Z. A. Jordan's paper focuses on two widely debated controversies about Marx which have played major roles in the contemporary development of Marxism and particularly in the disputes between Soviet and East European Marxists. One concerns the relation of 'dialectical materialism, to Marxian philosophy – more specifically, to the views of Marx himself as opposed to those of his friend and collaborator, Friedrich Engels. The second controversy, which Jordan selects for detailed analysis, has to do with the continuity or discontinuity of Marx's thought from the early to the mature stages of his career. A key factor in the revitalization of Marxist theory in recent years, and a significant impetus to deviation from Soviet orthodoxy, has been the discovery of Marx's humanistic philosophy of alienation as expressed in early unpublished writings such as the *Economic-Philosophic Manuscripts of 1844* and seemingly echoed in certain later writings as well, such as the recently translated *Grundrisse der Kritik der Politischen Ökonomie* of 1857–58. Jordan argues, against such recent interpreters as Robert C. Tucker and David McLellan, that Marx in his later work abandoned his early philosophy of alienation, though not the moral concern which underlies it and which today is often confused with it.

Ivan Sviták, himself a prominent Czech philosopher and a participant in the events he describes, presents the story of the origin and political failure of attempts to democratize post-war Czechoslovakia on the basis of an 'open' or non-Stalinist Marxism. His paper traces and analyzes the career of Stalinist Marxism in Czechoslovakia in three stages from 1945 to the present. The first stage, which lasted until 1948, was marked by the parallel development of Communist and social democratic variants of Marxist theory. After 1948 the latter version was suppressed and the ensuing twenty years saw the increasingly dogmatic development of Soviet-inspired, Stalinist Marxism and its successive conflicts with the domestic Marxist tradition, with various forms of 'revisionism', and finally with the reformist campaign for 'socialism with a human face'. The debacle of 1968 and the Soviet occupation which ushered in the third phase, though in one sense a disaster, in another gave promise for the future. For Sviták argues that 'open Marxism' was an 'illusion of the epoch', unrealistic because it failed to take account of existing power relationships and institutional realities in the U.S.S.R. and Eastern Europe. And if the Soviet tanks destroyed that illusion they also forever discredited Stalinist Marxism, so that the whole episode has produced a 'reform of consciousness' in Czechoslovakia which is prerequisite to any future political success.

A seemingly more fruitful experiment in humanistic Marxism in a different national setting is described in the paper by Mihailo Marković, a prominent member of the group of Yugoslav philosophers who established the widely read journal of liberal Marxist opinion, *Praxis*. Marković traces the formation and development of the *Praxis* group after World War II, explaining how and why the group turned from 'Marxism-Leninism' to the writings of Marx himself in a search for answers to specific problems facing Yugoslavia, and analyzing the social and political conditions that allowed the group to survive and to become until very recently the dominant force in Yugoslav philosophy despite increasing pressure from the government. Special attention is given to the group's apparently successful emergence in 1974 from a particularly virulent campaign against it conducted by hard-line Marxist-Leninist elements in Serbia. The tragic irony is that in the few short months since Marković's paper was written, the tide has turned dramatically and perhaps irreversibly against the *Praxis* group. Marković and seven of his colleagues were dismissed from the Philosophy Faculty of the University of Belgrade in January, 1975, and at this writing similar purges appear to be under way at the Universities of Ljubljana and Zagreb. The journal *Praxis* has lost its government subsidy and has ceased publication. Actually Marković's paper develops hypothetically some of the implications of such events for the future of Marxism in Eastern Europe. "If the *Praxis* group perishes," he writes, "that would mean simply that the intrinsic conflicts between revolutionary Marxism and the ruling bureaucracy is so deep and antagonistic that a peaceful resolution is not possible, even under the most favorable conditions." In any event, the humanistic Marxist theories outlined in the last section of Marković's paper may soon be without vocal support in Yugoslavia – and hence without significant open support anywhere in Eastern Europe.

2. Religion

Unlike philosophy, religion as a cultural phenomenon in pre-Communist Eastern Europe was supported by a vast institutional structure – the Church – which enlisted mass loyalties and consequently has weighed heavily on subsequent developments. Edward D. Wynot, Jr., shows the bearing of such historical considerations on understanding Church-state relations in Poland after the establishment of Communist rule at the end of the second World War. In the period between the two wars, Wynot argues, the relations of the Catholic Church and the Polish state under Pilsudski and others were never precisely determined. The result was that the government could redefine the situation to fit the needs of the moment; but at the same time the Church was left free from any binding commitments and instead stressed an uneasy but mutually beneficial co-existence with the regime. Wynot sees the attitudes and practices developed in the interwar years as exerting a major influence on Church-state relations in Poland after 1945. Instead of fighting a regime which stood for many things to which it was fundamentally hostile, for pragmatic reasons the Church supported the Polish Communists – who could, after all, provide the country with a Polish state and prevent its absorption into the U.S.S.R. As a popular and pervasive institution, moreover, the Catholic Church could render itself indispensable to the Communist state and perhaps exert a benign influence on the latter, as it had on its predecessor. The postwar *modus vivendi* of Catholicism and Communism in Poland, Wynot argues, should come as no surprise to anyone familiar with the pre-war developments.

The extent to which Soviet Russian anti-religious policy is also capable of forbearance when confronted with unfavorable historical and political realities is shown in Dennis J. Dunn's examination of Soviet treatment of the Catholic Church in occupied Eastern Europe during the war years. Drawing on both Vatican and Soviet sources, Dunn shows that the Soviets were far more lenient and restrained in their dealings with the Catholics, both Latin and Uniate, in the occupied areas of Poland than with the same groups in the U.S.S.R. itself. In seeking to explain this relative tolerance, Dunn cites four considerations which, with appropriate changes, might also be found relevant in understanding Soviet policy today: (1) the higher priority of other, chiefly political, matters of concern to the Soviet authorities; (2) the reluctance further to arouse a Western public opinion sympathetic to Catholicism; (3) the growing recognition by the Soviet government of the utility of organized religion as an arm of state policy; and (4) fear of Nazi Germany, which shared occupied Poland with the Soviets and maintained diplomatic relations with the Vatican.

With the paper by Vasyl Markus we move to an examination of religion inside the U.S.S.R. itself, and specifically to the first of three timely reports on Soviet religious groups that are frequently neglected: the Ukrainian Uniate Catholics, the Moslems, and the Roman Catholics of Lithuania. The Uniates are unique among the three groups in having been officially prohibited from practicing their religion: the Uniate Catholic Church was legally absorbed by the Russian Orthodox Church, at the order of the Soviet government, after World War II. Markus analyzes the various responses of Uniates to their imposed conversion, ranging from outward acquiescence and a *pro forma* acceptance of Orthodoxy to the active resistance mounted by a radical underground movement in the Western Ukraine. He concludes that Catholicism in the Ukraine, though without any legal existence, continues in many guises to enlist the sympathies of a large part of the population.

In considering Soviet Islam – a religion with accepted legal status – Alexandre A. Bennigsen and S. Enders Wimbush find an apparent anomaly. The official Moslem church is quiescent and is loyal to the Soviet regime. Yet Soviet authorities continue and even intensify the large-scale – albeit cumbersome and ineffectual – anti-Islamic campaign which they have been waging for half a century. The explanation of this paradoxical situation, the authors believe, lies in the existence of an unofficial, semi-clandestine Islam, which draws heavily on nationalistic customs and sentiments. This informal Islam requires no places of worship or clergymen (though it co-exists peacefully with the established Moslem Church) and for that reason is difficult to combat. Its reality and influence are indicative of the difficulties for Soviet policy which are created by the concurrence of non-Marxist religious traditions with non-Russian nationalism in the Soviet Union.

The current intensity of such difficulties is portrayed graphically in the final paper by Bohdan R. Bociurkiw. The latest and most powerful surge of religious dissent in the U.S.S.R. has come from the Roman Catholics of Lithuania, who after years of relatively silent endurance have become increasingly vocal in expressing their opposition to Soviet persecution. Bociurkiw reports on and analyzes both the open protests of religious and lay leaders of the Lithuanian Catholic Church and the corresponding underground movement as represented chiefly by a new *samizdat* ('self-published') newspaper, *Chronicle of the Catholic Church in Lithuania.* Though the nationalistic element is very evident in Lithuanian Catholic dissent, Bociurkiw also points out that in this case religious dissent has been instrumental in bridging the gap between religion and the intellectuals. He suggests that it may thus serve as an ideological and organizational framework for the articulation of non-religious dissent as well.

Hence in Lithuania as elsewhere in Eastern Europe, philosophy and religion remain sensitive and unsettled areas. Not only the cultural but the political future of each country is closely bound up with the complex interplay of orthodoxy and dissent in its philosophical and religious life, and for that reason philosophy and religion continue to demand the serious attention of students of Eastern Europe.

RICHARD T. DE GEORGE
JAMES P. SCANLAN

LIST OF CONTRIBUTORS

Richard T. De George, University Professor of Philosophy at the University of Kansas, is the author of *Patterns of Soviet Thought* (1966), *The New Marxism* (1968), and *Soviet Ethics and Morality* (1969).

James P. Scanlan, Professor of Philosophy at the Ohio State University, is co-editor of *Russian Philosophy* (1965) and editor of *The American Bibliography of Slavic and East European Studies for 1970, 1971, and 1972* (1974).

Z. A. Jordan, Professor of Sociology at Carleton University, is the author of *Philosophy and Ideology* (1963), *The Evolution of Dialectical Materialism* (1967), and *Karl Marx: Economy, Class, and Social Revolution* (1971).

Ivan Sviták, formerly associated with Charles University and with the Philosophical Institute of the Czechoslovak Academy of Sciences, is now Professor of Philosophy at California State University (Chico). His works in English include *Man and His World* (1970) and *The Czechoslovak Experiment* (1971).

Mihailo Marković, formerly Professor of Philosophy at the University of Belgrade, was dismissed from his professorship along with seven of his liberal Marxist colleagues in January, 1975. His most recent works to appear in English are *From Affluence to Praxis* (1974) and *The Contemporary Marx* (1975).

Edward D. Wynot, Jr., is Associate Professor of History at the Florida State University. He is the author of *Polish Politics in Transition* (1974) and of two forthcoming works: *The Fall of Poland* and *The Anatomy of History*.

Dennis J. Dunn is Assistant Professor of History and Director of the Institute for the Study of Religion and Communism at Southwest Texas State University. His works include a forthcoming monograph, *The Catholic Church and the Soviet Government, 1939–1949*.

Vasyl Markus, Professor of Political Science at Loyola University of Chicago, is the author of *L'Ukraine Soviétique dans les Relations Inter-*

nationales (1959) and other works on national and religious minorities in Eastern Europe.

Alexandre A. Bennigsen is Directeur d'Études of the École des Hautes Études, Paris, and Visiting Professor of History at the University of Chicago. He has authored or co-authored a number of works on Moslems in the U.S.S.R., including (with Chantal Lemercier-Quelquejay) *Islam in the Soviet Union* (1967).

S. Enders Wimbush is a doctoral candidate in Political Science at the University of Chicago. He is co-author (with Alexandre A. Bennigsen and others) of a forthcoming book, *Great Russian Nationalism.*

Bohdan R. Bociurkiw, Professor of Political Science and former Director of the Institute of Soviet and East European Studies at Carleton University, is co-editor of *Ukraine: A Concise Encyclopedia,* Vol. II (1971) and of *Religion and Atheism in the U.S.S.R. and Eastern Europe* (1974).

PART I

MARXISM

RICHARD T. DE GEORGE

COMMUNISM AND THE NEW MARXISTS

Marx's views on the nature of Communist society and on the means of achieving it form an important part of Marxist theory. An examination of the status of these views in various versions of contemporary Marxism can therefore serve both as a means of evaluating the original doctrine and of comparing divergent contemporary positions. It is the aim of this paper, by means of such an examination, to provide an overview of contemporary Marxist theory.

For Marx, 'Communism' was the name (1) of a certain form of social organization, (2) of a movement which would bring about a society so organized, and (3) of a theory which both described the nature of the society to be achieved and the means of attaining it. Marx considered Communism to be the next stage of social development after capitalism. Negatively he characterized it as lacking such evils of capitalist society as alienation, exploitation, private property, division of labor, and classes. He described it positively as a society in which each would give according to his ability and receive according to his needs, in which each person would have the opportunity for his full all-round development, and in which men would live throughout the world in cooperative harmony with other men, enjoying the relative abundance made possible through the development of productive forces. He saw the movement which would bring about this state of affairs as international in character, carried on by the workers of the world, and resulting from the contradictions inherent in capitalism and from the conditions existing in capitalist societies.

All aspects of the theory formed a single piece for Marx. He consequently never considered, for example, whether the development of the economic base should take precedence over the elimination of alienation or over self-management by workers if the movement towards establishing Communism were first successful not in the advanced industrial nations but in less industrially developed or predominantly agricultural countries. The criticism of Marxism by non-Marxists based on the events of history are well enough known to need no recounting here. The fact that

De George and Scanlan (eds.), Marxism and Religion in Eastern Europe, 3–12. All Rights Reserved.
Copyright © 1976 by D. Reidel Publishing Company, Dordrecht-Holland.

such criticism has not dampened the enthusiasm of Marxists for Marx's
doctrine is also well known. What then are the present positions and what
is their relation to original Marxism?

To an outside observer it sometimes appears as if there are as many
different Marxist positions as there are Marxists. This is especially true
of France, where each Marxist – such as Louis Althusser, Jean-Paul
Sartre, and Roger Garaudy – is an individualist. Althusser places heavy
emphasis on Marxism as a science, though he does not follow the Soviet
line; Sartre's philosophical position has become a unique type of exis-
tentialistic Marxism, though in politics he is often associated with the
New Left; Garaudy is a Marxist-Leninist turned humanist, who has become known for promoting a Marxist-Christian dialogue. The position of
all three on Communism is not clear. Yet without denying differences
among individual Marxists, I shall distinguish and discuss the positions
on Communism of what I consider three major groups of contemporary
Marxists.

Each of the three groups can be distinguished not only by its ideas but
also to some extent by its geographical location, and so by its relation to
the type of society in which it flourishes. Each group is therefore obviously influenced in its interpretation of Marxism by the social conditions in which it finds itself, and by the problems which theoreticians in
those conditions must face, though we cannot simply on this basis assess
the reasons why it accepts certain aspects of Marxism while rejecting
others.

I do not claim that all Marxists can be fitted into my three groups,
though I think a large number of them can. I also readily acknowledge
that my characterizations of the three groups is more suggestive than def-
initive, and that the characterizing epithets are distinguishing traits only
in the sense that they indicate degrees of emphasis. The three groups are
composed of scientific dogmatists, critical humanists, and negative critics.
I shall call them respectively the 'scientific' Marxists, the 'humanistic'
Marxists, and the 'critical 'Marxists.[1] I shall look in turn at the views on
Communism of each of the three groups.

(1) By the term "scientific' Marxists" I shall refer to those Marxist-
Leninists who follow the Engels-Lenin interpretation of Marx's doctrine.
The group consists primarily of the Marxist-Leninists in the Soviet Union
and those who follow their lead. They insist on the scientific aspect of

Marx's work, place more emphasis on his later economic writings than on his earlier works, and they follow the development of dialectical materialism as formulated by Engels and Lenin.

In accordance with their 'scientific' approach, the 'scientific' Marxists emphasize the need for developing the economic base of society in the assurance that the social superstructure will follow necessarily. There is consequently more emphasis on the development of the scientific-technical aspects of the base than on all-round development of the individual or on human rights or on freedom of expression or on social self-management.

The fact that the October Revolution took place in a primarily agricultural country without igniting a revolution in the industrially advanced countries, the fact that the Party leads the people, and the fact that the Party, not the proletariat, led the Revolution have all been given their rationale in the Marxist-Leninist framework long ago. The 'scientific' Marxists claim that the stage of social development following capitalism has been achieved, that socialism or the first stage of Communism is a reality, and that the second stage is in the process of development. They hold this despite the fact that they enjoy socialism in one country (or at best in a few countries), and that the Soviet Union is still a long way from the humane goals of Communism.

As a whole this is the most ideological of the three groups of Marxists. Marxism-Leninism is considered the justifying theory of governmental and party rule, a guide to action, and a doctrine to be taught to and believed by all members of the society. In accordance with the Leninist doctrine of *partijnost'*, the Party considers itself the guardian and promulgator of the truth of Marxism, and as such attempts to direct the development of Marxist-Leninist theory. How has it fared?

In Soviet hands, Engels' scientific socialism has been extended into scientific Communism. In a country in which the Marxist laws of the development of capitalism never operated, it is the task of those concerned with 'scientific' Communism to uncover the laws of the development of society from socialism to Communism. But, thus far it is a theory in search of its formulation. For the laws which have been uncovered and described thus far are not laws of development in any recognizable sense; rather they are statements of goals or aims to be achieved – such as the law of the absence of antagonistic classes, the law of the relation of collaboration and mutual help among men, or the law of the planned and proportional character of economic development.[2]

The scientifically sorry state of 'scientific' Communism is recognized by the leaders of the CPSU, as is evident from the directives they issue of tasks to be completed by Marxist-Leninist theoreticians. These are dutifully repeated in *Voprosy filosofii* and then later by those Marxist-Leninists in other countries who follow their line. The directives we find, for instance, in *Voprosy filosofii* of October 1972 and March 1973 underlined the need to develop an adequate account of the laws of the scientific-technological aspects of the social base, the need to explain the dialectical interaction between these and the superstructural aspects of society, and the need to justify the active role of the superstructure, especially of the Party, in influencing the objective dialectic working itself out in the base.[3]

Such directives are not new, nor are the tasks mentioned. The repetition from Party Congress to Party Congress of the need to satisfy the same theoretical issues is a clear admission of the Marxist-Leninist failure in this area.

Nonetheless, what may be new is a seemingly greater willingness on the part of some Marxist-Leninists to admit the shortcomings of their theory of Communism. This can be seen, for instance, in the somewhat new *emphasis* in discussions of the time-scale needed for the development of Communism. Marx never gave a time-scale; and though he may have thought that the realization of Communism was closer at hand than it was, this is really beside the point. For, this interpretation goes, Marx uncovered the contradictions in capitalism and so saw the *logical* development, not the *historical* development, of the forces inherent in capitalism. That their working out takes a hundred or two hundred years or longer is no argument against the logical relations which he uncovered. This emphasis on the logical aspects of the concepts and categories which form the Marxist conceptual scheme is being emphasized by P. I. Kosolapov and others[4] more frequently within the last two or so years than before, evidently with two purposes. The first is to raise the analyses of the historical materialists to a higher level by encouraging them to distinguish between the logical analysis of the theory and its concrete application to historical events. The temptation, too frequently succumbed to by lazy Marxist-Leninists, has been simply to apply the formulae of base-superstructure and similar pairs to every situation in a quasi-automatic and *a priori* way. What has been lacking is the concrete search in empirical data for the specific links between reality and theory. The need for the intelligent application of Marxist theory and the development of a Marxist dialectical method which can be fruitfully used has been spoken of numerous times in the past, but remains as critical a need as ever. The second reason for the new emphasis may well be to free empirical research in the social sciences at least somewhat from their domination by the lazy application of historical materialist dogma, just as in the not too distant past physical science was freed from its dialectical materialist fetters, much to its advantage.

The 'scientific' Marxists are still dogmatic, prosaic, and dull. They are more ideological than philosophical, and are not taken as a serious model by many Marxists outside their fold because their theory does not satisfy the criteria of science. Much of it is *ad hoc*, and its internationalist, worker-oriented, and humanistic concerns are clearly seen to be related only to a society in some far distant future, having little to do with the actual state of affairs within the Soviet Union. The Soviet Union's nationalist concerns and Party domination of a bureaucratic statist system are evident. The Soviet-led Communist movement, to the extent that it exists, is not a workers' movement, and it is not humanistic; it is Party directed, conservative, and oriented toward the good of the Soviet Union.

(2) The 'humanistic' Marxists are found primarily in non-Soviet Eastern European countries, such as Poland, Yugoslavia, Czechoslovakia, and Hungary, where they often share the philosophic scene with 'scientific' Marxists. The 'humanistic' Marxists are characterized by their concern for the development of a humanistic type of socialism or Communism. They are openly critical of such defects as alienation, bureaucracy, and lack of freedom in socialist countries – both the Soviet Union and their own. Their number includes Leszek Kołakowski, Ivan Sviták, such Yugoslav creative Marxists as Mihailo Marković, Svetozar Stojanović, and Gajo Petrović, the followers of Georg Lukács in Hungary, and others such as Karel Kosík in Czechoslovakia. They repudiate the pseudoscientific aspects of Marxism which they associate with Stalinism,[5] though some would nonetheless claim that Marxism is scientific in the broad sense of being true knowledge. They are critical in their approach; but their criticism is primarily of the socialism they find in their own countries in comparison to what they believe is achievable. They generally feel that

capitalism has been adequately criticized and they leave the further criticism of capitalism to others. Their countries are in the process of building socialism and their efforts are creative and constructive in the attempt to improve their societies and to help achieve a truly humanistic socialism.

The 'humanistic' Marxists go to the early Marx as well as to the later Marx; but they interpret the later Marx more as a humanist than as a scientist. Given the choice between the need for developing the economic base of society on the one hand and on the other the need to create humane conditions of labor, eliminate or alleviate alienation, and increase the involvement of the people at all stages of life, production and government, they emphasize the latter over the former. A developed material base is of course necessary. But the humanistic aspects of society will not come automatically after it is achieved. As Kołakowski in *Toward a Marxist Humanism* and Stojanović in *Between Ideals and Reality* so eloquently affirm, these aspects must be developed simultaneously or they will not be achieved at all.[6] They have the example of the Soviet Union to prove their case.

The 'humanistic' Marxists in Yugoslavia hence promote self-management at all levels both in the economic sphere and in the sphere of government. They feel that the Party is not synonymous with the workers, that the workers must take things into their own hands, and that the Party's proper role is not to govern but to criticize and to serve as the conscience of society as it develops. Though their concern is primarily with the development of a humanistic socialism in their own countries, they see this as a possible model for societies beyond their own borders. This is clear, for instance, in Marković's *From Affluence to Praxis* with its general discussions of technology, politics, and the organization of the new human society.

The 'humanistic' Marxists are without doubt the most creative interpreters of Marxism. They have broken the bonds of dogma, they criticize the classics when they are wrong, and they are innovatively and constructively developing their theories in the light of present conditions. But their freedom and their creativity may be short lived; for the societies in which they criticize and in which they have tried to foster humanism have tended little by little to stifle them in one way or another. Kołakowski was forced to leave Poland; Sviták has left Czechoslovakia; Kosík has remained but has been silenced. In Yugoslavia the *Praxis* group has been under official attack for a number of years, and their continued freedom is problematical.[7] The union of theory and practice, of Communist theory and a Communist movement, here too, therefore, is at best tenuous.

(3) The group I call the 'critical' Marxists includes Herbert Marcuse, such members of the Frankfurt School as Horkheimer and Habermas, and those members of the New Left who go to Marxism for their vocabulary, theory, or inspiration. They are Marxists in Western Europe or the United States, intent primarily on carrying on and updating Marx's critique of capitalism and bourgeois society. Their main thrust is negative (e.g., Marcuse's book *Negations*) and their critique is radical. They attack 'the system' and all that it is said to stand for: bureaucracy, war, racism, the military-industrial complex, alienation, and exploitation. They are radical in the sense that they have as their stated goal the destruction or toppling of the system – completely and irrevocably.

But their Marxism is a Marxism without Communism. For they do not describe the good society or attempt to delineate its structure. Their primary good is freedom, and in the name of freedom they are loathe to impose the future on those who will inherit it. For some, the stage following the present will be one of anarchy, despite the fact that Marx rejected this alternative. But in general their views are summed up nicely by Horkheimer's statement: "One cannot determine what a free society will do or permit.... If society in the future really functions through free agreement rather than through direct or indirect force, the result of such an agreement cannot be theoretically anticipated."[8]

In holding a Marxism without Communism, the critical Marxists have given up both a positive vision of the future society and the belief in the possibility of developing an effective Communist movement. For they realize that the overthrow of the capitalism they so virulently castigate will not take place in the foreseeable future. Moreover, to the extent that they appeal to any group to effect an eventual overthrow it is not to Marx's workers, whom they see as allied to the status quo, and incapable, as Lenin pointed out, of rising above a trade-union mentality. They appeal to students, perhaps to intellectuals, to Blacks and Chicanos, to a lesser extent to some of the *Lumpenproletariat*; in all events they appeal primarily to those outside of the basic economically productive groups in society.

The 'critical' Marxists have the freest reign of expression, being limited by neither government nor Party. But with good reason they are taken the least seriously. For the chances of their making any serious impact on the economics or politics of the Western countries in which they reside seem small indeed. The 'humanist' Marxists are capable of exerting the largest influence in their lands, and hence are seen as the most dangerous by their governments. The 'scientific' Marxists are handmaidens of the Party, and subservient to it; they might be helpful in fulfilling the Party's work, but their lack of imagination and their failure to produce a meaningful development of scientific Communism render them ineffective.

The three groups reflect three different social conditions. All go to Marx and can correctly be said to be applying at least some of what he said to their own conditions. But the unity present in the original doctrine of the nature of Communism, of a world-wide workers' movement, and of the process by which the new society would be achieved has clearly given way to multiple interpretations and a division of theory from practice.

The fragmentation of Marxism into groups concerned primarily with what they consider the realities of their position – the claimed hegemony of the Soviet Union, the concern with forming a humanistic socialism in Eastern Europe, the dream of ending the oppressive system some Marxists see in the West – all these are partial views of mankind's development and of the production of a good world-wide society. They all fall short of the scope and unity of Marx's original vision. But without the scope and vision of the whole they all become simply competing theories, too closely tied to particular parts of the globe, and reflecting the fragmentation of the present state of the world. Despite the noble goals of the 'humanistic' Marxists and the empty rhetoric of the 'scientific' Marxists, the Marxist theory of Communism has fallen on bad times; if the *theory* of a Communist *movement* has not actually been abandoned, in none of its forms does it have the vigor, comprehensiveness, or electricity of the original; and in none of its forms is it united with a vigorous movement which gives any real promise of achieving a Communist society.

The 'scientific', 'humanistic' and 'critical' Marxists have shown that the three strands of Marx's doctrine of Communism – a desirable end, a workers' movement, and a law-laden theory of revolution – though related in his view are and always were separable. Their actual separation serves as a critique of the original doctrine. For the varying interpretations are not simply revisions of or deviations from the original doctrine. Rather they were required by the historical realities of the contemporary world. The choices between eliminating alienation and developing the economic base, between fostering humanism and allowing economic laws to work themselves out with iron necessity, between peaceful coexistence and continuous revolution, between primitive Communism and a non-Communistic though relatively rich democratic society – all of these are choices which Marx never foresaw and never faced. History forced his successors to face them. Moreover, the abundance of goods and culture, which Marx envisaged that Communism as a world-wide phenomenon would enjoy, no longer seems within man's grasp. The evils of pollution and the other noxious by-products of industrialization, the development of nuclear power, the breakneck advancement of technology and its con-comitant problems, the actual or threatened chronic world-wide shortage of food and energy, and the relentless rise of the worlds' population all call for new interpretations of the good society and of the means to attain it. They are circumstances which could not have been foreseen by Marx; and contemporary Marxist theoreticians have only begun to face up to them.

In the weaker, fragmented versions of contemporary Marxism, Com-munism is clearly value-laden, no longer inevitable, and still in need of further critical analysis. There is still much that is worthwhile in Marx's theory of Communism – the values it espouses, the evils it condemns, the contradictions it uncovers, the new directions it points to. For these rea-sons Marxism is still attractive. But its possession of a coherent doctrine of Communism as a world-wide society of justice and plenty, or as a dynamic and necessarily successful movement toward that end, is no longer one of Marxism's attractions or strong points. Most of the new Marxists have realistically settled for less.

REFERENCES

[1] The terms 'scientific', 'humanistic' and 'critical' are used in widely differing ways in Marxist literature. I use them here to describe the position of three groups with respect to their theories of Communism, and not necessarily to other aspects of their views, e.g., to their theories of knowledge. An obvious fourth group would be the Chinese Maoist Marxists, whom I would tend to dub the 'primitive' Communists. But I do not treat them in this paper due to my lack of a sufficient number of recent sources, as opposed simply to the works of Mao and to second hand reports.

2 *Filosofskaja enciklopedija*, Moskva: Gosudarstvennoe naučnoe izdatel'stvo 'Sovetskaja enciklopedija', 1962, vol. II, p. 358. For a fuller discussion see Richard T. De George. 'Philosophy', in *Science and Ideology in Soviet Society* (ed. by George Fischer), New York: Atherton Press, 1967, pp. 67–72.

3 See 'Istoričeskij materializm segodnja: problemy i zadači', *Voprosy filosofii* (1972), no. 10, pp. 4–9; I. T. Frolov, 'Sovremmenaja nauka i gumanizm', *Voprosy filosofii* (1973), no. 3, pp. 5–6; and V. Ž. Kelle, 'KPSS-partija social'nogo tvorčestva', *Voprosy filosofii* (1973), no. 8, p. 47. As an indication of how the Soviet line is followed by other Marxist-Leninists, see the article by the East German philosopher Kurt Hager, 'Politika partii i zadači Marksistsko-leninskoj filosofii', *Voprosy filosofii* (1974), no. 3, pp. 5-14.

4 P. I. Kosolapov, 'Socializm v teorii i na praktike', *Voprosy filosofii* (1972), no. 5, pp. 20–21; 'Istoričeskij materializm segodnja', *op. cit.*, p. 7. For the East German version, see Erich Hahn, 'O xaraktere zakonomernostej duxovnoi žizni obščestva', *Voprosy filosofii* (1974), no. 3, pp. 23–31.

5 See, for example, Mihailo Marković, 'Humanism and Dialectic', in *Socialist Humanism* (ed. by Erich Fromm), London: Allen Lane, 1967, p. 83; and his *From Affluence to Praxis*, Ann Arbor: The University of Michigan Press, 1974, p. 59. For other Marxist critiques of the scientific claims of Marxist-Leninists, see Herbert Marcuse, *Soviet Marxism: A Critical Analysis*, New York: Columbia University Press, 1958, and Jean-Paul Sartre, 'Materialism and Revolution', in *Literary and Philosophical Essays*, New York: Criterion Books, Inc., 1955, pp. 191–208.

6 Leszek Kołakowski, *Toward a Marxist Humanism*, New York: Grove Press, 1968, pp. 140–41; Svetozar Stojanović, *Between Ideals and Reality*, New York: Oxford University Press, 1973, pp. 156–200.

7 See the Introduction above for further indications of the *Praxis* group's status.

8 Max Horkheimer, 'The Authoritarian State', *Telos*, 1973, no. 15, pp. 12 and 17.

Z. A. JORDAN

CONTEMPORARY PROBLEMS OF DIALECTICAL MATERIALISM

As we use the term today, 'dialectical materialism' refers to a comprehensive system of beliefs which can be divided into a metaphysical doctrine, a theory of knowledge, and an evolutionary philosophy of science. As a metaphysical doctrine, dialectical materialism is concerned with the question, 'What is the ultimate substance of the world?'; as a theory of knowledge, it tries to resolve the issue, 'How do we come to know the world?'; and as an evolutionary philosophy of science, it investigates the problem, 'What are the laws of change which explain how more and more complex phenomena have evolved from simple ones and how the world has come to be what it is?'. Since 'philosophy of science', in the present day terminology, means the inquiry into the logical structure of scientific knowledge, dialectical materialism may be better characterized as a speculative cosmology in the sense in which A. N. Whitehead used the term, giving to his *Process and Reality* the subtitle *An Essay in Cosmology*. Speculative cosmology attempts to construct a categorial framework in which every element of our experience can be described as part of an orderly and lawful universe. Dialectical materialism emphasizes that this categorial framework is "formed in the process of historical development of science on the basis of social practice" and reflects the pervasive interconnection and interdependence of all phenomena.[1]

The roots of materialistic monism stretch as far back as the Ionian school of ancient Greek philosophers. But dialectical materialism – the philosophical basis of the world outlook and program of the Communist Parties – has a much more recent origin. Its beginnings should be traced back to the publication of Friedrich Engels' *Anti-Dühring* in 1878, the most important source of dialectical materialism as we know it today. Engels claimed his dialectical materialism was a philosophy grounded in the sciences; it combined a materialistic monism with a cosmology formulated in terms of dialectics, viz., "the science of the most general laws of all motion", in nature, history and thought.[2]

While Engels' *Anti-Dühring* and, later, his *Dialectics of Nature* provided

De George and Scanlan (eds.), Marxism and Religion in Eastern Europe, 13–43. All Rights Reserved.
Copyright © 1976 by D. Reidel Publishing Company, Dordrecht-Holland.

the foundations of dialectical materialism, other philosophers, writers and political leaders contributed to its elaboration and constant transformation. The history of dialectical materialism since Engels' death is relatively well known and it is not my intention to deal with its recent modifications in the Soviet Union and elsewhere. The modifications may be politically and ideologically significant but philosophically their interest is negligible.

The most important contemporary problems of dialectical materialism do not spring from the content of its codified systematization but from the question of whether the codified systematization itself is historically and logically justifiable. This question has been prompted by two widely-debated controversies about Marx. One concerns the relation of dialectical materialism to the Marxian philosophy, and the other has originated in the diverse interpretations of the development, continuity and consistency of Marx's thought at the early and mature stages of his life, to which the publication of some manuscripts of Marx has given rise. These works, *Economic and Philosophic Manuscripts of 1844*[3] and the *Foundations of the Critique of Political Economy (Rough Draft)*,[4] were not extensively discussed until the 1960's, and their impact continues to be felt.

I

Dialectical materialism is considered to be the common property of Marx and Engels but can be, and is, presented with hardly any reference to Marx. Its present-day version is the work of Engels, Plekhanov, Lenin and Stalin, and its elaborate codification is the achievement of Soviet philosophers. Hence, it can be called 'Soviet dialectical materialism', and thus distinguished from other interpretations of Marx's philosophy that are designated by the same name. Ever since the dispute between Eduard Bernstein and Karl Kautsky about the propositions essential to Marxist socialism, other writers have called in question Engels' claim that dialectical materialism was, indeed, the philosophy of Marx. This growing doubt found its most systematic and comprehensive expression in Georg Lukács' *History and Class Consciousness* and Karl Korsch's *Marxism and Philosophy*, published almost simultaneously in Germany in 1923.[5] Both Korsch and Lukács used the term 'dialectical materialism' to refer to the philsosophy they believed to be Marx's original and undistorted thought. They regarded it as a method rather than as a substantive theory, but they did not feel they caused confusion by using the traditional name for its designation, since dialectics remained for them the most important characteristic of the Marxian philosophy. In fact, however, Lukács and Korsch offered an interpretation of Marx's thought incompatible with the one derived from the writings of Engels, Plekhanov and Lenin, and initiated a radical re-examination of Soviet dialectical materialism. The goal of *History and Class Consciousness*, Lukács wrote, was to provide "an exposition of Marx's theory as Marx understood it" and to defend it against Engels himself.[6] Korsch was not as explicit as Lukács and yet noted that Engels added to the economic determination of all socio-historical phenomena an even more final "determination of Nature".[7] Thus, both of them claimed that Marx and Engels held different views on some important points and both of them saw the main source of these differences in Engels' dialectics of nature. While they discarded dialectical materialism as a cosmological or metaphysical doctrine, Korsch and Lukács never wished to question the materiality of the external world.[8]

'Dialectics' can be understood in two different senses. It can be used to refer to a cosmic force, an all-pervasive power of change, subject to laws which Hegel discovered in the realm of thought and which are extended to all phenomena without exception, to history and society as well as to nature. Or 'dialectics' can mean a specific form of the development of ideas and a process of history, inapplicable to the relationships among natural objects. In the latter use, 'dialectics' is never adequately defined and may mean the relation of interaction between subject and object in the historical process, a way of looking at the world that emphasizes change through conflict, a tension between opposite tendencies resulting in their supersession, the appearance of unintended consequences or a regular succession of action and its reversal that reveals, in Engels' words, "the progressive movement from the lower to the higher". The former concept of dialectics was adopted by Engels and Lenin, and the latter by Lukács and Korsch who maintained that dialectics was a philosophical method for the investigation and reconstruction of society which cannot be applied to nature.[9] From their point of view, Engels' transformation of the laws of dialectics into cosmological principles distorted Marx's basic insight contained in his materialistic conception of history. Historical materialism was dialectical in view of its assumption that social-historical development resulted from the interaction between changes in the social reality and changes in thought, and embodied the principle of interdependence between theoretical and revolutionary activity.[10] Furthermore, historical materialism was, indeed, dialectical materialism since it involved a reciprocal determination, on the one hand, between the material conditions of existence of a social class and its class consciousness, and, on the other, between class consciousness of a social class (theory) and its purposive action intended to transform the world (practice or *praxis*). Instead of being a set of speculative principles, dialectics was a method for the analysis of the position and function of the proletariat in society and the proletariat's instrument in its struggle for supremacy and social emancipation. Here was a human activity, both theoretical and practical, having all of society as its object. The activity was theoretical, because it did not accept social facts as independent realities but viewed them as aspects of the historical process; it was practical, because social facts were the outcome of human interaction and should be under human control.

The distinctive concept of Lukács' and Korsch's view of dialectics is the notion of totality, which signifies the subordination of every phenomenon to a social and historical whole. A totality is not a mere abstraction but an objective reality, operating upon people from without and within. "Concrete totality . . . governs reality," wrote Lukács, and Korsch expressed a similar idea in the proposition that Marx's philosophy was "a materialism whose theory comprehended the totality of society and history, and whose practice overthrew it". The category of totality is indispensable because facts are truly known only if they are perceived as parts of a concrete whole and because every significant change manifests itself only in relation to a concrete totality. Social phenomena are transformed by the way they are perceived and they are perceived in terms of some specific categories of mediation which – even though they vary from one social class to another and are subject to historical change – alone integrate facts in a totality. The form in which the essence of things is manifest reveals itself only in the context of a concrete whole.[11]

In so far as men identify themselves with a social-historical totality, it acquires through them reason and will, and, thus, tends to realize itself by surpassing its preceding stages. The totality makes ideals real by uncovering the direction and purpose of historical processes. Hence, dialectics enables us to bridge the abyss dividing the world of Nature and the moral world, and to establish the unity of theory and practice. The distinction between theory and practice in the Marxian sense is not coextensive with the distinction between theoretical and practical knowledge in the ordinary and scientific usage since Plato and Aristotle. In the *Critique of Judgment* Kant distinguished the 'technically practical' and the 'morally practical'. The former expression refers to the application of theoretical knowledge for practical purposes, and the latter to what can be done but never be theoretically grasped, what is expressed in moral precepts and constitutes the subject-matter of practical philosophy.[12] Marx's use of the term 'material practice' or '*praxis*' in the strict meaning of the word applies only to a human action which, through a transformation and penetration of the physical or social world, is practical in the moral sense, imposes the actor's will and purpose upon it, and, in Marxian terminology, contributes to the humanization of man and his environment. If the social reality is never given or ready-made, social theory must deal with men as the producers of their own conditions and forms of life. Moreover, if men are the makers of their circumstances, the outcome of their productive activity depends on critical self-reflection, on the social reality into which they are born, and on what they wish to make of it. Theory and practice are not distinct; they emerge from and complete one another.

Lukács' and Korsch's reinterpretation of dialectical materialism produced a flood of condemnation in the Communist Parties, especially in the Soviet Union and Germany. George Lichtheim rightly observed that the denial of the relevance of Marx's philosophy to natural science removed the keystone from the construction of Soviet dialectical materialism.[13] But in Western Europe the writings of Korsch and Lukács remained unknown to most scholars until the 1960s, when they were republished and translated into other European languages to reinforce the recent trend towards a Hegelianized Marxism. Hegelianized Marxism derives from Engels' belief that since Hegel discovered the dialectics of things in the dialectics of concepts, the Hegelian system was a "materialism idealistically turned upside down in method and content", and, thus, the theoretical premise for the new materialist outlook of Marx.[14] The contemporary Hegelianized Marxism, based on Lukács' interpretation of Hegel, is incompatible with Engels' naturalized Hegelianism. According to Lukács, Marx's philosophy follows directly from the insight of Hegel

who, inspired by Kant's revolution in the theory of knowledge, maintained that Reason can only comprehend the order it has itself created.
Reason can acquire knowledge of the world as a whole only to the extent
it refuses to accept the reality that reveals itself empirically, conceiving of
it instead as formed by constructive thought in accordance with what the
world ought to be.[15]

II

The dispute about the two conceptions of dialectics – the dialectics of
nature and dialectics restricted to the realm of history and society – should
be distinguished from the second controversy which has been joined following the publication of the *Manuscripts* and the *Grundrisse* – i.e., the
controversy as to the continuity or discontinuity of Marx's thought at the
different stages of his life. The two disputes have a common link in Marx's
original interpretation of the *Phenomenology of the Spirit* in the *Manuscripts*,[16] based on the belief that Hegel's great discovery in the *Phenomenology* was his conception of history as "the outcome of man's own labor"
and as a process of the self-generation of man. This developmental process
proceeds by the ever-recurring succession of the three stages: the objectification of man's generic powers, their estrangement as objects, and the
supersession of estrangement in the act of speculative comprehension.[17]
Marx's interpretation of Hegel's *Phenomenology* is evidently associated
with his own view of social reality as the product of human interaction
and of history as "nothing but the activity of man pursuing his aims".[18]
   The distinctive feature of the *Manuscripts* is the critique rather than the
approval of Hegel's general and social philosophy.[19] Marx was immensely
impressed by Feuerbach's criticism of Hegel, used it to contrast Hegelian
idealism with his own anthropological realism,[20] and drove it home by
pointing out that Hegel failed to distinguish alienation (*Entfremdung*)
from objectification (*Vergegenständlichung*); consequently, Hegel misrepresented a social phenomenon which must be exposed by a critique of
society as a mere problem of speculative philosophy which may be resolved by speculative means.[21] Marx's criticism of Hegel was enhanced
by the discovery of the class struggle and the horrors of early capitalism
which provided a striking contrast with the myth of the rule of Reason
and Freedom, announced by Hegel in his *Philosophy of Right* and *Philosophy of History*. Together, they produced in Marx what Louis Althusser

calls *une coupure epistémologique*, a break with the conceptual framework of German idealism and the theoretical principles of the Young Hegelians.

An even more distinctive feature of the *Manuscripts* is Marx's analysis of the process of economic activity as a social process of producing the means to satisfy human needs, and the conclusions he derived from this investigation concerning the historical determination and limitations of classical political economy. Implicit in the analysis is an awareness of the peculiar nature of the material with which political economy deals. In the words of the Preface to *Capital*, it "summons as foes into the field of battle the most violent, mean, and malignant passions of the human breast, the Furies of private interest". Marx's study of economic theories culminated, at that stage, in the proposition that "political economy has merely formulated the laws of alienated labor" and that the political economist, like the philosopher of Hegel, was "an abstract form of alienated man" (*eine abstrakte Gestalt des entfremdeten Menschen*) who "sets himself up as the measuring-rod of the alienated world".[22] The part of the *Manuscripts* in which Marx discussed his philosophy of alienation has most impressed contemporary readers and, at the same time, has raised new questions concerning the development of Marx's philosophical and social thought.

The significance of the *Grundrisse* for the understanding of Marx is not as easy to discover as its admirers are wont to claim. The *Grundrisse* is the most complete presentation of Marx's economic theory of capitalism prior to *Capital*, and, in particular, deals with some socio-economic problems that cannot be found in the earlier works, for instance, the economy of time, leisure time, and technological progress that might one day replace, in Marx's opinion, surplus labor as the source of wealth. Furthermore, Marx discussed in the *Grundrisse* such topics as pre-capitalist economic formations, the credit system and the competition on the world market which in *Capital* were assigned to "its eventual continuation"; the *Grundrisse* thereby represents Marx's final opinion on the subject. Most students of Marx pay no attention, however, to the economic and sociological content of the *Grundrisse* and cite it solely as evidence that Marx never abandoned his philosophy of alienation as formulated in the *Manuscripts*. While there are some passages in the *Grundrisse* where the concept of alienation is discussed, implicitly or explicitly, it is the term 'alienation', and not its concept, that remains unchanged. The alienation of the worker in his product (that is, the loss of the object produced by the worker and its appropriation by the capitalist), which in the *Manuscripts* seem to be the origin of all other forms of alienation, is abandoned, and the scope of the concept of *Entfremdung* is restricted to the "alienation of the individual from himself and from others" to dispense with any speculative assumptions.[23] The comprehensive philosophical doctrine of alienation, formulated in the *Manuscripts*, with its detailed description of three or four forms of *Entfremdung* or *Entaüsserung*,[24] is conspicuous by its absence in the *Grundrisse*, *Capital* and also *Theories of Surplus Value*, for it is clearly recondite as well as redundant within the economic and sociological theory of capitalism expounded in these works. I will try later to justify this claim.

III

The *Manuscripts* and other works of the young Marx, which in the opinion of some writers attain a mature synthesis in the *Grundrisse*, have initiated another sharp controversy about Marx's philosophy. Most participants in this new dispute recognize that the thought of the young Marx, best exemplified by the *Manuscripts*, and the thought of the mature Marx, the author of *Capital*, show considerable and striking differences in their content and style. These differences can be explained in several ways, of which three are most frequently adopted. The contrast between the young and the mature Marx may be resolved by discounting either the former or the latter and claiming that the thought of only one of them is entitled to acceptance as Marx's authentic or enduring heritage. According to the third school, there is no break between the philosophy of the young and the mature Marx, whose works display a remarkably consistent development, and do not necessitate the choice of one theme of Marx's philosophy at the expense or exclusion of another.[25] The third solution is combined with the belief that familiarity with the philosophy of the early Marx is indispensable to the understanding of his mature work.

The various answers to the questions, 'Did Marx have two philosophies or only one?' and 'If he had only one, which is the more significant and enduringly valuable?' cannot be examined in this paper in detail. It is necessary, however, to discuss briefly the general issues raised in the dispute.

Those who support the view that Marx's early thought should be interpreted from the vantage point of his destination dismiss Marx's early philosophy as a biographical document and a testimony to his struggle against and break with his German philosophical inheritance, in order to establish a new science of history and society. Louis Althusser is perhaps the most consistent and certainly the most extreme representative of this school of thought which is favored by many Marxist philosophers in the Soviet Union and Eastern Europe as well as by such Western scholars as Herbert Marcuse, Auguste Cornu, Sidney Hook, and Daniel Bell. This interpretation is not as absurd as its opponents claim, since the formulation of historical materialism in *The German Ideology* can be considered independently of Marx's early investigations and critique of Hegel's philosophy. "There is indeed", Jean Hyppolite observed, "a body of doctrine which stands by itself and requires no interpretation in terms of the development of the earlier studies." [26] In the opinion of Soviet philosophers, the problem of alienation in the writings of Marx cannot be separated from the building of Communism. Since the transformation of the capitalist society into a classless Communist society is the central theme of his later works, the thought of the mature Marx provides the key to the understanding of the thought of the young Marx in general, and of his philosophy of alienation in particular. By this view, dialectical materialism (in Engels' formulation) is the logical outcome of pursuing historical materialism to its ontological foundations which were discovered in materialistic monism and the dialectics of Nature.

According to the opposite school of thought, the authentic philosophy of Marx can be found in the *Manuscripts*, the *Grundrisse*, and selective excerpts from Marx's other works. Its protagonists form a very diverse group. It includes Catholic writers (Jean-Yves Calvez and R. P. Bigo), psychoanalysts (Erich Fromm) and political scientists influenced by psychiatric theories (Robert Tucker), former orthodox Marxist-Leninists (Roger Garaudy and, with some qualification, Adam Schaff), Marxologists in Poland and Yugoslavia, and Western authorities on Marx (Iring Fetscher, Jean Hyppolite, or Maximilien Rubel). Very few of them actually dismiss the mature Marx altogether, but they reinterpret him in the light of the thought of the young Marx. Furthermore, they are convinced that the latter should be read from the viewpoint of Marx's early philosophy, with its concern for the human individual, since the works of the maturity are otherwise bound to be misunderstood or misinterpreted.[27]

Even though they may accept, in one way or another, the continuity of
Marx's thought, as the supporters of the third school do (George Lukács,
Heinrich Popitz, or Ernest Mandel), they tend to see Marx mainly as a
philosopher and maintain that the young Marx spoke the truth more
plainly and forcefully than the mature Marx.

Roughly speaking, the philosophy of Marx is interpreted today in two
mutually exclusive ways.[28] Firstly, there is the orthodox approach which
adopts the traditional framework of materialistic monism, regards dialectics as a cosmic force rather than a philosophical theory of social action,
and considers knowledge to be essentially a reflection of the external
world and objective social conditions. This assertion of naive realism in
the theory of knowledge[29] is associated, somewhat inconsistently, with
Hegel's belief that there is a privileged standpoint from which the ultimate
reality can be known, undistorted by the illusion of the senses, speculative
errors, or ideological presuppositions. Secondly, there is the approach
based upon the premise that the material and social world around us is
man-made in the historical process of continuous objectification of human
biological and social capacities. Contrary to the orthodox approach, the
second interpretation does not take the world of objects for granted but
claims that the physical and social world is constantly moulded and transformed by man's theoretical and practical, cognitive and productive activity. Reality is the outcome of specifically human actions of a whole
succession of generations, each of which stands on the shoulders of the
preceding one, continues the traditional activity in changed circumstances
and modifies the old circumstances with changed activity. This sociological interpretation emphasizes the critical function of philosophy, the
unity of theory and practice, and the role of practice in the humanization
of the physical and social environment. Since it is much less known than
the orthodox approach, I will examine more closely its basic assumptions
and main propositions, including Marx's philosophy of alienation, which
has presently overshadowed all other disputes about Marx and dialectical
materialism. It has also reopened the question of the relevance of the
Marxian heritage for contemporary man and society.

IV

In the sociological interpretation of Marx's philosophy the concept of

Nature holds the central place. 'Nature' or 'matter', as used by Marx both in his early and mature writings, means just the mass of undifferentiated materials (*Naturstoff*) in which labor is realized and which man shapes into things in order to adapt them to his needs and purposes. The labor-process combines the labor of the hand with that of the head, although "they part company and even become deadly foes" at a later stage of social development. Marx calls all things which are merely separated from connection with their environment 'objects of labor' (*Arbeitsgegenstände*) and those which undergo alteration by means of labor he calls 'raw materials'. If Nature comprises both objects of labor and raw materials 'Nature' means not only soil or water but also fish taken from the river, timber felled in the virgin forest or ores extracted from the earth.[30] It is self-evident that matter is prior to human activity[31] and that production is essentially the imposition of a form on materials provided by Nature in which either the same laborer performs all the functions or there is a collective laborer, a combination of workmen, transforming materials into a social product. Marx followed in the footsteps of Hegel who maintained that in forming a thing we not only confer externality upon it, but also take possession of it.[32] But from the principle that to impose a form on a thing is to make it one's property and the embodiment of one's personality, Marx derived consequences that never occurred to Hegel.

Unless we visualize man in the fictitious, purely animal state, all material production – the activity that adapts natural resources to human needs – is invariably social and the appropriation of Nature by the individual is always within and through the mediation of a definite form of society or social organization.[33] "In production", Marx wrote, "men not only act on Nature but also on one another"; they cannot produce unless they cooperate and mutually exchange their activities. "In order to produce, they enter into definite connections and relations with one another and only within these social connections and relations does their action on Nature, does production, take place."[34] Furthermore, since labor involves acting on the physical world, social labor is responsible, on the one hand, for the continued transformation of environment and, on the other for changes in man himself. As Marx put it, man acting on the external world "develops his slumbering powers and compels them to act in obedience to his sway".[35] The relationship of mutual determination between the

activity of one man and that of another and between his labor-power and
the object of labor constitutes a dialectical relation in Marx's sense. It is
evident, therefore, that a dialectical relation can only hold between man
and Nature or man and society, but never between natural objects or
processes alone. A dialectical relation does not obtain unless it is mediated
by the activity of man.

Marx's study of the process of labor, of classical political economy and
social history gave him a more realistic grasp of man's relation to Nature in
his everyday life than any *Naturphilosophie* could provide. He maintained
that when Nature is taken in abstraction from man, it is "devoid of sense"
for man. "The labor process . . . is human action with a view to the production of use-values, appropriation of natural substance to human requirements; it is the necessary condition for effecting exchange of matter
between man and Nature; it is the everlasting Nature-imposed condition
of human existence, and therefore is independent of every social phase of
that existence, or rather, is common to every such phase."[36] Since Marx
accepted the constitutive function of consciousness in human activity and
recognized the fact that the human individual is always a social individual,
Nature was for Marx a man-formed Nature, moulded by man's needs,
drives, and abilities. Since only Nature modified by previous human activity is given in experience, we can never come to know Nature as it exists
by itself and, therefore, objective idealism, metaphysical materialism or
any other doctrines claiming knowledge of the ultimate reality are equally
unjustifiable. Nature consists of things and relations articulated by man's
action, of things-for-us, and not of things-in-themselves. Furthermore,
Nature has human significance (*Wesen*) only for social Man, cooperating
and working together; hence Nature as the object of labor is invariably
socially-made Nature that never remains the same.[37] It is the ever-his-
torically-changing totality of socially-formed objects, each of them a product of man's work and the state of society. Marx's philosophy neither
has nor could have any metaphysical foundations; its general principles
are derived from the analysis of labor-process and the observation of man
in his social and economic relationships. For this reason, Marx was in a
position to investigate the relation of man to Nature and of man to man
in empirical terms, and formulate a theory of social action that was also
a theory of human emancipation.

A theory of human emancipation is necessary for two main reasons.

The division of labor liberates man from his dependence on Nature but, by the same token, puts him at the mercy of society. Marx grudgingly accepted the truth of Adam Smith's argument that the division of labor leads to an ever-increasing abundance of production and is the source of the diversity of "natural talents in different men". But while "the division of labor is ... a skillful deployment of human powers for social wealth," it also "reduces the capacity (*Fähigkeit*) of each person taken individually [sc. to have control over his life]".[38] Furthermore, the division of labor has the consequence that intellectual and manual labor, production and consumption, enjoyment and toil devolve on different individuals. Thus, there arises a conflict of individual and communal, particular and common interests, and as long as this conflict persists, productive labors of the individual produce an "alien power ... which enslaves him instead of being controlled by him".[39] Man comes to experience society as a force as blind as the elemental forces of Nature and, at the same time, becomes totally dependent on it for the sustenance of his biological needs and the satisfaction of his specifically human requirements.

It has already been pointed out that for Marx physical reality becomes a significant element of human experience only at the level of social Man. Nature as the object of social labor, and society as the totality of social relationships within which individuals produce, are an externalization and objectification of man's generic nature or species essence. The strange notion of *Gattungswesen*, which Marx adopted from Feuerbach's *The Essence of Christianity*, recurs frequently in the *Manuscripts*, where Marx tried to translate this speculative idea into an empirical language but, having failed, abandoned it altogether, from *The German Ideology* onwards. Briefly, 'species essence' refers to those human characteristics which prompt collective and cooperative action and through which the individual is provided with the means for his physical subsistence as well as increasingly acquires his distinctively human characteristics. "The human essence is no abstraction inherent in each single individual. In its reality it is the ensemble of the social relations."[40] The result of production is, in fact, the objectification of cooperating individuals and the social product of them all, although they need not be aware of it nor know how they did it.[41] 'Objectification' refers to the realization of labor (*die Verwirklichung der Arbeit*), to the performance of work by which human activities are transformed into things of use and, as they

embody "the power of the united individuals", they become external to
all and each of them.[42] In a socially made world, an isolated individual
views social reality as independent of himself and holding an overwhelm-
ing power over him, instead of as being the unintended product of many
men interacting and communicating with one another. 'Alienation' means
the outcome of the objectification of labor into a physical thing if and
only if the objectification is concomitant with the worker's loss of the
object produced by himself and its appropriation by another man. When
producers recognize that the labor embodied in the product of labor is no
longer their own united labor-power, it becomes an autonomous, alien,
and inhuman force that is hostile toward and independent of them, and,
as such, beyond the reach of their control.[43] Hegel thought that all objectification is alienation, the two merely being different stages of a single
process, and that alienation is an inherent characteristic of all intellectual
and spiritual creation.[44] For Marx, at least in his early period, objectification becomes alienation only in specific social and historical conditions
which are transient and not eternal, because they result from the blind
operation of market laws and can be overcome by collective action. Furthermore, alienation is not a circumstance that is part of every creative
activity, but a power destructive of man's freedom and his very existence.
The inhumanity of the alienated labor-power (that is, capital) is the consequence of the laws governing capitalist production which benefit the
master of labor at the expense of the laborer and, as they mortify his body
and ruin his mind, are hostile to his interests and well-being.

                                    V

Alienation is a concept characteristic of the early writings of Marx, and
not of his mature works, where neither the concept nor the term 'alienation' has a prominent place. It is a concept that more than any other is
believed to express Marx's humanism and moral concern. 'Humanism'
in the Marxian sense designates a philosophy which makes man the measure of all things, sets a high value on his personal worth, and supports
the right of all men to the whole range of material and spiritual values that
become available through human labor, intelligence and inventiveness.
Humanism also involves an ethical doctrine. It asserts that men should not
be treated as means, and that he who does treat them so, also reduces

himself to a mere means. The reverence for the worth of man, the Kantian principle of moral philosophy, led Marx to accept the categorical imperative that man is an end in himself. This categorical imperative is both a moral maxim and a rule for action to overthrow all conditions that make the exploitation of man by man possible, that turn him into a thing, and put him under the domination of another man.[45] Consequently, Marx's humanism is a naturalistic humanism. In the Marxian context, 'naturalism' means, above all, the belief that man, being part of Nature, depends on the external objects and his bodily needs are as essential to him as those of his mind.

Although the humanistic philosophy of Marx is stated inadequately and only in his early works, these works need not be known in order to discover that *Capital* involves a humanistic moral outlook or that without this knowledge *Capital* would be read as a straight economic treatise.[46] Marx was not a moral philosopher, either in *Capital* or in the *Manuscripts* (alienation is a value-loaded concept but it does not support by itself any distinctive moral theory). However, throughout his life, Marx was a critic of society and his moral indignation at the world of early capitalism, at its economic exploitation and political enslavement, is as unmistakable in the *Manuscripts* as in *Capital*. His social critique was based, on the one hand, on his sociology of morals, inherent in the basic proposition of historical materialism, that morality is socially conditioned, and, on the other, on his strong moral convictions concerning a truly human life, life worthy of and proper to man. His moral concern was not made explicit, because he used the words 'human' and 'inhuman' as if they were descriptive predicates and because he failed to state the principles of ethics which would contextually define the meaning of these terms as value predicates, conveying some definite moral ideas. Although Marx never worked out his moral philosophy, the moral beliefs of his youth continued, throughout his life,[47] to influence his view of man and society; they are responsible for his peculiar mode of expression in which the descriptive, the evaluative, and the directive use of language are combined. This conclusion has some implication as to why Marx assigned such an important place to the philosophy of alienation in his youthful writings and made no use of it, for explanatory purposes, in his mature work.

There is a grain of truth in Althusser's assertion that the early works of Marx are philosophical (or ideological, in Althusser's terminology) and

the works of maturity are scientific. But Marx's philosophy of alienation
is not entirely ideological. In the *Manuscripts*, and even more in *The
German Ideology*, Marx tried to reconstruct the Hegelian concept of alienation (which, with the exception of some restricted uses in social and
political philosophy, is inapplicable outside the creative work in art, literature or philosophy) into a sociological concept for the analysis of human
interaction in general and economic production in particular. The disregard for the philosophy of alienation in the works of maturity cannot
be explained in terms of an epistemological break. The term 'alienation'
appears in the *Grundrisse*, *Capital*, and *Theories of Surplus Value*, although
its use is restricted to alienation in the process of production, self-alienation, and alienation from others.[48] It is employed to describe the experience of, and effects upon, the worker in relation to the structural characteristics of the capitalist mode of production, based on the appropriation of the surplus product and the application of advanced technology,
itself an achievement of capitalism. The concept of the alienation of the
worker in his product becomes, therefore, part of the conceptual framework of the economics and sociology of capitalism and has only a genetic
connection with the early Marx's philosophy of alienation. This philosophy had to be abandoned once Marx no longer wished to analyze the
human predicament in the modern world – the poverty and wretchedness
in the midst of plenty and refinement – but to investigate alienation as a
social phenomenon, inherent in the social-economic structure of modern
society rather than in the philosophical reflection on the nature of thought
and its relation to reality. This development is foreshadowed in the *Manuscripts* where Marx's critique of Hegel's philosophy was prompted by the
realization that Hegel's concept of alienation had no empirical significance.

The *Manuscripts* may, indeed, be viewed as a tentative step towards the
transition from speculations about the generic human being to the empirical study of societies.[49] Marx argued that for Hegel the essential characteristic of man was self-consciousness and that the different forms of
alienation were, consequently, only different forms of abstract and vacuous
thought about alienation to be distinguished from the phenomenon of
alienation itself. While in the empirical world, *Entfremdung* "can only
become manifest through the real practical relationship to other men",
the Hegelian concept of alienation remained in the realm of pure or

speculative thought and had nothing to do with "the actual alienation of the human being".[50] Since Hegel confused man's activity with mere thinking, he also confused the thinker's abolition of empty abstractions with the abolition of alienation by emancipatory practice.[51] The same determination to relate alienation to the facts of social life is apparent when Marx adopted Adam Smith's definition of capital as "a certain command over all the labor or over all the produce of labor which is in the market", concluding that if the product of labor did not belong to the worker and confronted him as an alien power, this power was the capitalist, the master of labor, and nothing else. "Not the gods, not Nature, but only man himself can be this alien power over man."[52]

VI

Marx's conception of man, which underlies his philosophy of alienation, was formulated in opposition to two other views of man held at that time, namely, the idealistic view and the materialistic philosophy of man. Marx argued against the materialists that if man is a product of matter and physical forces which operate in accordance with the laws of mechanics, as Hobbes, Lamettrie or Holbach had maintained, or is a product of education and environment, as Helvétius and Robert Owen had claimed, man can neither change his environment nor make progress. Marx accepted as self-evident that social change is real, progress exists, and that human nature is mutable. Hence, both formulations of the materialistic conception of man had to be rejected.

Marx also disagreed with the idealistic view of man which was represented by Hegel and the Young Hegelians at that time. For Hegel, man was not "a determinate finite object", that is, a natural object or an organism, and the part of man he shared with other animal species was not human at all. Mind was man's genuine reality, "his true and essential being". As a mind, man was endowed with self-consciousness and creativity; they alone constituted his distinctive characteristics. It is in virtue of being spirit, Hegel wrote in the Introduction to his *Lectures on the Philosophy of Religion*, that "man is man".[53] Marx was quite right when he maintained that in Hegel "man appears only in the shape of mind" and "the essence of man equals self-consciousness". Consequently, for Hegel, man's world-creating activity was restricted to the philosopher's abstract thought – one specific and relatively unimportant kind of man's labor. "The only labor which Hegel knows and recognizes is abstract mental labor." [54] In describing man as a spiritual being, Hegel not only ignored man's bodily nature but also misrepresented "the real man . . . man with his feet firmly on the solid ground," who is not a philosopher's invention. On their part, Hegel's epigoni – the Young Hegelians and the True Socialists – were in essential agreement with Hegel and the Old Hegelians. For Bruno Bauer, self-consciousness was distinct from the minds of men and its development towards universality was a caricatural realization of Hegel's conception of history. The True Socialists had no interest in men but were concerned with "the interests of Human Nature, of Man in general, who belongs to no class, has no reality, who exists only in the misty realm of philosophical fantasy". [55]

For Marx, both the materialists and the idealists were in error. Man is a mind in a body, a unity of matter and spirit. He opposes Nature but only as one of Her forces in order to appropriate materials provided by Nature without which he cannot survive. He is a living and sentient natural being and this means that, on the one hand, he is endowed with the powers of life, inherent in him as predispositions, abilities, and drives (*Anlagen, Fähigkeiten, Triebe*) and, on the other, he depends on the external objects, independent of himself, for his existence. Although he has to rely on the physical environment for the satisfaction of his needs as much as an animal or a plant, man's forms of activity make it manifest that he has distinctively human powers. The animal merely uses Nature, but man makes it serve his ends. In contradistinction to the brute which acts to secure the requirements of life only when it is compelled by biological needs that remain constant, man produces even when he is free from biological necessity and, in fact, he only truly produces when he can engage in the activity proper to the human species. Marx adopted Feuerbach's idea that animal species have generic characteristics and that these characteristics are manifested in their specific life-activity (*Lebenstätigkeit*). The human being differs from the brute by his life-activity in that the animal does not distinguish its individual existence from its membership in a species, while man is aware of this difference, can reflect and act upon it. For this reason, man, but not the animal, has consciousness in the strict sense and, with consciousness, a twofold, inner and outer life. Feuerbach wished to assert thereby that man is aware of other men as human beings, lives and acts with them socially, and is "I and Thou," viz., "can put himself in the place of another."[56]

Being conscious of themselves and other human beings, men need not follow the path prescribed by Nature, but can pursue purposes of their own. "What distinguishes the worst architect from the best of bees is this, that the architect raises his structure in imagination before he erects it in reality. At the end of every labor-process, we get a result that already existed in the imagination of the laborer at its commencement".[57] Owing to his ability to act purposefully in co-operation with others, man acquires the power to control Nature and consciously make history. A fundamental condition of all history, says Marx in *The German Ideology*, is the gradual emergence of needs and the production of the means to satisfy them which give rise to ever newer needs. This dialectical multiplication of needs and the means of satisfying them confers upon labor a liberating quality, giving man the opportunity to work himself out of the animal state.[58] The rise of man is, ultimately, due to the fact that environment affects man and man modifies environment. Consequently, the truth of old materialism – that man is a product of circumstances and education – must be supplemented by the proposition that "man's physical and social environment is the outcome of man's activity". As Marx concisely put it: "Circumstances make men just as men make circumstances."[59]

Marx's naturalistic conception of man owes more to idealism than to materialism. Marx believed as strongly in the creativity of man as did Hegel, he only accounted for it in an entirely different way. For Marx, man is not passive in his relation to the physical and social environment, as the materialists described him, nor is he a detached observer, pure reason and thought, as Hegel and the Young Hegelians claimed him to be. Man not only reacts to external stimuli but acts spontaneously and creatively[60], and his creative character is not restricted to his mind, as it was for Hegel. Marx used the terms 'labor' and 'production' synonymously and in a very comprehensive sense to refer to any conscious purposive or planned activity, from the most lowly forms of productive labor to the highest achievements of art, literature, law, morals, science or philosophy.[61] There is a historical continuity between the two extremes, since each and all of them express man's social nature, enable him to transform the environment and himself, and acquire an external embodiment in the works he creates together with his fellow-men. This historical continuity also springs from the fact that productive labor is a fundamental form of activity on which all other forms of it depend.[62] Labor is not a curse, although it is a torture to be a laborer, a means of creating surplus-value. Through labor, man can pull himself up by his own bootstraps, as it were, out of his animal existence into society, and, through society (the product of his activity which makes possible the progressive achievements of science and technology) to realize his still undeveloped potentialities.

Material activity, released by sense perception, and not philosophical reflection or the Hegelian Reason, mediates between man and Nature. Sense perception itself should not be considered as primarily a cognitive act, for cognition is not a primary activity of man. Man gains knowledge about reality by acting upon it and trying to change it and, consequently, the relation of cognizing subject to the cognized object is secondary and subordinate to the relation of the producer to the product. *Praxis*, the spontaneous and creative activity that imposes man's own aims upon the environment, can be analyzed into perception and a mode of action, appropriate to the realization of a set purpose, in which the awareness of this intention replaces instinct. All objects in our environment are first and foremost objects of our life-preserving activity, and only secondarily are they objects of cognition. Similarly, concepts are not reflections of objects or sets of classificatory, descriptive characteristics that connote the objects themselves; they are representations of socially and historically man-formed objects and designate his relation to some selected segments of the environment which satisfy or fail to satisfy specific human needs and are the cause of pleasure or pain.

VII

Marx's theory of alienation was formulated to answer the puzzling questions which must have arisen in his mind when he tried to relate his philosophical assumptions, with respect to man and society, to his observations of the social world of the mid-19th century. His philosophical assumptions implied that the social world was man-made, but man experienced it as an alien and inhuman power which he did not control and which, on the contrary, oppressed his life. His philosophical assumptions also implied that social evolution was bringing progress and improvements of all sorts, making men increasingly rich in genuinely human qualities. Although the division of labor was raising the productive power of labor, increasing the wealth, and refining society, it was impoverishing the worker and turning him into a machine. The proletarian, "the man who, being without capital and rent, lives purely by labor", was tormented by heavy work and a long working day, starved to death by low wages, and brutalized by forced labor that benefited others, his degrading wretchedness being "in inverse proportion to the power and magnitude of his production". From the point of view of political economy, the worker was only "a working animal . . . a beast reduced to the strictest bodily needs", and "a mere thing or an article of trade".[63]

Marx's philosophy of alienation was intended to explain why the 19th-century world differed enormously from what his philosophical assumptions would lead us to believe. Marx maintained that the state of the world around him was in accord with the principles of political economy, although the economists themselves were unaware of the consequences these principles entailed as well as indifferent to the plight of the laborers. They assumed that the increase of wealth was always beneficial to all and, hence, that the interests of the worker never stood opposed to the interests of society. In the eyes of Adam Smith and Ricardo, poverty was "merely the pang which accompanies every childbirth", the birth in this case being the emergence of a superior mode of the production of wealth. For Marx, labor was harmful and destructive, if the increase of wealth was its exclusive purpose. Whenever wealth was pursued for its own sake, the interests of society and the workers were incompatible, and "the increasing value of the world of things proceeds in direct proportion to the devaluation of the world of men".[64] Thus, the question, 'Why is the increase of wealth, which is produced by the worker, the cause of the increase of his poverty and degradation?' became the central problem in the *Manuscripts*.

Marx's insight into the connection between the increase of wealth and poverty was a sharp denial of the claims made by classical political economists, and Marx had to justify his contention against their arguments. "Hitherto", Marx wrote in an attempt to expose the errors and blindness of his opponents, "political economy proceeded from the wealth that the movement of private property was supposed to create for the nations", and, thus, became "an apology of private property". Proudhon and other socialist writers brought into prominence "the poverty bred by the movement of private property", which political economy concealed, and, thus, they disclosed "the contradictory nature of private property". Political economy, Marx concluded, should proceed "from the fact of poverty and misery", and not from that of wealth, since otherwise the incompatibility of social justice and private property would remain incomprehensible.[65] Although the existence of poverty and misery arouses moral indignation, it does not provide a starting point for a more adequate theory of political economy which would explain want and destitution in a world of ever-growing wealth. Since Marx was unable at the time to construct such a theory and challenge the classical political economists on their own ground, he had no choice but to argue against Adam Smith, Say, and Ricardo on the basis of moral rather than economic principles. Poverty was the necessary effect of wealth, because wealth presupposed the separation of the workers from their means of production and, under these conditions, wages tended to fall towards the subsistence or starvation level. This trend resulted from the mode of production which Marx described in terms of alienated labor. In Marx's terminology, labor is alienated when the laborer no longer owns his product, his labor-power is reduced to "wage-earning activity" (*Erwerbstätigkeit*) and "self-acting commodity" (*selbsttätige Ware*), and he himself is turned into "a spiritually and physically dehumanized being" (*eine ebenso geistig wie körperlich entmenschtes Wesen*).[66] Marx contrasted alienated labor with labor as a free manifestation or enjoyment of life (*freie Lebensaüsserung, Genuss des Lebens*) and life's prime want (*das erste Lebensbedürfniss*), that is, with his ideal of man's social nature. He believed that this ideal could be derived from the concept of communal life (*Gemeinwesen*), because men were originally members of a community and became individuals only through the process of history. Probably all influential conceptions of man involve this sort of naturalistic fallacy or openly combine descriptive and evaluative characteristics (unless they remain within the confines of physical anthropology), and the conception of man of the young Marx is no exception.[67] If this is the case, it is no wonder that Marx's philosophy of alienation, based on normative premises, led to moral condemnation of the system of production in which men were prevented from living and acting as social beings, but it did not and could not explain the system it pronounced to be inhuman.

The philosophy of alienation in the *Manuscripts* makes use of the concept of the essential human nature which Marx sharply criticised and rejected in *The German Ideology* and other later writings. 'Man' may be either a general term, referring to human individuals, or a collective term, designating the society of men; in the tradition of Feuerbach, to which Marx belonged, 'man' is used in the second sense. Marx spoke of "the return of man to himself as a social, that is, truly human being" (*ein gesellschaftlicher, d.h., menschlicher Mensch*) and emphasized that a mode of existence is not human unless it is social. He opposed the concept of social man and the human world to that of man "viewed as an isolated monad", that is, "separated from the community" – man as a member of civil society composed of "atomistic, mutually hostile individuals".[68] 'Social' means the characteristic predicated on the cooperation of several individuals, regardless of its end, mode, or the conditions under which it takes place.[69] The proposition 'man is essentially social' means, first of all, that men depend on the material conditions of existence and no moral preaching prevails against this determination. Being dependent on the environment, they must cooperate with one another for the satisfaction of their needs, and then their needs connect them with each other by the relations between sexes, between the rulers and the ruled, the relations of the division of labor, production, exchange, and so forth. Since each individual is determined by all the others with whom he is directly or indirectly associated and this reciprocal bond changes throughout history, man has no fixed essence to be distinguished from his accidental characteristics. "The difference between the individual as a person and what is accidental to him, is not a conceptual difference but a historical fact", and has a different significance at different times.[70] What may appear as an incidental characteristic at some time or other is as much the outcome of the social relationships and corresponding productive forces as are the characteristics the philosophers call the 'essence of man'. There is no Man distinct from real men, no human nature other than man's social relations of production which, in the words of the *Communist Manifesto*, are "continually subject to historical change consequent upon the change in historical conditions". In particular, it is absurd to believe that the essence of an animal or human individual is that mode of life and activity in which "its 'essence' feels itself satisfied". If man's nature reflects the structure of society, then all its manifestations are equally expressions of man's essence. In *The German Ideology* Marx emphasized that human nature is entirely constituted by the interaction of concrete individuals, and, according to the Sixth Thesis on Feuerbach, men are what they actually do.[71]

Marx resorted to a normative concept of social man in support of his humanistic outlook and used it as an absolute standard for the evaluation of the alienated world, since he was unable at that time to oppose the doctrines of classical political economists in other ways. He could not provide an analysis of wealth created by commodity production; he had no labor theory of value of his own and no theory of surplus value; he did not clearly understand the distinction between constant capital and variable capital from which the proposition about the fall of the average rate of profit was to be derived. Since Marx was not able until much later to inquire into the social origins of alienated labor, he derived alienated labor from his philosophical anthropology and view of ideal society that fulfilled what he regarded as the essential requirements of human nature.

In the *Manuscripts* Marx argued at first that alienated labor was the inevitable consequence of private property, but later came to the conclusion that private property was the outcome of alienated labor, just as the gods are the effect of man's intellectual confusion and not its cause.[72] This conclusion gave rise to the question – "How does man come to alienate his labor? How is this alienation rooted in the nature of human development?"[73] Although the question remained unanswered in the *Manuscripts*, the course of further investigation concerning the socio-economic causes of alienated labor was set. This investigation required the abandonment of the partly Hegelian and partly Feuerbachian conceptual framework that is a peculiar feature of the *Manuscripts*; the concepts of generic man, self-consciousness, human essence, the dialectics of negativity or species being might have been useful in a philosophical discussion and moral evaluation of the social conditions in the capitalist society, but were inappropriate for an economic investigation of them. The search for the answer to the question, 'How does man come to alienate his labor and what is the historical and social significance of this development?' began in *The German Ideology* where the causes of alienation were traced back to the division of labor, commodity production, formation of social classes, property relations within the mode of production based on the antagonism of capital and wage-labor, and class-dominated state power. From that stage onwards the term 'alienation' was not abandoned but its use was entirely changed. 'Alienation' did not mean any longer 'the estrangement from man's essential nature' or 'the loss of the product of labor' or 'the surrender of an inalienable part of man's person'; the state of alienation was not derived from man's generic nature or discovered by comparison of the prevailing conditions with the ideal ones. Alienation became a social-psychological concept, rooted in the historical development of the pre-industrial to capitalist society, reflecting the impact of the division of labor, class struggle, and technology on the social relations of production in the experience of the individuals involved. Since alienation was derived from the nature of social labor in industrial society rather than from the requirements of human nature in ideal society, and since the necessity of social labor is independent of the mode of production, social-economic alienation, in one form or another, is bound to survive capitalism. Unlike alienation in the philosophical or ethical sense, socio-economic alienation cannot ever be entirely overcome (contrary to what the *Manuscripts* seem to imply), although it can be reduced, especially by increasing leisure time at the expense of working time (as the *Grundrisse* and *Capital* seem to indicate). The range of activities and enjoyment they provide to the individual, Marx claimed in a striking passage of *Grundrisse*, depend on economy of time, and, thus, "economy of time . . . remains the first economic law on the basis of communal production".[74]

The abandonment of the philsophy of alienation does not imply that Marx gave up the moral concern which underlies this philosophy and which today is often confused or equated with it. Marx's critique of capitalist society was inspired by moral indignation, as manifest in the *Manuscripts*, in the *Grundrisse* and *Capital*. But these works differ radically in their language, assumptions, conceptual frameworks, and mode of analysis. No comprehensive knowledge of the economics and sociology of Marx is necessary to recognize the fact that his modified labor theory of value and his theory of surplus value gave a better account of the facts than his philosophy of alienation. This philosophy, tainted by its speculative origin and normative content, was superseded by a new, more comprehensive and powerful economic and sociological theory.

There are Marxian scholars who maintain that this conclusion is utterly mistaken, since the disappearance of the philosophy of alienation from the mature system of Marx is only apparent. As one of them put it, "alienation remains his [Marx's] central theme, but it has gone underground in his image of society." [75] In view of what has been said earlier about the reconstruction of the concept of alienation in the mature works of Marx, and about the indisputable advance of Marx beyond the compass of his early studies, it is hardly possible to treat seriously the contention that the whole work of Marx is a continuing meditation on central themes of the *Manuscripts*. Those who hold such a belief reflect the interests, trends, and moral malaise of the present times rather than the thought and concern of Marx.

REFERENCES

[1] M. Rosenthal and P. Yudin (eds.), *A Dictionary of Philosophy*, Moscow: Progress Publishers, 1967, pp. 67–68.

[2] Frederick Engels, *Anti-Dühring*, Moscow: Foreign Languages Publishing House, 1959, p. 194; *Dialectics of Nature*, Moscow: Foreign Languages Publishing House, 1954, p. 353.

[3] Karl Marx, *Ökonomisch-Philosophische Manuskripte*, were published in an English translation in Moscow: Foreign Languages Publishing House, 1959, under the above-given title and will be referred to as *Manuscripts*.

[4] Karl Marx, *Grundrisse der Kritik der politischen Ökonomie (Rohentwurf)*, Berlin: Dietz Verlag, 1953, referred to below as *Grundrisse*. An English translation of this work is available under the title *Grundrisse: Foundations of the Critique of Political Economy (Rough Draft)*, London: Allen Lane, 1973, and will be referred to as *Foundations*.

[5] Lukács and Korsch were aware that their books were related to the aftermath of World War I, especially in Germany and Eastern Europe, but they were anxious to influence revolutionary political thought and social movement all over the world. Despite important similarities their views diverge on a number of salient points. Nevertheless, Korsch wrote, "Lukács and I are objectively on the same side in our critical attitude towards the old Social Democratic Marxist orthodoxy and the new Communist orthodoxy. This is, after all, the central issue" (*Marxism and Philosophy*, London: NLB, 1970, p. 92). Their basic agreement included their views on the philosophy of Marx.

[6] Georg Lukács, *History and Class Consciousness: Studies in Marxist Dialectics*, Cambridge, Mass.: MIT Press, 1971, pp. XLII–XLIII. For a more detailed criticism of Engels see pp. 131–33, 198–200.

[7] Karl Korsch, *Marxism and Philosophy*, p. 80. Korsch was more outspoken in his later work and openly opposed the claim that Marx's historical materialism sprang from and was theoretically dependent upon metaphysical materialism. See Karl Korsch, *Karl Marx*, New York: Russell & Russell, 1963 (first published in 1938), pp. 167–71 and *passim*.

[8] When Jean-Paul Sartre writes of Engels that he "a tué la dialectique en prétendant la découvrir dans la nature," (*Critique de la raison dialectique*, Paris: Gallimard, 1960, tome I, p. 690), he has ranged himself on the side of Korsch and Lukács. For the critique of dialectical materialism as a sociomorphic projection into the cosmos of certain ways of viewing social life, see my *Evolution of Dialectical Materialism: A Philosophical and Sociological Analysis*, London & New York: Macmillan and St.

Martin's Press, 1967. pp. 205 ff., and the contributions of Philip G. Frank and Ernst Topitsch, which are cited there. More recently, Jacques Monod, the French biologist, has argued that dialectical materialism is one more attempt to re-establish the animistic covenant between man and Nature that is traceable back to mankind's infancy and is expressed in the belief that "natural phenomena can and must be explained in the same manner, by the same 'laws', as subjective human activity, conscious and purposive." (*Chance and Necessity: An Essay on the Natural Philosophy of Modern Biology*, New York: Vintage Books, 1972, pp. 30–31).

[9] Dialectics can be extended, however, to scientific theories of Nature, since natural science is a product of human activity and is rooted in society and history.

[10] Korsch, *Marxism and Philosophy*, p. 82.

[11] Lukács, *History and Class Consciousness*, pp. 5–15, 149–59; Korsch, *Marxism and Philosophy*, p. 68; cf. pp. 51–52, 63, 83.

[12] Immanuel Kant, *Kritik der Urteilskraft*, in *Werke*, ed. Ernst Cassirer, Berlin: Verlegt bei Bruno Cassirer, 1922, B. 5, p. 240; *The Critique of Judgment*, Oxford: Clarendon Press, 1952, p. 9; Nicholas Lobkowicz, *Theory and Practice: History of a Concept from Aristotle to Marx*, Notre Dame-London: University of Notre Dame Press, 1967, pp. 124–27.

[13] George Lichtheim, *From Marx to Hegel and Other Essays*, London: Orbach & Chambers, 1971, p. 57. Cf. Korsch, *Marxism and Philosophy*, pp. 109 ff.

[14] Frederick Engels, *Ludwig Feuerbach and the End of the Classical German Philosophy*, in Karl Marx and Frederick Engels, *Selected Works in Two Volumes*, Moscow: Foreign Languages Publishing House, 1951, vol. II, p. 336, 364; *Karl Marx: A Contribution to the Critique of Political Economy*, in *Selected Works in Two Volumes*, vol. I, p. 338.

[15] Lukács, *History and Class Consciousness*, pp. 111ff.

[16] Marx called the *Phenomenology* "the birthplace of the Hegelian philosophy" and this observation is of considerable significance. The *Phenomenology* and *Philosophy of Right* had a more enduring and significant influence on Marx than *Science of Logic* and the *Encyclopedia*. The *Phenomenology* is also the prime source of Lukács' Hegelianized Marxism. According to Lukács, the *Science of Logic* contained a new logic of totality and of the relations of the parts to the whole, but its first formulation in the *Phenomenology* remained, really, unsurpassed even by Hegel in his later works (*History and Class Consciousness*, pp. 141–42, 215, fn. 54, 25, fn. 14). Walter Kaufmann observed that the basic idea of the *Phenomenology* is that "a philosopher should not confine himself to views that have been held but penetrate behind these to the human reality they reflect" (*Hegel: Reinterpretation, Texts and Commentary*, London: Weidenfeld and Nicolson, 1966, p. 133). Kaufmann's comment makes it easier to understand why the *Phenomenology* was for Marx and Lukács Hegel's highest achievement. This cannot be said either of Engels or Lenin for whom *Science of Logic* and the *Encyclopedia* were the most important works of Hegel and the fountainhead of their naturalized Hegelianism.

[17] Marx, *Manuscripts*, p. 149. In a less respectful comment, this triad becomes an instance of "the consecrating formula... of pure reason, separated from the individual" which is realized by affirmation. negation, and negation of the negation. (Karl Marx, *The Poverty of Philosophy*, Moscow: Foreign Languages Publishing House, n.d., p. 101.)

[18] Karl Marx and Frederick Engels, *The Holy Family or Critique of Critical Critique*, Moscow: Foreign Languages Publishing House, 1956, p. 125.

[19] The opposite view, which emphasizes the endorsement of Hegel's philosophy at the expense of its critique, has had the most influence on the *Manuscripts'* reception in recent years.

[20] See Z. A. Jordan, *Philosophy and Ideology: The Development of Philosophy and Marxism-Leninism in Poland Since the Second World War*, Dordrecht: D. Reidel Publishing Company, 1963, Ch. 18; *The Evolution of Dialectical Materialism: A Philosophical and Sociological Analysis*, Ch. II, 3.

[21] Marx, *Manuscripts*, pp. 149–50. Lukács made the same error in his *History and Class Consciousness*; he himself later discovered it and recognized it in the preface to the 1967 German edition of the book. In the *Grundrisse* Marx ascribed Hegel's conceptual confusion to bourgeois economists who mistook the necessity of a particular stage of social development for a universal necessity of production. See *Grundrisse*, p. 716; *Foundations*, p. 832.

[22] Marx, *Manuscripts*, pp. 81, 149. Marx used 'abstract' in the Hegelian sense; Hegel meant by 'abstract' the quality of being partial and incomplete. He called 'abstract' whatever was considered from a specific and single standpoint, and unrelated or severed from connections to other things. 'Abstract' was a derogatory term and, if this emotive meaning predominated, it qualified a mode of thinking which Hegel and Marx regarded as philosophically inadequate.

[23] Karl Marx, *Capital: A Critique of Political Economy*, Moscow: Foreign Languages Publishing House, 1959, vol. III, p. 109 (cf. Ernest Mandel, *The Formation of the Economic Thought of Karl Marx*, New York and London: Monthly Review Press, 1971, Ch. 7); Marx, *Manuscripts*, pp. 72, 103; *Grundrisse*, pp. 79–80, 354; *Foundations*, pp. 162, 451.

[24] For a detailed distinction of the different forms of socio-economic alieration see Z. A. Jordan, 'Socialism, Alienation, and Political Power', *Survey* (July 1966), no. 60, pp. 126–29; Iring Fetscher, *Marx and Marxism*, New York: Herder and Herder, 1971, pp. 9–15.

[25] Lukács, and also Korsch, had adopted this view long before it became a controversial issue. See *History and Class Consciousness*, pp. XXVI, XLV.

[26] Jean Hyppolite, *Studies on Marx and Hegel*, London: Heinemann, 1969, p. 95. Since the inclusion of Herbert Marcuse in this school of thought may be challenged. it is advisable to support it by reference to his *Reason and Revolution: Hegel and the Rise of Social Theory*, Boston: Beacon Press, 1960, pp. 258ff.

[27] See e.g., Robert Tucker, *Philosophy and Myth in Karl Marx*, Cambridge: The University Press, 1961, p. 174.

[28] Raymond Aron believes that the two ways of interpreting Marxism "are not fundamentally incompatible," since "they have hardly anything in common but the name" (*Marxism and the Existentialists*, New York: Simon and Schuster, 1965, pp. 112–13). Aron's definition of the two approaches is too vague to allow any dividing line to be drawn and, above all, ignores the crucial difference of the theories of knowledge which underlie them. For this point see Jordan, *The Evolution of Dialectical Materialism*, pp. 27–34.

[29] For the criticism of naive realism that underlies the orthodox approach see Korsch, *Marxism and Philosophy*, pp. 76ff., 108–109, and my *Philosophy and Ideology*, Ch. 16.

[30] Marx, *Manuscripts*, p. 70; *Capital: A Critical Analysis of Capitalist Production*, Moscow: Foreign Languages Publishing House, 1958, vol. I, pp. 178, 508.

[31] Marx and Engels, *The Holy Family*, p. 65.

[32] Hegel, *Philosophy of Right*, #54, 56.

[33] Marx, *Grundrisse*, p. 9; *Foundations*, p. 87.

[34] Karl Marx, *Wage Labour and Capital*, in Marx and Engels, *Selected Works in Two Volumes*, vol. I, p. 83.

[35] Karl Marx. *Capital*, vol. I, p. 177; cf. Engels, *Dialectics of Nature*, p. 228: "Labour created man himself."

[36] Marx, *Capital*, vol. I, pp. 183–84; cf. 42–43.

[37] Marx, *Manuscripts*, pp. 103–104, 168–70.

[38] Marx, *Manuscripts*, p. 133.

[39] Karl Marx and Frederick Engels, *The German Ideology*, London: Lawrence and Wishart, 1965, pp. 43–45.

[40] Karl Marx, *Theses on Feuerbach*, in Karl Marx and Frederick Engels, *Selected Works in Two Volumes*, vol. II, Thesis VI, p. 366. In *The German Ideology* the words *Verkehr* and *Verkehrverhältnisse* ('intercourse' or 'association') are used to replace *Gattungswesen* and their place is taken in turn by *die gesellschaftlichen Verhältnisse* in Marx's later writings. *Gattungswesen* reappears in the *Grundrisse*, where, however, it refers to a stage of human evolution that is intermediate between a herdlike existence and a properly social or political life in the Aristotelian sense.

[41] Marx, *Grundrisse*, p. 137; *Foundations*, p. 226.

[42] Marx and Engels, *The German Ideology*, p. 87; Marx, *Manuscripts*, p. 69. 'Objectification' is *Vergegenständlichung* but Lukács and Marcuse use *Verdinglichung* ('reification') to discuss objectification in the Marxian sense. The two expressions are not synonymous, either in English or in German, and treating them as synonymous may and does cause misunderstandings among Marx's readers.

[43] Marx, *Manuscripts*, pp. 69–70, 83.

[44] Marx, *Manuscripts*, p. 151: "Hegel . . . conceives objectification as loss of the object, as alienation (*Entaüsserung*)"; Jordan, 'Socialism, Alienation and Political Power', p. 127.

[45] Karl Marx, *On the Jewish Question*, in *Writings of the Young Marx on Philosophy and Society* (ed. by Lloyd D. Easton and Kurt H. Guddat, New York: Anchor Books, 1967, pp. 225, 246; *Towards the Critique of Hegel's Philosophy of Law: Introduction, Ibid.*, pp. 257–58. See also Jordan, 'Socialism, Alienation, and Political Power', p. 122. 'Marxist humanism' is rarely defined by those who use the term and Adam Schaff is a welcome exception to this rule (*Marxism and Human Individual*, New York: McGraw-Hill, 1970, p. 168); his definition does not differ importantly from mine. George L. Kline ('Was Marx an Ethical Humanist?', *Studies in Soviet Thought*, vol. 9 (1969), pp. 91–103) claims that Marx's humanism has no ethical content, is humanism of ideals and not of principles, but he himself offers some evidence that undermines his conclusion. He has a strange bedfellow in Louis Althusser, *For Marx*, London: Allen Lane, 1969, pp. 221ff., who also claims that Marx's humanism is essentially an ideology.

[46] Tucker, *Philosophy and Myth in Karl Marx*, Ch. XIV.

[47] See Eugene Kamenka, *Marxism and Ethics*, London: Macmillan, 1969, Ch. II, where the interpretation offered above is discussed in greater detail. Marx analyzed 'human' and 'inhuman' as if they were descriptive predicates in *The German Ideology*, pp. 475–76.

[48] Self-alienation and alienation are also concepts of Hegel's social and political thought (*Philosophy of Right*, #65–70, 153, 264); they go back to, but are independent of, his philosophy of alienation in the *Phenomenology*. 'Alienation' in *Philosophy of Right* means the disruption of the individual's unity with the social substance (*die sittliche Substanz*), that is, with his political, social and cultural institutions, through

which alone man achieves universality. The universal and essential nature of man implies certain inalienable (*unveraüsserlich* means also unsaleable) rights, *die Menschenrechte* in Marx's terminology, and these rights cannot be separated from or surrendered by any individual if he is to remain a person. Hegel used the term *Entaüsserung* to refer to this disruption of the unity with the social substance and to the surrender or loss of inalienable rights (as far as I am aware, *Entfremdung* does not occur in *Philosophy of Right* at all, although it does in the *Phenomenology*, where it is used synonymously with *Entaüsserung*), and discussed the alienation from one's personality, rationality, morality or religion. The Marxian concept of the alienation from others closely resembles the Hegelian split of the individual from the social substance and the Marxian concept of self-alienation seems to be derived from the Hegelian idea of the loss of inalienable rights that turns a person into an object, deprives him of self-determination or makes him dependent upon the will of others. The alienation of labor-power is unobjectionable to Hegel. Hegel regarded the alienation of productive capacity as a contract and, as the alienation is restricted in time and in other respects, the surrender is not a loss of anything inalienable (*Philosophy of Right*, #67, 80). For Marx labor as wage labor was deprived of its human dignity and could hardly be distinguished from forced labor and slavery (Manuscripts, pp. 72, 81). For a brief but enlightening discussion of Marx's view on the rights of man see Easton and Guddat (eds.), *Writings of the Young Marx on Philosophy and Society*, pp. 31–32.

[49] Cf. Lawrence Krader (ed.), *The Ethnological Notebooks of Karl Marx*, Assen: Van Gorcum & Company, 1972, p. 85.

[50] Marx, *Manuscripts*, pp. 79–80, 149, 151, 153, 166.

[51] Marx and Engels, *The German Ideology*, p. 654.

[52] Marx, *Manuscripts*, pp. 79, 80.

[53] Hegel, *Vorlesungen über die Philosophie der Religion, in Sämtliche Werke* (ed. by H. Glockner), Stuttgart: Friedrich Frommann Verlag, 1965, B. 15, p. 19; *Encyclopedia*, #377 ff.; *Philosophy of Right*, #182–95. For a more detailed presentation of Hegel's concept of man see Karl Löwith, *From Hegel to Nietzsche: The Revolution in Nineteenth-Century Thought*, London: Constable, 1965, pp. 307–310. Marx's statement "society produces man as man" (*Manuscripts*, p. 103), seems to be a reformulation of Hegel's dictum in *Lectures on the Philosophy of Religion*.

[54] Marx, *Manuscripts*, p. 152.

[55] Marx, *Manuscripts*, pp. 150, 153, 155–56; Marx and Engels, *The Holy Family*, pp. 105–117; *The German Ideology*, pp. 29–31; *Manifesto of the Communist Party*, in Marx and Engels, *Selected Works in Two Volumes*, vol. I, p. 55. For Marx's criticism of Max Stirner's concept of man see *The German Ideology*, pp. 284–85, 315–16.

[56] Ludwig Feuerbach, *The Essence of Christianity*, New York: Harper Torchbooks, 1957, pp. 1–3; Marx, *Manuscripts*, pp. 75–76; Marx and Engels, *The German Ideology*, p. 42. Feuerbach's "I and Thou" seems to be a different formulation of Hegel's statement "An *I* which is a *We*, and a *We* which is an *I*", although Hegel's statement is metaphysical rather than anthropological or sociological (*Phänomenologie des Geistes*, Frankfurt am Main: Suhrkamp Verlag, 1973, p. 145; for an interpretation of the quoted passage see J. N. Findlay, *Hegel; A Re-examination*, New York: Collier Books, 1962, pp. 94–95). It should be noted that Marx's criticism of Malthus' theory of population is ultimately derived from the differences between man and the brute. There is a universally valid law of population for plants and animals but none for man. "Every historic mode of production has its own laws of population, historically valid within its limits alone" (*Capital*, vol. I, p. 632; cf. p. 529).

[57] Marx, *Manuscripts*. p. 156; *Capital*, vol. I, p. 178.
[58] Marx and Engels, *The German Ideology*, pp. 39, 87. That the multiplication of needs differentiates man from animals is a view that Marx might have adopted from Hegel's *Philosophy of Right* (≠189–95).
[59] Marx and Engels, *The German Ideology*, p. 50.
[60] Marx, *Manuscripts*, p. 156.
[61] Marx, *Manuscripts*, p. 103. In the Marxian usage, only 'productive labor' or 'material production' refer to the economic process by which the material means of satisfying human needs are produced.
[62] Marx and Engels, *The German Ideology*, p. 87.
[63] Marx, *Manuscripts*, pp. 28, 30, 31, 67, 69–73, 112; *Wage Labour and Capital*, in Marx and Engels, *Selected Works in Two Volumes*, vol. I p. 77; Marx and Engels, *The German Ideology*, p. 312.
[64] Marx, *Manuscripts*, pp. 29, 69; Marx, *The Poverty of Philosophy*, p. 119.
[65] Marx and Engels, *The Holy Family*, pp. 49–50.
[66] Marx, *Manuscripts*, pp. 30, 67, 85.
[67] Karl Marx, *Aus den Excerptheften: Die entfremdete und die unentfremdete Gesellschaft, Geld, Kredit und Menschlichkeit*, in Karl Marx und Friedrich Engels, *Studienausgabe* (ed. by I. Fetscher), Frankfurt am Main: Fischer Bücherei, 1966, B. II, pp. 252–53, 261. The famous phrase 'life's prime want' occurs in the *Critique of the Gotha Program* (Marx and Engels, *Selected Works in Two Volumes*, vol. II, p. 23), but the concept of labor which it expresses underlies the critique of capitalism in the *Manuscripts* (p. 72 and *passim*). Labor is bound to be alienating unless it is a spontaneous and free activity that develops the producer's physical and mental capacities. Richard T. De George, starting from a different point of departure, has also reached the conclusion that both the Marxian and contemporary Soviet concept of man involve normative assumptions ('The Soviet Concept of Man', *Studies in Soviet Thought*, vol. 4 (1964), pp. 261–276). He rightly points out that the main differences between the Soviet and Western views of man seem to lie in the evaluative rather than descriptive characteristics that are used in the construction of the concept.
[68] Marx, *Manuscripts*, pp. 82, 102, 103, 104–105 and *passim*; *On the Jewish Question*, in Easton and Guddat (eds.), *The Writings of the Young Marx on Philosophy and Society*, pp. 235, 237, 247.
[69] Marx and Engels, *The German Ideology*, p. 41.
[70] Marx and Engels, *The German Ideology*, pp. 87, 481–82.
[71] Marx and Engels, *The German Ideology*, pp. 32, 50, 54, 84; *Capital*, vol. I, p. 609. Marx referred to Feuerbach's *Grundsätze der Philosophie der Zukunft* as the source of the view that a characteristic is essential if it provides satisfaction, but I was unable to locate it in that work. Marx's own belief that labor is an enjoyment of life is a specific version of the view he seems to criticize in *The German Ideology*.
[72] Marx, *Manuscripts*, pp. 67, 80.
[73] Marx, *Manuscripts*, p. 82.
[74] Marx, *Grundrisse*, p. 89; *Foundations*, pp. 172–73.
[75] Tucker, *Philosophy and Myth in Karl Marx*, p. 176; cf. David McLellan, *Marx's Grundrisse*, London: Macmillan, 1971, p. 12.

IVAN SVITÁK

MARXIST PHILOSOPHY IN CZECHOSLOVAKIA:
THE LESSONS FROM PRAGUE

"Märtyrer ohne Wirkung, das ist
etwas Sinnloses."

KURT TUCHOLSKY

I. STALINISM IN CZECHOSLOVAKIA

Philosophy usually is a much more important discipline in the left wing tradition than in the tradition of power elites, which regard a worldview only as impractical speculation. For the political Left philosophy as a rule represents an arsenal of ideas and is correctly appreciated as a considerable potential force because the Left can rely not on power, but only on the strength of reason, ideas, and judgment. Philosophy is the natural ally of the political Left. This is true of the democratic tradition of humanism, the tradition of the working class movement, and also of the first phase of revolutionary Communism in the U.S.S.R. In this last instance, however, philosophy was negated in a peculiar way during the Stalin era because it was transformed into both an instrument for controlling the masses and an irrational mythology.

Young people are always attracted by philosophy, but this is doubly true of times when the world is fundamentally reorganized as was the case toward the end of the last world war. For the young people who grew up toward the end of the war, philosophy (or rather ideology) assumed key importance because it facilitated their political orientation and supplied answers to the most urgent social and political problems of the postwar world. The people who became about twenty years old by 1945 did not look to a worldview for the Olympian peace of Platonic reflections or for the depths of their own existence, but rather for some sort of safeguard of values and a guarantee of the significance of the social changes they were living through. Under these circumstances, it was perhaps inevitable that it was Marx's social philosophy which became the decisive ideological force for the young Czech generation, although the ideological spokesmen of this generation were not able to realize that they were accepting the

De George and Scanlan (eds.), Marxism and Religion in Eastern Europe, 45–62. All Rights Reserved.
Copyright © 1976 by D. Reidel Publishing Company, Dordrecht-Holland.

Stalinist forgery of Marxism instead of the genuine original. The surrender
to Stalinist ideology was as rapid and spontaneous as the subsequent
emancipation was troublesome and slow. Ideology is not a conscious lie,
but an illusion of the epoch, a radical simplification which is always based
on people's everyday experience. It was not Hegel's adventure of dialectics,
but that consistent interpretation of history, that dreadful clarity of the
analysis of capitalism which attracted the young Czechs to Marxist philosophy. Socialism appeared as an unquestionable truth, appealing by its
obviousness to the total man. Youth does not realize the limits of truth
because a young person accepts either the total truth or nothing at all.
Youth does not have a sense of compromise and lacks the very premise
of tolerance – that is, the consciousness that "our thinking is conditioned
thinking" (Max Frisch).

Tolerance represents only the later developmental phase of mature and
strong personalities. If someone regards his own view as a panacea, he
must force its acceptance upon others and thus become an inquisitor
precisely because he must exculpate, rehabilitate, or justify himself before
history by his deeds. It is therefore not surprising that disillusionment
took place only after the young Czech generation had gained experience
with the new faith during approximately the next ten years. The year
1956 confirmed its conviction that it had fallen into a trap. The history of
Czech thought in the 1950's and 1960's reflects above all this dramatic
transformation of social consciousness, the intellectual development of
this generation against the background of the Cold War and the frequent
radical ideological changes which accompanied the zigzag road of emancipation from Stalinist ideology. To put it in simplified terms, the history
of Czech thought during the past three decades is the road from Masaryk
to Stalin and back which, according to the criteria of full-blooded Stalinism, logically appears as submission to revisionism.[1] In order to be able to
describe any view as a revision of another view, however, we must accept
a priori the former view as the criterion of reality and truth. As a result,
the very designation of an opinion as revisionism constitutes a pseudo-
problem obscuring the fundamental issue – the truth about reality itself.

If the revision of a previously held view is regarded as a mistake, however, we must reject intellectual development, accept the stagnation of
principles, and violate a basic rule – namely, that people's ideas and
actions must be judged in the light of the reality produced by their ideas

and not according to the motivations underlying their actions. Insofar as we are able to see what happens, to understand history and express it, then we are outside of ideology and it does not make much difference to us whether we are classified as orthodox or revisionist. On the other hand, if we affirm ideology – that is, secularized religious faith – in the purity of its primary principles, then every revision is *a priori* a mistake even if it is not in conflict with the facts. Revisionism thus always is a pseudo-problem or a mortal sin, but nothing else. If we want to describe the development of Czech thought, it would be best to discard the ambivalent term 'revisionism' and to evaluate only what actually happened and what was really intended. This however is impossible because under the conditions of a totalitarian regime the value of thought does not depend only upon whether or not it is true, but also upon whether or not it contains criticism. So long as orthodoxy is institutionally (by laws and the Constitution) insured, we cannot, unfortunately, get rid of the pseudoproblem of revisionism, precisely because we cannot free ourselves of the institutional basis of orthodoxy which generates revisionism. The development of the Stalinist ideology in Czechoslovakia thus appears as any other ideological development, namely as the sequence of revisions which are necessitated by actual historical development, and which transform (frequently into comical paradoxes and antinomies) the ideological foundation of the movement.

According to Marx, ideology – that is, false consciousness – does not develop because it has no logic but is only a continuity of errors. A logician is the slave of facts, a romantic is the slave of dreams, and an ideologist is the slave of his own false consciousness. In other words, what appears as an independent development of thought, as a development of ideology, is nothing other than a continuous revision, then a revision of the revision, then a revision of the revised revision, a revised revision of the revised revision and so on – until the consistency of thought and reality which ideology wants to express is so small that philosophy degenerates into simple apologetics. If the real link with reality vanishes from it, living philosophy becomes academically acceptable and the fruitful connection of ideas with deeds is sacrificed to the consistency of dogmas which is scrupulously guarded by censorship and police power. And this is precisely the situation which stimulates the genuine philosophers to action, which transcends the academic horizon and which is existentially important because it destroys the false consciousness of reality (that is, ideology) and replaces it by implacable truth which is as limpid as water. Ideologies offer an ideal in accordance with which one can act with a feeling of security; they offer a map of the universe and a total transformation of society and man – an ideological authority which frees the individual from responsibility and, in addition, offers him a total understanding of the world. Ideology is a secularized religion, it is a substitute for the relinquished faith in the absolute.

So long as the supporters of the salutary ideal do not have torture chambers and armies at their disposal, they are harmless. As soon as they assume power, however, and have the opportunity to translate their ideas into reality, not only do the 'idealists' begin to change into terrorists, but also the function of ideology is transformed into a political myth which sanctions any despotism. The Czechs and Slovaks did not defy this rule. In Czechoslovakia also, Marxism – originally a mortal enemy of any ideology – was transformed into an instrument of Stalinist bureaucracy when it became state ideology, and when the philosophy of the revolutionary movement became the doctrine of the reactionary practice of a bureaucracy. It is absolutely erroneous to see in this transformation of Marxism into Stalinism a betrayal of original ideals or a degeneration of ideas; because what appeared on the surface as ideologically a seemingly insignificant shift in emphasis in the interpretation of the doctrine, was not caused by the moral degeneration of leaders or the apathy of the masses, but was a parallel to the fundamental transformation of the social structure and an epiphenomenon of the formation of the new class. For Lenin's generation of revolutionists, socialism still represented a classless and stateless society which could not be built in one country. For the next generation of bureaucrats the problem of the nature of the Soviet state vanished in the false consciousness of the theory of 'socialism in one country'. Stalin coped with the Gordian knot of the isolated revolution by smashing the heads of those who saw a Gordian knot in the isolated revolution. In both the U.S.S.R. and Czechoslovakia, socialism as a vision of a classless society vanished and only a myth of the New Man remained – a myth whose destruction took twenty years.

Stalinism as the practice of socialism in one country was a mockery of international and humanistic ideology of socialism, and represented a strong dose of the dialectics of contradictions between intentions and results. The 'trick of history' also killed millions of Hegel's adherents, on the right and on the left – the former in the battle of Stalingrad, the latter in the Siberian concentration camps. In light of the Soviet parody of socialism the policy of Western European social democratic parties was, of course, revisionism – as was every Communist but non-Stalinist position, both to the right and to the left of the Soviet point of view. Authentic Marxism has thus become, in the Soviet interpretation, revisionism – that is, a heretical deviation, regardless of the facts that the first workers' upheavals in Western Europe (and also in Bohemia) took place fifty years before the foundation of the first Russian Marxist organization, and that the Czech social democratic movement had already had twenty years' experience with Marx when the young Lenin began to organize the first cells in Petrograd. 'Revisionism' thus had a long tradition in Czechoslovakia; and during the interwar period, which brought the Bolshevization of the left wing of the Czech working class movement, the Communist Party preserved the character of a mass political party and a lawful movement; in other words, something which the Czech communists – even against their will – had in common with 'social democratism'.

Under normal circumstances, common sense would necessarily reach the conclusion that the tactics employed by three per cent of the proletariat in the Russian sea of illiteracy and despotism could not be repeated by one third of the Czech nation representing the working class of a democratic state; in other words, Leninism appeared as a specifically Russian phenomenon which could not be exported. Stalin, however, did not let himself be guided by the common sense of the Czech Communists, and as soon as they came to power, he forced them to accept Stalinist practice and theory. For this reason, those ideas which did not fit into the program of organizing a totalitarian state were periodically declared to constitute revisionism. In the torrent of insults described as discussions, the terms 'Zionism', 'social democratism,' 'bourgeois nationalism,' 'Titoism,' 'Trotskyism,' and 'revisionism' were more or less employed as codes signaling a simple fact that somebody had deviated from the road safeguarded by the police, having been confused by his normal common sense, genuine socialist ideas, or the illusion that bureaucracy was indeed interested in implementing Marx's tenets. It is, of course, difficult to determine to what extent the revisionists deviated from the party line, but it is certain that their views have always been labeled by the party apparatus

as non-party, hostile, and dangerous opinions. The question whether or
not such views represented a revision of Marx's ideas is not of great importance. But they were deemed non-party views, if they opposed the
given policy, and bureaucracy had to make a decision on them.

After T. G. Masaryk there were not many Czech thinkers who had
something to say to the world. From the older generation there perhaps
were only Václav Černý, Jan Mukařovský, Zenek Nejedlý, Jan Patočka,
and Karel Teige whose work met with a response outside Czechoslovakia.
The younger group of Marxist philosophers, the present middle generation, perhaps met with a bigger response but only because under the
social conditions prevailing in Czechoslovakia in the 1960's the post-
Stalin ideology found itself in such a ferment that it became interesting as
a document of disintegration of the previously homogeneous ideology,
as a lethal mutation of Marxism. Regardless of what the philosophers
thought of it, the process of disintegration of Czech 'Marxism' (or, to put
it more accurately, Stalinism) was only a marginal event in the cold war
and strictly a local affair. It is for us an unflattering truth, but it is so, although in the euphoria of the year 1968 the ideology of 'socialism with a
human face' would almost seem to be a panacea for mankind.[1]

Three decades of intellectual development of this middle generation of
Czechoslovak philosophers are marked by a remarkable spiral of transformations, which after dramatic changes culminated approximately
where the process began after World War II. The contradictions between
system and method in the philosophy of Marxism led the ideologists of
Czech reformism to the politically erroneous and materially eclectic conclusion that 'Marxism' (that is, Stalinism) was in fact an open system
which is capable of absorbing Western philosophy, science, and psycho-
analysis. The Soviet occupation – the absolute failure of reformist policy
and philosophical revisionism – signified the end of 'open Marxism' and
thus also a new confrontation of 'Marxism' (that is, Stalinism) with new
views – not only with the bourgeois democratic ideology, but also with
the New Left and its Marxist (though non-Stalinist, but class) analysis of
given conditions. Following its adventure with dialectics, Czech thought
again regains common sense, which shows the Czech state as a totalitarian
dictatorship, and turns away from the forgeries perpetrated by 'Marxism'
(Stalinism). Czech philosophy thus acts as an intermediary in furnishing
the experience that the end of an ideological monopoly also means the

end of Stalinism, which has already lost all ground in Czechoslovakia and can only fade away and rot. This is not a tragedy, but a positive process of emancipation from illusions and the destruction of myths. If there are still philosophers in Czechoslovakia today, they are the people who repeat with Feuerbach: "Keine Philosophie – meine Philosophie".

II. DIALECTICS OF METAPHYSICS

> No one was the object of such lethal hatred or such terrible police and political persecution as the independent left wing or any Communist or communizing movement critical of Stalinist practice and dogma.... From time to time the press could publish statements by bourgeois politicians, but this was unthinkable for activists of the non-Stalinist left.
>
> LESZEK KOŁAKOWSKI,
> *History and Responsibility*

The development of Stalinism breaks down into three qualitatively distinct phases. The first phase – short but very important (1945–1948) – gave birth to the theory of the Czechoslovak road to socialism as a complex of measures enacted by the coalition government of non-Communists and Communists. Marxism was still expounded in Czechoslovakia at the time in two different (Communist and social democratic) variants, and democratic socialism was accepted as the future prospect by a considerable majority of the nation. The year 1948 signified a radical change in this development because democratic socialism as an ideology and social democracy as a political party, as well as the non-Communist working class movement, all vanished from the scene and were excluded from participation in political life. Soon afterwards the Communist theory of a specific road to socialism was condemned as Rudolf Slánský's revisionist deviation. We thus witnessed in Czechoslovakia the repetition of the phenomenon, well-known from the history of Soviet Communism, that the defeated political platform was retroactively classified as revisionism, although this platform represented the official party line during the preceding period. The Communist Party of Czechoslovakia maintained until 1950 that the Czechoslovak road to socialism constituted a creative application of Marxism to Czechoslovak conditions.

This radical change in philosophy was carried out by radical students who disrupted the lectures of non-Marxists, positivists, and existentialists, with the result that the conflict between 'Marxism' (that is Stalinism) and 'non-Marxism' was settled not by the force of arguments, but by police force. The malicious twist of history saw to it that within a mere twenty years the radical purgers of Czechoslovak universities were removed from their academic positions in exactly the same way. It is difficult to say what was the relative strength of Stalinist 'Marxism' and social democratic ideology which also referred to Marx. It is certain, however, that Marxism both with and without quotation marks represented the main intellectual tendency among the young postwar intelligentsia and, as a program of socialist reforms, had been supported by the majority of the nation long before the Communist Party declared this slogan to be its election program. The degenerative trends in Czech Stalinism were neither evident nor crystallized at the time, and the program of socialist reconstruction was accepted also by the non-socialists. The Communists thus did not come to power with their own ideological program calling for the liquidation of civil liberties; rather they assumed the role of advocates of the programmatic principles of the social democratic party – that is, they stole the other party's program, used it as a pretext for gaining mass support, and replaced it by their own goal of totalitarian dictatorship only when they sat firmly in the saddle.

The second developmental phase of Czechoslovak Stalinism covers twenty years (1948–1968). This entire period can be regarded as three variations of one and the same conflict between orthodoxy and heresy, dogmatism and revisionism, criticism and apologetics – the conflicts which shaped the entire middle generation of reform Communism. The fundamental difference between this and the previous generation lies in the fact that the disputes between factions were the disputes within Stalinism ('Marxism') and that any theoretical platform outside Stalinism was driven underground. Besides the official ideology of Communism no other philosophy was allowed to speak out; other philosophies could not be publicized or exercise influence on students, and could only vegetate outside the academic institutions. Moreover, any public propaganda was punishable as a criminal act. Under these conditions, Stalinism was the only possible, privileged, monopolistic philosophy; this meant that shades of political orientations were reflected only in an indirect way, in the subtle form of abstract nuances and changed meanings which was attributed to dialectics or science, ontology or materialism, man or history.

The controversies were carried out in a disguised form, but their intensity was by no means small. The disputes on the philosophical issues of "revisionism" must be regarded as paraphrases of much more important problems discussed in the Politbureau. Under conditions of monopolistic dictatorship, every dispute outgrows its strictly specific importance and becomes part of political ideology in general. It must therefore be classified by the apparatus as correct or incorrect because the prerogative of making such decisions underlies the very monopoly of truth, that is, the leading role of the party, the thought control exercised by the bureaucratic apparatus. Although the disputes on the conception of dialectics may seem futile and ridiculous outside ideology proper, they are significant within ideology because a potential political action is seen behind the philosophical deviation. The heresy of revisionism must be periodically exterminated because the heretics must be potential enemies of the existing power relationships. Indeed they are such enemies. And vice versa, the heresies of revisionism must be periodically initiated from above because revisionism promulgated from above is not revisionism at all, but orthodoxy. It is simple, is it not?

During the twenty-year rule of Stalinism this problem recurred in three analogical cycles (1948–1955, 1956–1962, 1963–1969): first as an indistinct conflict between Soviet philosophy and the domestic tradition of Marxism (it was not apparent in the seeming uniformity of the 1950's); then in a more open form as a conflict between dogmatism and revisionism; and finally as a reformist tendency of crystallizing 'socialism with a human face' against the rigid neo-Stalinist ideology. This last attempt, namely the attempt to open Stalinist ('Marxist') philosophy to the world, to the West, and to other philosophical viewpoints of the twentieth century ended in a disaster. Nevertheless, the catharsis was worth it because Stalinisms of all varieties were finished off, so far as the Czech nation is concerned, once and for all.

During these twenty years, the main institutional pillars of Stalinist philosophy were set up in Czechoslovakia and the principal tendencies among the entire middle generation slowly crystallized. The ideological centers of philosophy were in Prague: the Philosophy Institute of the Czechoslovak Academy of Sciences, the Party College, and the Faculty of

Philosophy at Charles University. Politically the most important institution among them was the Party College, located in the police building at
Ruzyně and nicknamed therefore the "Ruzyně Sorbonne". Although its
publications did not contain any startlingly new views, it seems that it
was precisely this institution which by its more enlightened training of
cadres paved the way for Dubček's attempt to liberalize the party. The
Faculty of Philosophy concentrated on the history of Czech philosophy
and logic; in other words on the marginal disciplines. It was more closely
supervised and could not openly advocate revisionism among the students.
The Philosophy Institute became an ideal seed-bed of revisionism both
because thirty workers at the institute had privileged access to books and
because the climate in the Czechoslovak Academy of Sciences was far
more permissive than anywhere else. The university departments of Marxism-Leninism were staffed with retired, meritorious, but absolutely in-
competent comrades and the instruction accordingly was mocked at by
the students because of the manifest idiocies of the lecturers. An enclave
of authentic Marxism arose in the Philosophy Institute.

The differences in the Stalinisms of these three ideological centers were
quite considerable. In the Philosophy Institute of the Czechoslovak Academy of Sciences during the 1960s, the Hegelian trend, essentially derived
from Lukács, Goldmann, Sartre, Schaff, and Kołakowski, was constantly
gaining in importance. There was, however, another conspicuous orientation basis at the Institute embodied by Richta's team of technocrats and
representing rather positivistic scientific viewpoints, which also predominated at Charles University. The third principle tendency at the Philosophy Institute was closely linked to art, the post-Marxist, existentially-
phenomenological, non-Stalinist orientation to the philosophy of man,
alienation, and history. All these tendencies demonstrate how diversified
and heterogeneous was the current of 'revisionism' shortly before all its
varieties were carried away by the flood of the Soviet occupation and
driven into the same underground into which the representatives of reformism had relegated their teachers some twenty years earlier. Kosík's
Dialectics of the Concrete, unfavorably received by the apparatus, Richta's
Civilization at the Crossroads, rewarded with a state prize, and the unpublished, but illegally circulated *Unscientific Anthropology* are the books
which were born in the Institute at the same time. They are the fruit of the
same intellectual ferment of the 1960s and yet the first one of them reflects

the views of the reformist intelligentsia, the second the views of party technocrats, and the third the view of the new democratic student Left. How many abysses there were within the 'same' revisionism!

During the two decades of Czech reformism the Philosophy Institute always was the focus of attention. When the political development reached the point of crisis, it was therefore quite comprehensible that the Institute was the primary target of all three principal purges organized by the party apparatus. In the first purge of independent minds which took place after the stormy year 1956, the attack concentrated on the officially listed deviations and their perpetrators (Kosík, Tondl, Sviták). In the second purge, strong sanctions were already employed against the deviationists (Kolman and Sviták in 1964) and in the third purge the inundation of 1968 carried away most of the institute members and replaced them by collaborationists. In addition to these actions initiated and stimulated by the party apparatus, life in the institute was variegated by petty scandals in which politics intermingled with philosophy. The background of these scandals is too colorful to be portrayed here. The dividing line between the philosophers appeared to lie in their attitude toward the leading role of the party, or (to put it in plain English) in their willingness or unwillingness to be informers, or (to put it in philosophical terms) in their attitude toward orthodoxy and revisionism.

There seemed to be substantial differences of opinion between the more liberally and the more technocratically minded Stalinists. The decisive criteria of distinction, however, were to be found outside strictly philosophical terms – in the objective irreconcilability of 'Marxism' (that is, Stalinism) with philosophical, literary, or artistic culture. The fundamental viewpoints of philosophers (and artists, scientists, writers) as expressed in their ideological statements and political intentions were the derivatives of the positions taken by various groups (classes, strata) in the production process itself. While the viewpoints of various factions seemed irreconcilable in the 1960's, the Prague Spring at once revealed the decisive dividing line between the party elite and the nation. This objective dividing line did not depend any longer on the interpretation of Marx's tenets, on the changing views of intellectual factions, or on the intrigues of cliques of apparatchiks. The criterion of distinction lay in the bitter reality of the political apparatus of the totalitarian dictatorship and Stalinist economy – an apparatus which mercilessly divides entire nations into members of the privileged elite and the mass of producers controlled by it. This division, which became clear to the public only during the democratization process, was drastically simple: it antiquated the formerly employed criteria of distinction as childish and simplified the political roles of the elite and of the nation as brutally as the police of the totalitarian dictatorship does. Under these conditions, the reformers could win only with the methods which are effective against gangsters, and not with the methods of democratic coquetry. One Stalinist hanged would have been of greater value to Dubček than the Action Program of 1968.

When the fictitious criteria of distinction between the ideological shades of Stalinisms were transformed by history into the realistic criteria of distinction between the irreconcilable objective situations in which various groups and classes found themselves, both ideological variants of 'Marxism' (that is, Stalinism) turned out to be equally powerless, although it seemed that the reformed ideology of Communism was already within reach of the palms of victory. The differences between the party and nonparty intelligentsia were temporarily erased in the 1960's, and the old henchmen of the Stalinist era could again regain their prominent positions in literature and philosophy – as the spokesmen of the anti-Stalinist opposition! To be sure, the essential criteria of distinction consisted and consist in social existence and not in the consciousness of people, or to put it differently, in the class antagonisms of Stalinist institutions and not in the views of daddy Novotný. The ideologists of socialism with a human face could not transcend the limits set by the nature of the regime of the totalitarian dictatorship. They tried to forget the elementary truths of both Marxism and politics, and succumbed to the false consciousness that they were able to inaugurate the era of 'conscience and reason' without disrupting the totalitarian dictatorship by a mass movement. History demonstrated that that was nonsense.

Only the Democratic Left, an unorganized but terrifying and rapidly growing force, did not succumb to the illusions of democratization, and was and is blamed for that by the reformers as if it had driven a wedge between the party and the people. To be sure, there never existed a unity between the apparatchiks and the masses, while there was an abyss between the workers and intelligentsia on the one hand and the power elite on the other. Seeing this abyss was no invention of malicious radical students: it was simply an elementary truth – like a blow to the solar plexus – which entered the consciousness of the people on the basis of twenty years' experience and not because in a local student periodical with several thousand circulation somebody wrote that what we wanted was democracy and not democratization. It is banal to say that the Democratic Left was supported by the force of truth alone, but it is so. Without an organization, without a political party, without any influence on press and television, the Democratic Left successfully launched a mass anti-totalitarian movement based on the unity of the working class and intelligentsia *against* the apparatchiks. It was precisely here that the Democratic Left parted company with both the reformers and the dogmatists because both factions were running out of breath. The occupation strengthened this anti-totalitarian movement to such an extent that 'national heroes' Dubček and Svoboda had to break the neck of the movement. They imposed martial law against their supporters and administered the fatal blow to national unity in the resistance to the occupiers. The Czechoslovak Democratic Left was, of course, regarded also by the reformed Stalinists as their sworn enemy because it refused to believe in the existence of round squares and in the reformability of the totalitarian dictatorship by some factions of the bureaucracy.

III. POLITICS AND PHILOSOPHY

> For a European, the problem is whether
> Europe can survive.
>
> T. S. ELIOT, 1946

With the Soviet occupation we entered the third and final phase of Stalinism in Czechoslovakia, the period of destruction of the myths of the Cold War and the new man, the period of emancipation of the national consciousness from all forms and masks which the interests of Czechoslovak and Soviet bureaucracy adopted in the various stages of the postwar era. Immediately before and after the occupation the Czechoslovak experiment (1968) contained the elements of all sorts of attitudes: radicalization and collaboration, hope and despair, activity and passivity, violence and non-violence, resignation and faith, apathy and enthusiasm, love and hatred, passion and reason. The new special interest groups and new interests gradually entered the historical stage in 1968: the reformist faction of bureaucrats in January, the intelligentsia as the representative of middle classes in April, and the working class (or to put it more accurately the nation) in August. Soon afterwards, however, they were expelled in the reverse sequence from the same stage. First the nation was betrayed by the 'restriction' of sovereignty (October 1968), then the intelligentsia lost its illusion about freedom of the press (January 1969), and finally the reformist faction of bureaucrats was removed from the scene (April 1969). As a result the power elite, the middle classes, and the nation sank in reverse sequence into that emotional apathy of the bitter winter of 1969 from which they had been roused in spring, 1968. As Stalinization, de-Stalinization, and re-Stalinization alternated in Czechoslovakia during the two preceding decades, so now, in the course of merely one year, the triads of reform, occupation, and resistance, and of revolution, invasion, and counterrevolution took their turns at a drastic speed. This bizarre *pas de trois* documented the specific nature of the modern revolutionary process in which the humanistic content of socialism must again merge with democracy, if it is not to succumb to the total degeneracy of Soviet neo-Stalinism.

The educational value of this lesson for the Czech nation was and is unique because it recalls that all ideological postulates of reformed Communism, that is, revised Stalinism, collapsed immediately after the false consciousness of bureaucracy had been confronted with the unfalsified reality of class conflicts. The reformers strove only for changes within the power elite and not for socialist democracy or activization of the masses. It looked as if, in implementing their policy, they forgot the elementary tenets of Marxism concerning the conflicts between classes and replaced them by vague illusions of the compatibility of the market economy, Soviet planning, and the possibility of making the institutions of the totalitatian dictatorship more democratic. The revisionist premises were not a deliberate fraud and in fact were not even designed to carry out a revision. They simply represented a tactical necessity, an improvised concession to the intelligentsia, and an eclectic mixture. From this antinomy of incompatible, but politically quite understandable objectives – to de-Stalinize ideology, but not to touch the institutional foundations of Stalinism – there arose that irresolvable crisis of Communists which claimed not only the prominent revisionists, but eventually the entire nation among its victims.

Stalinism has played out its role in Czechoslovakia and cannot be reformed in any form, that is, neither in the form of socialism with a human face nor as the doctrine of open Marxism which constituted its theoretical core. Open Marxism was a purely ideological illusion of the epoch, geographically predestined to be the self-deception of East European intellectuals who attempted to formulate a humanistic version of authentic Marxism, taking into account the big power interests of the U.S.S.R. Unfortunately, this is not possible because a compromise breaks down in its practical implementation during a crisis. The theory of open Marxism tried in vain to by-pass, with the help of the young Marx, the fact that the institutional foundations of Stalinism were and are unchanged both in the U.S.S.R. and Czechoslovakia, and that no camouflage with terms can cover up the organic defects of the system itself. Open Marxism, or to put it more accurately, somewhat de-Stalinized Stalinism made it impossible to understand both the internal problems of East European countries and the big power chauvinism of the U.S.S.R. Open Marxists created theoretical conflicts on the highest plane of abstraction, but they were not able to see the actual problems where they were and are, namely as police terror, as the class narrow-mindedness of the bureaucratic elite, and as the direct interest of the apparatus in maintaining the status quo.

These trivial problems which every human being with common sense can grasp without any theory – as he perceives a punch in the teeth – manifested themselves in the pseudotheoretical robe of philosophy, were coded in ad hoc terminology and obscure abstractions. They dealt with incredible banalities which had to be resorted to only because what could not be stated in plain language should at least look scientific to the censor's inquisitive eye. The ideological make-up of the reformers who suddenly recalled the human face of socialism became worthless as soon as the spring rains washed away the make-up and revealed the true inhuman face. What matters in the conflict between two or three world political blocs is not the various interpretations of Marx's tenets, but the power relationships between the classes, groups, nations, and races. It was precisely that ideological reproduction of reality, so ridiculed by Marx, which the post-Stalinist ideologists offered in their Action Program, at their auction of Marx's economic and political principles. Open Marxism – this Sartrian chimera which haunted the banks of the Moldau in the 1960's – has not brought real intellectual progress anywhere. It only attracted to the banks of the silver-foaming river those Cossack motorized horses which not only were travesties on the old prophecy – that the situation would not improve in Bohemia until the Cossack horses drank from the Moldau – but also fulfilled the much gloomier vision of Karl Marx that unless Europe carries out its own socialist revolution it will have to invigorate itself with Kalmyk blood.

The Czechoslovak experiment with socialist democracy disclosed the chasms which existed and exist between the apparatus, the intelligentsia, and the nation; between the party directives, the intelligentsia's aspirations, and radical actions; between Dubček's reformers, Vaculík's signatories, and the people. While the reformist self-deceptions rapidly evaporated, after five years it has become even clearer than ever before that the political controversies during the Prague Spring must be viewed as conflicts between the classes, strata, groups – as a conflict of the nation with the power elite of party bureaucracy. The Action/Auction program itself was put up at auction, but the platform of the Democratic Left based on the alliance of the working class and intelligentsia against bureaucracy and technocracy is still topical. The strategy of the Czechoslovak New Left combining socialism with democracy counts on the tremendous political potential of the unity of workers and intelligentsia *against* the totalitarian dictatorship of the bureaucratic apparatus, and is therefore incompatible with any Stalinism – no matter whether it is Dubček's or Husák's, Gottwald's or Novotný's version. This strategy does not see in the Prague Spring a defeat of traditional Czech democracy, but does see a conflict between the two bureaucratic cliques of the totalitarian dictatorship. It must therefore appear as 'Chinese'. If truth speaks Chinese, let us learn Chinese. The Prague Spring does not represent a defeat of the Democratic Left, because the ideas advocated by a few individuals of the 'New Czechoslovak Left' have now become the general property of the nation.[2]

The definite merit of the Czechoslovak experiment lies in the destruction of Stalinist mythology in the consciousness of the nation, which will turn out to be a victory in defeat in every future crisis of the Czechoslovak totalitarian dictatorship. The Communist reformers were defeated, but did not completely lose the game because the alternative leadership has not been physically liquidated and can, under changed conditions, re-emerge as a political force. What definitely lost is the apparatus of the Communist Party, the apparatus of police terror, controlled thought, and the centralized economy. In a future crisis, democrats and Communists, socialists and Christians will again stand side by side. In contrast with the 1968, spring, however, they will realize that their common enemy is the power elite – regardless of the masks and changed clothes which it will wear to maintain its power. Although the reform of consciousness does not yet signify the destruction of the totalitarian system, it is an indispensable prerequisite of political action. In this sense, the Soviet machine guns shooting at the National Museum have done much more for Czech emancipation from the Stalinist infection than all the reformers put together because, from the pedagogical standpoint, the bullets of the machine gun are very effective.

The second permanent merit of the Czechoslovak experiment lies in the independent action of the Czech Democratic Left, that is, in the birth of the anti-totalitarian movement and in the formulation of some sort of embryonic democratic program which went far beyond the scope of the Action/Auction Program promulgated by the reformers. This promising movement – so close to the Soviet voices of the protesting intelligentsia – essentially constitutes a nucleus of the rational, democratic, socialist opposition. It is a movement fighting for civil liberties and human rights which does not confine itself to demanding cultural freedom for writers, but is becoming a nationwide movement incompatible with the tamely conceived technocratic reform which wants to replace the decline in freedom by a higher standard of living.

Finally, the third permanent merit of the Czechoslovak experiment is somewhat paradoxical. While the occupation of Czechoslovakia has not increased the risks of a third world war, it strengthened the will to compromise which would put an end to the Cold War. It seems that the Soviet sphere of interest will be acknowledged simply because the Russians have kept that part of Europe for a quarter of a century. The occupation of Czechoslovakia has helped Brezhnev in making the détente more favorable for Russia. It is a sad thing for us to state, but it is so: the détente symbolizes the normalization of the abnormal. The acknowledgment of the status quo must be interpreted as a Soviet success and as the beginning of the 'Finlandization' of Western Europe. Fortunately, historical forces which act against the colonialism of the Soviet state will not be brought to a halt and the détente will make further changes possible. As far as Eastern Europe is concerned, each détente improves the chances of bureaucrats and each increase in tension reduces them. The détente, however, does not represent an automatic improvement, if we ourselves do not contribute to it. The normalization of the abnormal must eventually be replaced by the abnormal change in the normalized abnormality – the democratic revolution.

REFERENCES

[1] For bibliographical and other data on recent Czech philosophy see the following books:
a. Bochenski, Joseph M. (ed.), *Guide to Marxist Philosophy. An Introductory Bibliography*. Chicago: The Swallow Press, Inc., 1972.
b. Kusin, Vladimir V., *The Intellectual Origins of the Prague Spring*, Cambridge: Cambridge University Press, 1971.
c. Lobkowicz, Nikolaus, *Marxismus-Leninismus in der ČSSR*, Dordrecht, Holland: A. Reidel Co., 1961.
d. Parrish, Michael, *The 1968 Czechoslovak Crisis: A Bibliography, 1968–1970*, Santa Barbara, California: Clio Press, 1971.
e. Zumr, Josef, 'Philosophie der Gegenwart in der Tschechoslovakei', in *Contemporary Philosophy* (ed. by R. Klibansky), Firenze: La Nova Italia Editrice, 1971.
f. Zumr, Josef, 'Československá filosofie přítomnosti', *Filosofický časopis*, vol. 16 (1969), no. 4, pp. 417–427.
g. Lobkowicz, Nikolaus, 'Philosophy in Czechoslovakia since 1960', in *Studies in Soviet Thought*, vol. 3 (1963), no. 11, pp. 11–32.
h. Berger, Peter L. (ed.), *Marxism and Sociology. Views from Eastern Europe*, New York: Meredith Press, 1968 (contributions by Miloš Kaláb and Bedřich Baumann).
i. Oestreicher, P. (ed.), *The Christian-Marxist Dialogue*, London: Macmillan, 1969 (contributions by Milan Machovec and Milan Průcha).
j. Kosík, Karel, 'The Concrete Totality', in *Telos*, Fall, 1968,No. 2, and Fall, 1969, No. 4.
[2] Very few people have expressed this fact more accurately than Raya Duneyevskaya, Trotsky's former secretary and the author of the book, *Marxism and Freedom*: "Without engaging in revolution, the Czechoslovak New Left did touch the raw nerve of Communism – in this case, Czechoslovakian as well as Russian Communism. They did this by questioning the concept of the vanguard, not to mention omniscient, role of the Communist Party. Here Dubček refused to budge. On the contrary. He was not only adamant about the 'leading role' of the Party. He not only claimed total credit for the new road of 'democratization.' And he not only opposed the creation of new opposition parties. He also staked out the claim that 'the greatest majority of the best creative minds in the country is in the Party.' This, then, defines the next battleground of ideas. Hence, the importance of the fact that the philosopher, Ivan Sviták, and others, who raised the question of opposition parties, the role of the Communist Party, raised them as inseparable from their philosophic foundation, on the one hand, and the needed unity of worker and intellectual, on the other. In raising the fundamental question of philosophy and revolution, the party and spontaneity, the unity of worker and intellectual, they have indeed laid the foundation of a new relationship of theory to practice. Thereby they have gone far beyond anything raised by the New Left in 'the West'." Raya Dunaevskaya, *News and Letters*, 1968.

MIHAILO MARKOVIĆ

MARXIST PHILOSOPHY IN YUGOSLAVIA:
THE *PRAXIS* GROUP

I. THE SIGNIFICANCE OF THE PRAXIS GROUP

Yugoslav philosophy in the Sixties and the beginning of the Seventies has been a curious social phenomenon.

Public lectures in philosophy have attracted unusually wide audiences. Philosophical books and articles are read in all social strata. Some issues of the journals *Praxis* and *Filozofija* as well as some philosophical debates are spoken of as most important cultural and, in a certain sense, political events.

It is a commonplace that philosophy is divorced from concrete social life and actual practical social needs. As a matter of fact, philosophy is often uncommitted, often apologetic or very abstract, or it lags considerably behind social processes whose deeper meaning it tries to reveal. Minerva's owl flies out only at dusk, when things already have taken place, when the necessary experience is already there. A characteristic feature of the philosophy which has been developing in Yugoslavia during the last two decades is its tendency to anticipate social processes, to reflect critically and in very concrete terms on the present, not only in the light of the past but also of a possible future.

Concrete, critical thinking is always a challenge to some existing authority, the more so if the ability of that authority to direct things and to realize its projects depends upon its full ideological control of the field. That is why Marxist theoreticians have difficulties not only with bourgeois power (the legitimacy of which they tend to destroy) but even more with past revolutionary power (which they legally support) as soon as they really begin to think – that is, begin to think freely. The Yugoslav *Praxis* group has taken the risk of complete freedom in analysing the present-day world and its own society. This fact accounts for both its unusual vitality and its being the target of official ideological attacks over the last ten years.

The fate of the group is not an exceptional event. There is a long line of

De George and Scanlan (eds.), Marxism and Religion in Eastern Europe, 63–89. All Rights Reserved.
Copyright © 1976 by D. Reidel Publishing Company, Dordrecht-Holland.

predecessors and contemporaries, indeed the most creative Marxist
philosophers of this century, who have been rebuffed and occasionally
persecuted by their own party: Lukács, Bloch, Korsch, Kołakowski,
Kosík, Fischer, Marek, Il'enkov, Léfèbvre, Garaudy, Schaff, Heller,
Marcuse, and many others. What is nevertheless exceptional about the
Praxis group is that it has managed to resist so long while never giving up
any of its principles and convictions; whereas in all the preceding cases the
party bureaucracy was able either to compel its theoretical *enfant terrible*
to engage in self-criticism (Lukács, Schaff) or else to isolate him completely
from the movement (Kołakowski, Léfèbvre, Garaudy) and sometimes to
silence him for a long period (Korsch, Kosík, Il'enkov). None of this has
happened in Yugoslavia, owing to a fortunate constellation of various
factors to be analysed later. *Praxis* philosophers still teach in universities
although the authorities have repeatedly demanded since 1968 that some
of them be eliminated.[1] They continue to publish their books although
the doors of most publishing houses are closed to them. They continue to
publish their journals, *Praxis* and *Filozofija*, with little money and much
enthusiasm. They keep up lively links with many important figures in
Yugoslav cultural life and enjoy strong support within their communities,
although the Establishment has made great efforts to isolate them and
drive them within the narrow walls of an intellectual reservation. In order
to cut off their international links the authorities have revoked passports
from some of them, but a spirit need not travel in space to touch another
spirit.

Most Yugoslavs naturally do not understand what the fuss over
philosophers is all about. Some watch with amusement as Goliath fails
once more against little David. But an enlightened minority, which is
likely to play a key role in the future development of Yugoslav socialism,
expects from the outcome of this conflict to obtain answers to some crucial
questions: are Marxist intellectuals in socialism ever able to preserve their
right to free, independent, critical thought when they find themselves
under pressure from political power? Is the avant-garde of the socialist
movement ever ready to tolerate true, creative, non-dogmatic, non-
apologetic Marxism (let alone other forms of critical thought) after the
seizure of political power? Consequently, is bureaucracy in socialism
merely a deformed vanguard which is pathologically self-assured but not
yet totally alienated from the mass movement, and therefore able to

overcome its arrogant and authoritarian style of management when offered firm revolutionary resistance? Or is bureaucracy a new oppressive class which tries to utilize isolated fragments from Marx's writings for the purpose of ideological mystification of reality, but otherwise must regard every true Marxist revolutionary as its natural enemy? In any case, what are the chances of preserving certain basic liberties in socialism after they have been enjoyed on a mass scale for more than two decades? What are the chances of preserving the principle of self-management (even in its initial limited form) after it has become the ideological backbone of the whole system?

The destiny of the *Praxis* group is of such crucial importance because there are reasons for optimism if it survives. The historic lesson from this unique experiment would be that no matter how strong is the desire of bureaucracy under socialism to rule in an easy way, without any public challenge, it can be compelled to accept the existence of criticism and to live with it. Intellectuals must take the liberty of critical thinking instead of waiting for an enlightened power that will kindly invite them to think freely. In the relation between a bureaucrat's arrogance and an intellectual's cowardice, it is the latter that reinforces the former. Furthermore, one of the decisive factors that contributes to the transformation of the revolutionary vanguard into a bureaucratic elite is a general readiness to surrender, to escape, to accept the role of an object. Perhaps the only way to preserve a revolutionary socialist movement is to reduce the authority of the vanguard immediately after the abolition of the old power, and to oppose energetically every symptom of arbitrariness, autocracy, and aggressiveness toward those who think differently.

If the *Praxis* group perishes, that would mean simply that the intrinsic conflict between revolutionary Marxism and the ruling bureaucracy is so deep and antagonistic that a peaceful resolution is not possible, even under the most favorable conditions. The conditions in this case are exceptionally favorable indeed. Yugoslavia is still the most democratic socialist country. Its leadership, very early after the revolution and while still very young, was compelled to see in *the other* – Stalinism – what it could become itself. In a genuine effort to avoid bureaucratization it introduced initial forms of self-management and a considerable measure of political and academic freedom. Those democratic forms must be preserved if the country is to continue to enjoy its self-respect and a

special economic and political status among non-socialist countries. On
the other hand, by any standard the *Praxis* group is not a victim to be
dealt with easily. Most of its members participated in the partisan war and
have spotless backgrounds. Their scholarly reputation ranks high. They
have not committed any illegal act; everyone knows that the reason they
are persecuted is that they have publicly expressed certain truths about
their own society. If, in spite of all these obstacles the bureaucracy
decides that it must effectively silence this voice by force, that would be a
proof that the interests of the bureaucracy in preserving its full unques-
tioned authority is incompatible with the interest of all progressive forces
in further developing Marxist theory and in experiencing all the practical
consequences of its basic philosophical ideas.

II. DEVELOPMENT OF MARXIST PHILOSOPHY IN
YUGOSLAVIA 1945–1964: FORMATION OF THE PRAXIS GROUP

Marxist philosophy in Yugoslavia emerged with the rise of the socialist
revolutionary movement before and during World War II. The whole
preceding history of philosophy is relevant for contemporary philosophical thought in Yugoslavia only to an insignificant degree. Two important
spiritual sources in the past, however, are (1) a very old tradition of
resistance to sheer force, expressed especially in beautiful epic poems
about struggles for liberation against the Turks and other foreign invaders, and (2) nineteenth century socialist thought, which combined a
general revolutionary orientation with a concrete approach to the existing
backward, rural society in the South Slavic countries of that time.

School philosophy was not very attractive to the young generation that
took part in the war of liberation and in the struggle against Stalinism
after 1948. With few exceptions professors of philosophy in Yugoslav
universities were mere followers of influential European trends. A socially
committed philosophical thought was needed, one able to open up the
prospect of settling grave social issues. Marxism seemed the only existing
philosophy that was likely to satisfy that need.

For a brief time, until 1947, the only interpretation of Marxism that was
available was 'dialectical materialism' as elaborated by Soviet philosophers. But very soon, even before the conflict with Stalinism in 1948, the
most gifted students of philosophy in the universities of Belgrade and

Zagreb began to doubt whether what they found in the fourth chapter of the *History of the Communist Party of the Soviet Union (Bolsheviks)* was really the last word in revolutionary philosophy. It sounded superficial, simplified, dogmatic and it lacked any criticism of the existing forms of socialist society.

This very beginning throws considerable light on what followed. Those students who would later constitute the core of the *Praxis* group were mature people; they had held a range of responsible functions in the partisan army before they came to study. An attitude of inferiority and awe before Soviet achievements was entirely lacking. "We made our own revolution and have the right to behave and to be treated as equals." But the job of a revolutionary theory is to anticipate further development rather than to glorify the past. If socialist revolution requires a whole epoch, the initial episode of which is the overthrow of bourgeois power, Marxist theory cannot be construed as something ready-made and fixed; rather it must gain a new form with each important practical step.

The year 1948 marked a great turning point. The fall of such an over-whelming authority as Stalin, the fourth classic, cleared the ground for a much freer, more independent, and critical approach to all problems. For a generation which actively fought Stalinist dogmatism, realizing how it damaged Soviet philosophy, the basic motive for all subsequent work would remain the relentless search for truth rather than loyalty to any established authorities or institutions. The principle that 'the progressive is true' was transformed into 'the true is progressive'. Marxism lost the character of an ideology; no single individual and no organization would again have the right to determine and impose an official interpretation of the thought of the classics of Marxism. The accusations of 'revisionism' would become pointless as the essential task would no longer be the *defense* of a sacrosanct classical heritage but its further *development*, involving the principle of revisability or transcendence. The fall of the fourth classic could not occur without repercussions for the three pre-ceding ones: their texts would no longer be regarded as ultimate truths which can only be interpreted, commented upon, and confirmed by new data, but rather as more or less fruitful guide lines for further inquiry.

The most important ethical experience of 1948 was the realization that not all means can be justified by the mere fact that they serve to attain a supposedly revolutionary goal. The old Jesuit doctrine was widely used by many pragmatically minded revolutionaries and was not questioned so long as it meant that violence was often necessary to achieve radical social change, or that a revolutionary must not tell the truth about his organization's activities in front of the class enemy. Now socialists used the most absurd lies and threats of physical force against other socialists in order to subordinate them "in the interests of the international workers' movement". It has turned out that the definition of a really revolutionary goal presents a much greater problem than was suspected. And even if a goal is not controversial in its abstract conceptual form, it can be profoundly deformed in the process of its practical realization if unsuitable means have been chosen. Use of inhuman, unjust means deforms the agents profoundly and makes them utterly deviate from what they believed was their end. It has become clear that if one wants to avoid being caught up in myths and hypocritical ideological justifications of stupid or tyrannical actions one has to apply the same ethical criteria both to ends and to means, and to evaluate each action according to both consequences and motives.

A major change in political philosophy has been the reevaluation of demands for the unity of all revolutionaries, both in theory and in practice. Unity (even 'monolithic' unity) used always to be highly esteemed by Marxists. Since the days of the *Communist Manifesto* it was believed that united proletarians were the only social force able to topple an extremely powerful and firmly entrenched capitalist elite. However, the issue of unity appeared in 1948 in an entirely new context. It became obvious that an abstract demand for unity was purely formal; the concrete problem was unity on the basis of certain principles and policies. Now, these principles and policies are either imposed by one central authority or reached by agreement among several equal partners. Only the latter alternative leads to an increase of freedom, initiative, and self-determination of all the parts of a united whole. The differences that may be generated in this way, due to specific living conditions of particular social groups and nations, do not necessarily lead to a disintegration of the whole; rather they enrich it, increase total creativity, and accelerate the rate of development. This synthesis of monism and pluralism, of the principles of unity and individuality will remain one of the basic constitutive principles in various spheres of Yugoslav social life, and in particular in the formation and development of the *Praxis* group itself.

The Fifties were a period of reinterpretation of Marx's philosophy and modern science, a period of building up the theoretical foundations of a new philosophy which, while remaining in the tradition of Marx, was sharply opposed to the rigid, dogmatic schemes of *diamat* and at the same time tended to incorporate the most important achievements in post-Marxian philosophy and culture.

A thorough study of the classical works of Marxism – especially of Marx's early manuscripts – in a new perspective led to the rediscovery of a profound and sophisticated humanist philosophy which, for a long time, was either ignored or dismissed as Hegelian by a great many Marxist philosophers. It became clear that the problems which Marx was grappling with – *praxis*, conflict of human existence and essence, true needs and basic human capacities, alienation, emancipation, labor and production, and others – far from being sins of his youth, underlay all his mature work and furthermore are still the living, crucial issues of our time and indeed of the whole epoch of transition.

It did not take long to realize that in the writings of the classics of Marxism there were no answers to many problems of our time. How can it be explained that socialist revolutions did not occur in developed industrial countries of the West but in backward rural societies of the East? What really is a revolution if after an apparent revolution a bureaucratic society can emerge? How is socialism to be built in a relatively underdeveloped country? What does it mean for the state to wither away? How is a non-market modern economy possible? What is *Marxist* logic, ethics, esthetics? Is there a Marxist anthropology? What is the essence of man with respect to which one speaks about alienation? If that essence is universal, how is history possible? If it is particular, how can we escape relativism? If man is a being of *praxis*, and *praxis* is (among other things) labor and production, how can the standpoint of *praxis* be a standard of critical evaluation? How can we reconcile the principle of determinism, according to which historical processes are governed by laws independent of human consciousness and will, with the principle of freedom according to which it is men who make their own history? What is the axiological ground for such normative dialectical concepts as *totality, development, self-actualization, negation, transcendence*? How can we conceive of the category of *matter* without either renouncing materialism or falling back upon absolute, pre-Kantian dualism?

These and many other questions had to be thoroughly studied and discussed. Asking good questions resulted, on the one hand, in an opening out toward the whole of existing culture and, on the other hand, in creating a proper intellectual community capable of a creative collective effort.

In the years of orthodoxy immediately following the war and political revolution, Western culture was considered decadent and declining in almost all respects (with the exception of ideologically neutral fields such as the exact sciences and technology); but the picture became much more diversified and pluralistic in the early Fifties. Curiously enough, that happened in the worst days of the cold war, when intolerance and ideological prejudice reached the level of sheer madness in McCarthyism and in Stalin's campaign against cosmopolitanism – indeed against any appreciation of foreign science and culture. On the contrary, in Yugoslav cultural life at that time ideological criteria tended to be replaced by aesthetic and scholarly ones. Socialist realism was generally abandoned as a caricature of a Marxist approach to the arts. A thoroughgoing process of emancipation from ideological censorship took place at first in music, painting, sculpture, and architecture, then in literature, and eventually in all other fields. In the social sciences, especially in disciplines which at that time were suspected of being 'bourgeois sciences' (!) such as sociology and psychology, the pendulum even went to the other extreme when in reaction to 'historical materialism' certain primitive forms of empiricism were revived which by that time were considered passé in the West.

In philosophy a measure of general criticism of the basic assumptions of various existing trends of Western philosophy was always present, but that did not exclude a genuine interest in the concrete contributions of analytic philosophy, phenomenology, existentialism, and others. Under these influences much serious work was undertaken in philosophy of language, methodology of science, axiology, philosophical anthropology, and metaethics – disciplines and problems which were completely outside the framework of orthodox Marxist philosophy.

A fortunate circumstance in those formative years after 1948 was the fact that the new, postwar generation quickly found suitable forms for a collective intellectual life. In 1950 the Serbian Philosophical Society was created. Later similar philosophical societies emerged in all the other republics. Since 1958 there has also been a Yugoslav Philosophical

Association. During the decade of the Fifties dozens of philosophical conferences were held on problems which were considered essential at that time: the nature of philosophy, the relationship between philosophy and science, ideology, truth, alienation, the young and old Marx, Marxist humanism. These discussions were conducted in complete freedom and sincerity, in an atmosphere of genuine dialogue among several different Marxist orientations. A basic polarization occurred between those who continued the line of orthodox Marxism – i.e., a mere defense and justification of the classical writings of Marx, Engels, and Lenin – and those who radically opposed any orthodoxy, insisting on further development of what is, in our time, still living and revolutionary in the classical sources.

The former orientation laid emphasis on the philosophy of the natural sciences, trying to employ recent achievements in that field to confirm an Engelsian conception of *Naturphilosophie*. Outside the domain of their interest were Marx's critique of political economy and especially the early humanistic writings of Marx. Therefore the basic philosophical problem remained for them the relation of matter and mind. The main objective of their research program was the establishment of the most general laws in nature, society, and human thought. This in fact was the program of the whole orientation of dialectical materialism.

The other orientation rejected 'dialectical materialism' as a dogmatic and essentially conservative orientation that at best leads to a generalization and systematization of existing scientific knowledge, but does not contribute to the creation of a critical epochal consciousness which is capable of directing practical social energy toward liberation and humanization of the world. From this point of view the basic philosophical problem is the historical human condition and possibilities for a radical universal emancipation.

Within this humanist orientation there was from the beginning a clear distinction between those who tended to develop Marxism as a *critical science* and those who construed it as essentially a revolutionary *utopia*. From the former standpoint the essential limitation of dogmatism was its ideologization of Marx's doctrine. In order for this to be demystified it was necessary not only to return to classical sources and to reinterpret them, but also to develop a high degree of objectivity and criticism in dealing with contemporary problems; to reestablish the unity of theory and practice and to mediate the *a priori* philosophical vision of man as a

'being of *praxis*' and Communism as a dealienated human community
with concrete knowledge about existing historical conditions and tendencies. According to this view Marx had transcended pure philosophy
and created an all-embracing critical social theory. Such an approach
required the development of a general method of critical inquiry –
dialectic.

From the latter standpoint it was believed that the essential philosophical limitation of dogmatism was a positivist reduction of philosophy to a
quasi-objective science. It is the nature of science to divide, fragment,
quantify, reduce man to an object, study equilibrium rather than change,
see changes only as variations of a fixed pattern. It was considered desirable, therefore, sharply to separate philosophy from science, to put science
into brackets as insufficiently relevant for the study of human alienation
and emancipation. According to this view the philosophical thought of
Marx expressed in his early writings was in fact utopian thought about the
future, about what *could be*. Such utopian thought is radical due to its
implicit invitation to abolish existing reality. Scientific knowledge, on the
other hand, remains within the boundaries of actually existing objects:
that is the source of its conformism.

Although the representatives of these two tendencies used to clash
whenever they met (and they have continued to disagree on some points
up to the present) they also considerably influenced one another and
began to coalesce. What united them and at the same time opposed them
to orthodox Marxists was their resolute criticism of dogmatism, resistance to Engelsian *Naturphilosophie*, high appreciation for the humanism
underlying all Marx's work, and a self-critical attitude with respect to
both the Marxist heritage and the reality in which Marxist ideas were
being implemented.

A decisive debate between the humanists and the orthodox Marxists
took place at the symposium *Problems of Object and Subject, Practice
and the Theory of Reflection*, organized by the Yugoslav Philosophical
Association at Bled in August, 1960.

During this lively and at moments dramatic debate, orthodox Marxists
tried to save the theory of reflection, the cornerstone of the epistemology
developed by Soviet dialectical materialists and the Bulgarian philosopher
Todor Pavlov. The main objections addressed to this theory were: First,
it ignores the whole experience of German classical philosophy and goes

back to the eighteenth century dualism of a material object *in itself* and a spiritual subject. Second, there is an implicit dogmatism in the view that reflection is the essential property of all consciousness: how can we challenge products of mind which by definition are reflexes of reality – i.e., are true? Third, the theory is false because, as a matter of fact, consciousness, far from passively accompanying and copying material processes, very often anticipates and projects not-yet-existent material objects. The attempt to define the theory of reflection by saying that in such cases we deal with 'creative reflexes' made the impression of an *ad hoc* convention by which the concept of reflection was expanded in such a way as to become totally uninformative.

During this debate the view prevailed that the central category of Marx's philosophy was free, human, creative activity – practice. Dualism of matter and mind, object and subject was superseded by showing how these categories can be derived from the notion of *practice*. Objects we speak meaningfully about are not just given in themselves, they are objects of a historic human world, transformed by our practical activity, mediated by our previous knowledge, language, needs, and indeed the whole of human culture at a given historical moment. The subject is not just a locus of reflection of external reality but a complex historical being, who not only observes and infers but also projects what is not yet there but could be. Only within this context does the category of reflection become meaningful, only when it has been practically established that certain products of mind have their antecedent correlates in physical reality may they be considered reflections.

The Bled debate marks the end of the period of formation of the theoretical grounds for a new activist interpretation of Marxism. Orthodox Marxists completely withdrew from philosophical societies and journals and played quite an insignificant role in philosophical life during the Sixties. On the other hand, humanists felt that after settling fundamental theoretical issues, a step towards more concrete activism had become urgent. Once it became clear that the role of a revolutionary philosophy cannot be reduced to a rational explanation of the existing reality, socialist as well as capitalist, that its essential task is the discovery of the essential limitations of the existing world and of the historical possibilities abolishing these limitations, it became necessary to transcend the initial abstract critical theory by a concrete, practically oriented social criticism.

Criticism reduced to a highly general analysis of alienation in the contemporary would have the character of an alienated criticism because it would abolish alienation only in thought, not in reality. Concrete criticism, on the other hand, could not have been reduced to capitalist society only, because many forms of alienation characteristic of capitalism were still present in post-revolutionary society: fetishism of commodities, appropriation of surplus value by the ruling elites, political alienation and state power, nationalism, and above all, a professional division of labor and an enormous gap between the creative activity of the minority and the mechanical, degrading labor of the vast majority. To project alienation only into the external bourgeois world would amount to speaking about one's own problems in an ideological, mystified way which would block further revolutionary activity. An authentic philosophical criticism had to be concrete in the sense of dealing with its own immediate historical grounds.

This new orientation was clearly formulated at the annual meeting of the Yugoslav Philosophical Association in Skopje, 1962, and in the collective work, *Humanism and Socialism*, produced by Zagreb and Belgrade philosophers (Supek, Petrović, Vranicki, Kangrga, Marković, Korać, Krešić, and others).

Between 1963 and 1968 a series of extremely lively and fruitful philosophical meetings took place.[2] The central themes discussed were the meaning and historical novelty of socialism, criteria of historical progress, concepts of freedom and democracy, a critique of professional politics and bureaucracy, analysis of the limitations of the existing forms of self-management, a critique of the market economy, personal integrity in a society dominated by politics, and the character of a new socialist culture.

An especially great role in the development of a philosophical social criticism was played by the Korchula Summer School[3], an informal summer meeting place of Zagreb and Belgrade philosophers and sociologists with the participation of internationally known Marxists and Marxologists such as Fromm, Marcuse, Bloch, Habermas, Goldmann, Mandel, Bottomore, Rubel, Axelos, Mallet, Marek, Kołakowski, Kosík, Cerroni, Lombardo-Radice, Heller, Fleischer, Wartofsky, Tucker, Birnbaum, and others. The same group of philosophers and sociologists who established the Korchula Summer School (Supek, Petrović, Vranicki, Kangrga, Grlić, Bošnjak and Kuvačić from Zagreb; Marković, Tadić, Korać,

Krešić, Milić, Stojanović, Golubović, and Životić from Belgrade) founded the journal *Praxis*, the first issue of which appeared in 1964, edited by Petrović and Supek. At that time the journal of the Yugoslav Philosophical Association, *Filozofija*, edited in Belgrade, had a rather academic character, being open to all philosophical problems and all existing orientations. A new editorial board in 1967 gave it an equally engaged and critical character. Selected articles from *Filozofija* and the domestic edition of *Praxis* are now being published in the international edition of *Praxis*.

III. DEVELOPMENT OF THE PRAXIS GROUP, 1964–1974, UNDER INCREASING PRESSURE FROM THE ESTABLISHMENT

Since most members of the *Praxis* group actively participated in the revolution and because the critique of Stalinist dogmatism coincided with the general policy of the country in the Fifties, the official reaction was more or less favourable. It is true that Big Brother's eye kept close watch and each philosophical meeting was attended by a few informers who would afterwards prepare detailed reports about what was said within the conference halls (and outside them). In 1957 a short period of improvement in Soviet-Yugoslav relations was used by an old dogmatist, Boris Ziherl, to attack 'revisionists' in a long article published in the Party newspaper *Komunist*. His main point was that a group of younger Marxist philosophers read Western philosophers uncritically and were creating confusion by attempting to incorporate some of those ideas into Marxism. However, at that time it was possible to publish an extensive reply in the same newspaper [4], and many of those who disliked Ziherl took this opportunity for rebuttal as an indication that the Party no longer supported him.

Several top leaders listened with mixed feelings to tapes from the Bled debate. They did not have any illusions about the mediocrity and sterility of orthodox Marxists – the losers; but there was something on the winning side which they held suspect – an apparent touch of 'idealism', a complete sense of autonomy and self-reliance, an unusual boldness in taking up ideologically relevant positions without even consulting the authorities, an exaggerated activism which seemed to neglect real conditions, a humanism that for some reasons sounded 'elitist'. It was already customary in those years around 1960 to characterize this dominant philosophical trend as an *abstract* humanism. The true meaning of the derogatory term was this:

instead of practically supporting and affirming the efforts of the Party to build a new society here and now, philosophers discuss such abstract problems as alienation, human nature, *praxis*, emancipation, self-realization, true human community, and similar themes that Marx dealt with only while he was young and immature. At that time politicians were not yet able to see how relatively harmless this *abstract* humanism was and how much more trouble they would have with humanism when it became *concrete*.

After 1963 *Praxis* philosophers established that forms of both economic and political alienation still exist in Yugoslav society, that the working class is still exploited, this time by the new elites – bureaucracy and technocracy; that a market economy will inevitably reproduce capital-labor relations; that self-management exists only at the micro-level in enterprises, local communities, and local organizations, and that consequently its further development requires a gradual withering away of professional politics and the formation of workers' councils at the regional, republican, and federal level; that the basic precondition for a really participatory democracy was first a radical democratization and later the withering away of the Party.

In the period 1963–1968 an attempt was made to mobilize loyal Party theoreticians to oppose those critical views by an ideological counter-criticism. But few able scholars were available and the counter-arguments were weak: the working class, being the ruling class in socialism, cannot exploit itself; Marx's critique of the market economy is not valid for a socialist market economy; the attack on bureaucracy is an anarchistic assault on organized society; the critique of the existing form of self-management is a critique of self-management in principle; integrated self-management at the republican and federal level is a form of statism; democratization of the Party in the sense of allowing a minority to continue to express and justify its ideas amounts to a demand to allow factions within the Party; and so on.

The year 1968 was a turning point. Mass student demonstrations in Belgrade on June 2 and 3 and the occupation of all buildings of the universities in Belgrade on June 3–10, followed by similar events in Zagreb and Sarajevo, initiated the greatest political crisis in Yugoslav postwar society and produced a permanent fear that critical philosophical theory under certain conditions might inspire a mass practical movement.

A series of measures were undertaken in order to reduce greatly the field of activity of *Praxis* philosophers. Most of those who were members of the Party were expelled or their organizations were dissolved. They were eliminated from important social functions. Funds for philosophical activities, journals, and other publications were cut off or became extremely scarce. Demands were expressed by top leaders that those philosophers who had exerted a 'corrupting', 'ideologically alien' influence on students – more specifically those from the University of Belgrade – had to be ousted from the University.

That in spite of all this the *Praxis* group was able to continue to work, to publish, and in a sense still to dominate the Yugoslav philosophical scene can be explained by a fortunate combination of several factors.

First and most important, after 1948 Yugoslavia had gone rather far in the process of democratization and rejection of the theoretical and practical forms of Stalinism. The achievements of this process can no longer be fully undone, since the mentality and life style of millions of people have changed irreversibly. A whole new generation has grown up in the meantime, as well as a new generation of liberal and pragmatic functionaries who are lacking the earlier fanaticism and ideological militancy and who would hate to be identified with Stalinists. There is a lot of foot-dragging when things reminiscent of old 'administrative' practices have to be done. No matter how little the principles of self-management are present in the higher political regions, self-management is a reality in the micro-cells of the society, i.e., in enterprises and also in university faculties.[5] One would have to violate the Constitution and the laws in order to usurp the rights of workers' councils to decide about matters of internal organization and of personnel policy.

Second, the *Praxis* group has had sufficient time between 1948 and 1968 to establish its scholarly and political reputation. In Yugoslavia as elsewhere, ordinary people are ready to believe that there are all kinds of internal and external enemies. But unlike people in some other socialist countries they are no longer ready to believe that socialists turn over night into enemies or that in reality they have always been anti-socialist, or that good comrades have to confess whatever has been demanded of them in some strange, inconceivable interest of the Party. Therefore all the abusive labels that were stamped on *Praxis* philosophers over the years – 'anarcho-liberals', 'opposition to the Party', 'extremists', 'enemies of self-management' (!), and so on – have come to sound much more like expressions of someone's anger than real descriptions. Another relevant circumstance is that the *Praxis* group plays an important role in maintaining a complex ideological balance in Yugoslavia. Its disappearance would inevitably strengthen right-wing nationalists (especially in Croatia) and pro-Stalinist hard-liners (especially in Serbia). The *Praxis* group played an important role in the struggle against those two dangerous conservative forces. In revenge, they would gladly settle accounts with *Praxis* and they keep offering their services to the Party; but the latter must beware of such allies. Because the ideological situation is different in different republics, and Yugoslavia continues to emphasize its federal structure, it is very difficult to synchronize pressure against *Praxis* in Serbia and in Croatia. Croat leadership cannot possibly expel *Praxis* professors from the University while at the same time tolerating dozens of those who in various ways were involved in the nationalist movement of 1971. Serbian leadership, on the other hand, finds itself in an awkward position when it attempts to drive out of Belgrade University the same kind of people who retain important functions at the University of Zabreb.

Third, the international status and reputation that the country has enjoyed in the world is also a serious limiting factor. It is absolutely essential for Yugoslavia to preserve its present political and economic relations with non-socialist countries. Those relations have been somewhat strained since the Party's 1972 crackdown on liberalism. Any further erosion of civil liberties and harsh repressive measures against intellectuals would be interpreted as clear symptoms of a retrogressive trend and of a return towards Stalinism. This would eventually jeopardize all the achievements of a long, consistent policy of non-alignment and opening out toward the world.

Fourth, and not the least significant, is the amazing solidarity not only within the group but also in the broader university community to which it belongs. There are well known devices used a hundred times over by which the Establishment reaches its objectives without actually using force. The essence of the technique is to disintegrate the victim morally and then to bring him to the point where he strangles himself with his own hands. This is usually achieved by a combination of measures: strong pressure is applied intended to scare possible supporters and to break the will of the victim; in the recent situation it included sharp, abusive attacks at meetings and via mass media; banning issues of the journal; threats that the Philosophy Faculty would be dissolved and that supporters as well as the main victims would lose their jobs; rumors that individuals in question are foreign spies and therefore soon to be arrested; and so on. This pressure is combined with opening up the prospect of a 'compromise' – i.e., splitting the issue into two elements, one of which must be sacrificed for the other to be saved: in this case, *Praxis* could continue but must change its editorial policies, or it must apply self-criticism to past errors; the Belgrade professors would be given scholarly jobs but they must resign from their teaching positions, or even that two of the eight must go so that six may remain. After sufficiently long and thorough pressure the victim usually feels isolated, becomes unnerved, and makes himself believe that by sacrificing something and by partial surrender he will be left in peace. But what he sacrifices is usually moral strength – the only weapon he has. And a surrender is never partial: bureaucracy takes its time and the principle of its absolute authority requires a corresponding principle of absolute surrender (which might technically be divided into several episodes).

None of those devices worked this time. The scenario was well known in advance; the usual errors were not made, and human relationships within the group, between the group and other intellectuals, and between professors and students withstood the test. After six years of hard pressure these relationships were even solidified. Student support from all three of the most important Yugoslav universities – Belgrade, Zagreb, and Ljubljana – played a very important role. Students threatened to strike if anything happened to their professors and it was indeed difficult to foresee what kind of processes, in the given economic conditions[6], might have been triggered by such a strike.

For all those reasons the activity of the *Praxis* group after 1968 was only reduced; it never stopped. A number of books were published in that period.[7] The journals *Filozofija* and *Praxis* survived. The sessions of the Korchula Summer School continue to take place each August.[8] The Philosophical Institute at the University of Belgrade has engaged a number of co-researchers on several research programs.[9]

Since 1971 this institute together with the journal *Filozofija* and the Serbian Philosophical Society has organized winter meetings which concentrate on most current theoretical issues.[10] These meetings take place in an atmosphere of considerable tension. The last one, in February 1974, ended with security agents searching the rooms of several participants, interviewing some, and confiscating the tapes intended for the publication of the *Proceedings* of the meeting. Eventually a participant, the poet Milan Ignjatović, was arrested and sentenced to three and a half years in jail for the speech that he delivered at the meeting.

IV. BASIC PHILOSOPHICAL VIEWS OF THE PRAXIS GROUP

1. *The Conception of Philosophy*

The *Praxis* group is composed of individual philosophers who not only specialize in different fields but also differ in certain basic conceptions. They must not be treated therefore as a homogeneous philosophical school. What unites them is much more a practical attitude than a theoretical doctrine, though this does not exclude the possibility of formulating certain basic views which could be endorsed by all.

Concerning the nature of philosophy, for example, it is not controversial in the *Praxis* group that the essential function of philosophy is to form a total critical consciousness able to enlighten and direct all human activity in a given historical epoch. Being *total* it differs from the fragmented knowledge of various scientific disciplines; being *critical consciousness* it is much more than a totality of positive scientific knowledge.

The main disagreement begins, however, when one embarks upon a more specific determination of the relation between science and philosophy. According to Petrović, Kangrga, and Zivotić it makes sense to speak of a 'pure' philosophy that is *a priori* with respect to science and fully independent of it. According to Marković, Supek, and Vranicki, philosophy in the tradition of Marx cannot be 'pure'; it develops from an initial abstract *a priori* vision towards an increasingly concrete and rich theory that tends to incorporate all relevant scientific knowledge.

2. *The Philosophical Starting Point*

The orthodox *diamat* view that the central philosophical problem is the relation of matter and mind has been generally rejected as abstract, historical, and dualistic. The central problem for Marx was how to realize human nature by producing a more humane world. The fundamental philosophical assumption implicit in this problem is that man is essentially a being of *praxis*, i.e., a being capable of free creative activity by which he transforms the world, realizes his specific potential faculties, and satisfies the needs of other human individuals. *Praxis* is an essential possibility for man but under certain unfavorable historical conditions its realization can be blocked. This discrepancy between the individual's actual existence and his potential essence – i.e. between what he is and what he could be – is *alienation*. The basic task of philosophy is to analyse critically the phenomenon of alienation and to indicate practical steps leading to human *self-realization, to praxis*.

This is believed to be the common ground of Marxist humanism. Undoubtedly it opens up a number of problems which are dealt with in various individual writings. Within the scope of this paper I shall mention only briefly a few distinctions which I have had to make in some of my works.

Praxis has to be distinguished from the purely epistemological category of *practice*. The latter refers simply to any subject's activity of changing an object, and this activity can be alienated. The former is a normative concept and refers to an ideal, specifically human activity which is an end in itself, a carrier of basic values, and at the same time a standard of criticism of all other forms of activity.

Praxis must also not be identified with *labor* and *material production*. The latter belong to the sphere of necessity; they are necessary conditions for human survival, and must involve division of roles, routine operations, subordination, hierarchy. Work becomes *praxis* only when it is freely chosen and provides an opportunity for individual self-expression and self-fulfillment.

How are we to conceive of potential human faculties? They must be universal, otherwise a general standard of criticism would be lacking and philosophy would have to be relativized, which is absurd. On the other hand, if they are unchangeable, history would lose all meaning and would be reduced to a series of changes in the realm of mere phenomena. The only solution is to conceive of universal faculties as latent dispositions which are the product of all previous history and which can be slowly modified or even replaced by some new, future ones – depending on actual life conditions over a long period of time.

But is human nature constituted only by 'positive' faculties such as creativity, capacity for reasoning, for communication, sociability, etc.?

How can we justify such an optimistic view? And how can we account for the tremendous amount of evil in human history? Again, the only solution is to modify Marx's optimism somewhat and to introduce an idea of the polarity of human nature. As a result of millennia of life in class society man has also acquired some 'negative' latent dispositions, such as aggressiveness, egoistic acquisitiveness, will to power, destructive drives. All these enter into a *descriptive* concept of human nature which can be tested by historical evidence. Which of the conflicting latent dispositions will prevail and what sort of character will be formed in each individual case depends upon the social surroundings, upon the actual historical conditions. Thus when a philosopher builds up a selective, *normative* concept of human nature he implicitly commits himself to a way of life, to the creation of life conditions under which certain desirable (positive) latent dispositions contained in his normative concept may prevail, while certain undesirable (negative) dispositions would be blocked or slowly modified, assuming socially acceptable forms.

On these grounds it becomes possible to distinguish between *true, genuine needs* and *false, artificial* ones, or between a true and an illusory *self-realization*. The concept of truth in this context is much more general than the customary epistemological concept. One of its dimensions is adequacy to actual reality (descriptive concept of truth). Another dimension is adequacy to an ideal standard, to an essential possibility (normative concept of truth).

3. *Philosophical Method*

Philosophers who agree on so many issues and have collaborated fraternally over such a long period of time, as is the case with the *Praxis* group, must presumably have some common general methodological assumptions. But it is not easy to establish what they are. One of the things that unite all Yugoslav Marxist humanists is their rejection of the orthodox conception of dialectic.

Orthodox Marxists ('diamatchiks') believed that they should continue Engels' work and try to find new scientific confirmation for 'the laws of dialectic' discovered by Hegel and 'interpreted materialistically' by the classics of Marxism (the three laws were the unity of opposites, the transition of quantity into quality, and the negation of negation).

Dialectic thus conceived became a static and formal method – a set of ready-made, fixed, *a priori* rules that could be applied to any given content, celestial mechanics as well as the history of a revolution. While rejecting this interpretation of dialectic, some *Praxis* philosophers lost all interest in the problems of philosophical method in general and dialectic in particular. As a consequence, one finds in their works quite sharp distinctions, absence of mediation between the opposites, a tendency to construe some key concepts such as human essence, alienation, revolution, human community, etc., as transcendental rather than historical categories.

Other *Praxis* philosophers consider the question of method decisive for a theoretical orientation. They are convinced that the dialectic is the proper method for a critical philosophy and they try to develop it, on the one hand, by a deeper study of Hegel's *Phenomenology of Mind* and *Logic* together with the implicit dialectic of Marx's writings and, on the other, by critical examination of other contemporary methods (analytic, phenomenological, structuralist). The defining characteristics of dialectic, in contrast to those other methods, are the following regulative principles:

(a) Reality should be approached as a concrete totality rather than as an association of parts to be analysed in isolation from each other. Such an approach reveals possibilities of radical change of the given system, not only of its modification.

(b) Making sharp dichotomous distinctions is only a first approximation in the process of conceptual inquiry; deeper analysis reveals mediating instances among opposites.

(c) A study of synchronic, structural relations must be supplemented by the study of diachronic, historic relations. Each apparently stable object is only a phase of its history; it can be fully understood only in the light of its origin and its future possibilities.

(d) What moves all objects is the conflict of inner opposite forces and tendencies; what moves thought is discovery of contradictions. All problems are contradictions of some sort; to solve the problem means to disentangle the contradictions.

(e) As distinguished from an external, rigid determination in the world of objects (and reified human beings), *praxis* is a specifically human activity and is characterized by self-determination, i.e., by a conscious, purposeful commitment to realize practically one specific, freely chosen possibility among a set of alternatives.

(f) What constitutes a radical qualitative change of an object is the abolition of its essential inner limitation ('negation of its negation').

Dialectic according to this conception is neither a structure of an absolute, abstract spirit (as in Hegel) nor a general structure of nature (as in Engels), but a general structure of human historical *praxis* and its essential aspect, critical thinking. This conception, in contrast to the orthodox one, allows room for its further self-development. To conceive or to create an object by this method means at the same time to enrich and make more concrete the method itself.

4. *Ontological, Epistemological, and Axiological Implications*

From the standpoint of a dialectic of praxis it does not make sense to speak about reality 'in itself', truth 'in itself', or values 'in themselves'. There certainly is an antecedent structured reality; without assuming its existence it would be impossible to understand how organized, coordinated activity is at all possible. But whatever we come to know and say meaningfully and concretely about material or cultural reality has been mediated by the specific, historically determined features of our practical activity.

For the same reason, to speak about truth 'in itself' is either to confuse an epistemological category (truth) with an ontological category (fact) or to assume the existence of some mystical extrahuman consciousness. As a measure of adequacy, truth is a human, historical category.

The same holds for 'values in themselves'. There is no ideal, ahistorical sphere to which they apply. There is not a Lotzean, Husserlian, or, more recently, Popperian 'third world'. The world into which man has not practically penetrated is blind, meaningless, truthless, valueless. Objects and processes become values only when they are relative to human needs, which again in their turn are a product of the whole of preceding history.

An opposite procedure from this projection of specifically human products into transcendental, extrahuman realms is their reduction to mere things, i.e., their *reification*. In ontology, reification shows as a tendency to regard human conscious activity as merely an epiphenomenon of some primary objective structure – Being, Matter, Nature, inexorable Laws – independent of human consciousness and will. However, in the human world (with which philosophy deals) all objective structures are, in one way or another, mediated by human activity and relative to it. For example, laws that govern historic processes are nothing but relatively permanent patterns of human behavior, repeated time and again while certain conditions are present. But conscious subjects can modify those conditions and change the patterns of their behavior. In *epistemology* reification appears as a tendency to regard the model of the natural sciences as the paradigm of knowledge in general. The transfer of concepts and methods of the natural sciences into the social sciences and the humanities results not only in gross simplifications but also in a specific sort of conformism whereby mechanical, unimaginative, uncreative, reified forms of human behavior (which are the result of extraordinarily dehumanizing conditions) are explained easily as the *natural* way of being. Analogously, in *axiology* reification takes the form of a behaviorist reduction of all purposive, goal-directed activity to a stimulus-response scheme, thus relegating all discussion of values to an archaic, prescientific era of theoretical development. This approach is capable of yielding interesting results only with rats and pigeons. It fails miserably in dealing with specifically human, that is spontaneous, free, creative, imaginative, self-improving action. For example, no revolution could be accounted for in terms of mechanistic or behaviorist assumptions.

5. *Practical Social Implications*

A philosophy based on the notion of *praxis* will naturally pay special attention to deriving practical consequences from its principles; furthermore these consequences essentially will be steps that have to be undertaken in order to make true the idea of man as essentially a *being of praxis*.

Under what social conditions, in what kind of social organization can human activity become the objectification of the individual's most creative capacities and a means of satisfying genuine individual and common needs?

This question is much more general than the one usually asked by Marxists who ignore the philosophical roots of Marx's economic and political criticism. All questions about specific social institutions, such as private property, capital, the bourgeois state, and so on, boil down to the fundamental issue of what happens to man, what are his relationships to other human beings, and whether he actualizes or wastes all the wealth of his potential powers.

In this radical perspective (*radical* because the root – *radix* – of all issues is man) the basic purpose of critical inquiry is the discovery of those specific social institutions and structures which cripple human beings, arrest their development, and impose on them patterns of simple, easily predictable, dull, stereotyped behavior. Thus the critique of various institutions of bourgeois society is a superficial, sectarian critique if it remains an abstract negation of one particular form of social organization (capitalism) from the point of view of another particular form (socialism). The essential point of a radical, universally human critique is that these institutions inevitably bring about various forms of economic and political alienation. Thus *private property* produces a privatized, egoistic, acquisitive type of man; *professional division of labor* pins down complex human individuals to fixed simple roles which employ only a small fraction of their potential abilities; the regulation of production by the *market* reduces both the producer and the product to mere commodities, substitutes the profit motive of production for the needs-satisfaction motive, and turns production into an uncontrollable competitive process governed by blind economic forces; the *state* divides citizens into ruling subjects and ruled objects, turns decision-making on issues of general social interest into a specialized, professional activity in the hands of an alienated elite; the *party* is a hierarchical political organization with very little equality or genuine participation, and it tends to create and preserve an artificial unity of will and of faith in an apparently just cause by ideological manipulation and compulsory discipline.[11]

An important practical implication of the dialectical method is the distinction between criticism as an "abstract negation", aiming at total destruction of the criticized object, and criticism as a 'concrete negation' – *Aufhebung* – aiming at the abolition of only those features of the criticized object which constitute its essential inner limitation, while preserving all those other features (properties, elements, structures) which constitute a necessary condition for further development.

Thus while it is in the nature of Marxist theory to offer "a relentless criticism of all existing reality" – characterization of the *Praxis* group approach which infuriates bureaucracy – this criticism invites not the destruction but the *transcendence* of its object.

The practical form of transcendence in history is *revolution*. The defining characteristics of a social revolution are neither use of violence, nor overthrow of a government and seizure of political power, nor economic collapse of the system. Marx himself spoke of a possible peaceful social revolution in England, Holland, and America. He also made very clear, explicit statements about seizure of power as being only the first episode of a long process of social revolution, and about political revolution (as distinguished from social revolution) as having a 'narrow spirit' and leading necessarily to the rule of an elite.[12] That economic collapse is also not a necessary condition of revolution follows from Marx's description of economic transition measures which a new proletarian government has to undertake after successful seizure of power.[13] These measures are cautious and gradual, intended to preserve the continuity of economic functioning.

The Marxian concept of revolution is constituted by three basic elements. The first is the idea of a *socio-economic formation*. Each concrete society belongs to a certain type, to a socio-economic formation (feudalism, capitalism, etc.) which has definite structural characteristics. The second is the idea of an *essential inner limitation*: some structural characteristics block any further development and prevent the realization of already existing historical possibilities of the given society. (For example, private property prevents the socialization of production and its rational coordination as a whole). The third is the idea of *transcendence*, and it is irrelevant whether physical force is used, or whether change takes place in one discontinuous cataclysmic act or by a series of gradual transformations. The only relevant condition is the *abolition of the essential inner limitation of the given socio-economic formation*.

From this point of view none of the twentieth century socialist revolutions has yet been completed. What have taken place so far in Russia, China, Cuba, Yugoslavia, and elsewhere have been only initial phases or abortive attempts. Private ownership of the means of production has not been transcended by really social ownership but has been modified into state and group property. Professional division of labor still largely exists, and work is as long, monotonous, stultifying, and wasteful as in capitalism. The market is no longer the exclusive regulator of production; it has been supplemented by state planning. But this latter way of regulating production is still far from being very rational and democratic, and it still preserves a good deal of profit motivation. The bourgeois state has not been transcended by a network of self-management organs but has only been modified into a bureaucratic state which allows a greater (in Yugoslavia) or a lesser (in Russia) degree of participatory democracy in the atomic units of social organization. The party (as a typically bourgeois type of political organization) tends to be perpetuated. True, the social composition of the rank and file membership of the 'Communist' party shows a shift toward the working class, but the organization is even more authoritarian and ideological indoctrination even more drastic. The fact that there is only one such organization which monopolizes all political power is hardly an advantage over bourgeois pluralism. Real supersession of political alienation will materialize only when all monopolies of power are dismantled, when authoritarian and hierarchical organizations such as the state and Party are gradually transcended and replaced by self-governing associations of producers and citizens at all social levels.

This whole conception is labelled 'anarcho-liberal' by some politicians who speak in the name of Marx and of the Yugoslav League of Communists. The irony of the situation is that these are the ideas of Marx, ideas with which the Yugoslav League of Communists attracted the best minds of a generation of partisans and rebels against Stalin's domination. These are the ideas explicitly formulated in the 1958 Program of that same League of Communists.

The mortal sin of the *Praxis* group seems to consist in taking these ideas seriously.

REFERENCES

[1] The situation of the *Praxis* philosophers in Yugoslavia has changed dramatically since these lines were written. See the Introduction to this volume. (Editors' note.)

[2] *Present-day Problems of Philosophical Anthropology*, Opatija, 1963; *Man Today*, Dubrovnik, 1963; *Moral Values of Our Society*, Vrnjacka Banja, 1964; *Art in a Technical Age*, Varazdin, 1965 – all organized by the Yugoslav Philosophical Association; *Marx and Our Time*, Arandjelovac, 1963; Novi Sad, 1964; Opatija, 1965 – all three organized by the Institute for the Study of the International Labor Movement; *The Relevance of Marx's 'Capital' For Our Time* – organized by the journal *Gledista* in Belgrade 1967 on the occasion of the centennial of Marx's *Capital*.

[3] The general themes of the first five sessions were: *Progress and Culture*, 1963; *The Meaning and Perspectives of Socialism*, 1964; *What Is History*, 1965; *Creativity and Reification*, 1967; *Marx and the Revolution*, 1968. The 1966 session was cancelled as a consequence of strong ideological attacks on the school.

[4] Marković, 'Savremena gradjanska filozofija i marksizam', *Komunist*, November 15, 1958.

[5] Predrag Vranicki, one of the leading members of the *Praxis* group, was elected Rector of Zagreb University in 1972 and reelected in June 1974 for a second two year term.

[6] By the end of 1973 there were half a million unemployed workers (in addition to over a million who had to seek work abroad) and as a result of an extremely high rate of inflation (25–30%) the standard of living of workers began to decline.

[7] Grlić, Zašto, 1968.
Krešić, Dijalektika politike, 1968; Političko društvo i politička mitologija, 1968.
Marković, Dijalektika i humanizam, 1968; Dialektik der praxis, 1968; Preispitivanje, 1972; From Affluence to Praxis, 1974.
Mićunović, Logika i sociologija, 1971.
Petrović, Wider der autoritären Marxismus, 1969; Philosophie und revolution, 1971; Čemu praxis, 1971.
Stojanović, Between Ideas and Reality, 1973.
Supek, Sociologie und Humanismus, 1970; Ova jedina zemlja, 1973.
Tadić, Tradicija i revolucija, 1972; Autoritet i osporavanje, 1974.
Vranicki, Historija marksizma, II ed. 1972.
Životić, Čovek i vrednost, 1969; Egzistencija, realnost i sloboda, 1972.

[8] The general themes were: Humanism and Power, in 1969; Hegel, Lenin and the New Left, in 1970; Utopia and Anarchism, in 1971; Equality and Freedom, in 1972; The Bourgeois World and Socialism, in 1973; Arts in the Modern World, in 1974.

[9] Current research projects are: Marxism and Bourgeois Philosophy, The History of Philosophy, Axiological Problems of Yugoslav Socialism, Philosophical Foundations of Science and Yugoslav Philosophy.

[10] The general themes of the winter meetings were: Liberalism and Natural Right, Tara, 1971; Nationalism and Human Universality, Tara, 1972; Philosophy, History and Literature, Vrnjačka Banja, 1973; Culture and Revolution, Divchibare, 1974.

[11] This view of the party as a specifically bourgeois form of political organization is not shared by all members of the Praxis group. A few of them are still members of the Yugoslav League of Communists. Some follow Lukács (from History and Class Consciousness) in believing that the proletariat can be organized as a party.

[12] Marx, 'Kritische Randglossen auf dem Artikel: Der König von Preussen und die Soziale Reform: Von einem Preussen', Vorwärts, August 7, 10, 1844.

[13] Marx, Communist Manifesto in The Marx-Engels Reader (ed. by Robert C. Tucker), Norton and Co., New York, 1972, p. 362.

PART II

RELIGION

EDWARD D. WYNOT, JR.

RELUCTANT BEDFELLOWS: THE CATHOLIC CHURCH AND THE POLISH STATE, 1918–1939

From the beginning of their association in the tenth century, the Roman Catholic Church and the Polish state have experienced an intimate and complex relationship. The Church served as the focal point for the continuance of Polish national and political, as well as spiritual and cultural, life after the state was threatened and finally destroyed in the eighteenth century. The re-emergence of an independent Poland in 1918 provided the Church with new opportunities for expanding its influence over Polish life, and its presence in Poland became especially pervasive between world wars. Accordingly, in this period the relations between the Church and the Polish state must be viewed on two levels, one representing the formal, official institutions of government and politics and the other concerned with the informal, more subtle and less evident ways in which Church and state interacted. Since the attitudes and practices developed in the interwar years exerted a major influence on Church-state relations in Poland after 1945, an understanding of this earlier period is essential to an appreciation of the situation in People's Poland.

The formal relationship of the Church to the Polish state and its legal position in Polish life were defined by the constitutions of 1921 and 1935, the complementary Concordat signed with the Vatican in 1925, and in numerous statutes and regulations formulated to suit specific situations. Yet this impressive array of documentation never determined precisely the true official position of the Church in Poland. Instead, it clouded the question of Church-state relations with ambiguities and inconsistencies which allowed the government to re-define the relationship in a manner that would correspond to the political circumstances and needs of a given moment, while leaving the Church free from any binding commitments.

The March Constitution of 1921 was the best example of this tendency to avoid taking an unequivocal stance on Church-state relations.[1] Although it was a liberal document heavily influenced by the French model, the first Polish constitution nonetheless rejected the complete separation

De George and Scanlan (eds.), Marxism and Religion in Eastern Europe, 93–105. *All Rights Reserved.*
Copyright © 1976 *by D. Reidel Publishing Company, Dordrecht-Holland.*

of Church from state. The general political uncertainties in Poland during the immediate postwar years, together with the pressing questions of minority and religious freedoms, forced the constitutional framers to stop short of formally recognizing Catholicism as the official state religion. Rather, the article devoted exclusively to the religion issue (Article 114) granted the Roman Catholic Church the status of 'primus inter pares' among organized religions in the country, and implied that both public and private life should be under its influence. Furthermore, the state specifically renounced any claims to interference in the administration of Church lands, organizations, or laws. In addition, religious training was made compulsory in all public schools, with its implementation to be determined by school supervisory authorities in concert with local religious leaders (Article 120). But the constitution carefully ignored the question of a formal legal, institutional definition of Church-state relations, instead leaving this delicate task to a concordat to be concluded later with the Vatican. Catholic spokesmen expressed a general disappointment with the overall 'liberal' provisions of the document, and especially regretted that the constitution had neither made Catholicism the state religion nor assigned exclusive responsibility for all Polish education solely to Catholic parochial schools. Nevertheless, despite these reservations they stated that the Church was only 'mildly dissatisfied' with the final result.[2]

The conclusion of a treaty agreement between the Holy See and the Polish government was required by the constitution to spell out the precise relationship between Church and state in various areas. The Vatican was particularly anxious to sign the concordat in order to insulate the Church from the sharp political fluctuations resulting from the already-evident political instability in Poland and the consequent vulnerability of the Church to state interference in the absence of a binding legal commitment. Perhaps Rome also wished to halt a discernible widening of the gap between Church and state, and felt that the negotiation and signing of a concordat would reverse the trend to separation of the two.[3] In any event, a new papal nuncio was sent to Warsaw in 1921 with orders to hasten the conclusion of an agreement, a process which seemed simple enough to Polish Church officials given the limited nature of their demands: the right of the Church to apply Canon law to all Catholics, and the consent of the state not to adopt any statutes which would conflict with Church doctrine, such as marriage-divorce laws.[4] However, the negotiations became enmeshed in the economic and political turmoil that plagued Poland in the early 1920's, and no real progress was made until Władysław Grabski's government made the conclusion of a concordat a leading priority.

The agreement signed in February, 1925 was extremely favorable to the Church.[5] The key provisions bound the state to assist the Church in defrocking errant clergy and collecting the compulsory Church tax from all Catholics (Article IV), and to omit Church property and possessions from any government actions unless they were essential in eminent domain situations (Article XIV). The state was given the power to veto appointments to high Church offices, but only for clearly political or national security reasons (Articles XI, XIX, XX). The general tone of the Concordat was so favorable to the Church that Catholic spokesmen unanimously approved it.[6] This was due in large part to the nature of the Polish legislature, or Sejm, that had shaped the treaty, for this body was dominated by parties either openly or informally pro-Catholic.

The establishment of an authoritarian regime by Marshal Józef Piłsudski in May, 1926 presented the Church with a novel situation. The creation of a politically stable government offered the chance to normalize Church-state relations on a durable basis. When it became apparent that Piłsudski's Sanacja, or 'cleansing', regime was determined to revise the constitution to reflect its authoritarian outlook, the Church exerted tremendous pressure upon the government in hopes of bolstering its legal position. A dramatic example of Catholic lobbying in this direction came in the 1924 Christmas Eve speech of August Cardinal Hlond, Primate of Poland, who exhorted the new document's authors to "Let God ordain your constitution. Take His word into account when drafting your statutes."[7] But the regime avoided re-opening debate in the delicate areas of religion and minority affairs because of the dangers such inflammatory issues posed both to its own inner cohesion and its hold over the general Polish community. Instead, the Sanacja decided simply to retain intact those provisions of the 1921 constitution relating to religion and the national minorities, and the new constitution signed into law in April, 1935 merely repeated verbatim the relevant articles. Yet it was far more authoritarian in tone, pleasing some Church officials but alienating others with its clear emphasis on the supremacy of the state and its official in-

stitutional organs and interests over community and political organizations and movements.[8]

The seizure of power by Piłsudski in 1926, and the succession crisis
resulting from his death nine years later, were major turning points in
Church-state relations. For they forced the Church to reconsider its position on active participation in Polish politics on a formal basis. Generally
speaking, Catholic political activity was based upon a deep belief in the
need to maintain a stable political, economic, and social system, free
from internal disorder. Consequently, the Church always had reacted vig-
orously against any threats to the existing government, attacking Leftist
movements with particular ferocity. Very often this attitude was expressed
in strongly conservative terms which were directed against what the Church
considered the twin threats to Poland of liberalism and democracy. Spokesmen for the Catholic Social School noted that "the system of so-called
parliamentary democracy, hitherto universally accepted, has not acquitted
itself very well in countless countries, forcing them into severe crises and
weakening their internal cohesion".[9] Another Catholic writer observed
that Poles must purge their social and economic, as well as political, life
of "everything that is favorable to Communism, especially the excesses
of liberalism."[10] While the hierarchy also distrusted totalitarian forces
on the extreme Right, it tended to view some of these with considerable
tolerance. This was true even of the Falanga wing of the National Radical
Camp, which provided Poland's native fascist party. Unlike most other
fascist movements, the Falangists openly wooed the Catholic Church;
they published a monthly entitled *Pro Christo*, and adopted the slogan
'God is the Highest end of Man' to express their view that Catholicism
formed the fundamental basis of the entire Falanga program. Not surprisingly, Catholic leaders considered the Falanga highly sympathetic
to the Church's most cherished goal: the incorporation of every aspect of
Polish life under its control or influence.[11]

Yet, although they were united on their ultimate ends, Catholic officials
were divided over which means to employ in their attainment, especially
after the 1926 Piłsudski coup. Until then, the Church had been a solid, if
unofficial, supporter of the National Democratic movement (Endeks) as
the best defender of the existing sociopolitical structure. Many of the
upper Catholic hierarchy joined the lower clergy as eager participants in
the movement's activities, particularly in the heavily non-Polish eastern

borderlands; in fact, several Polish bishops entered the legislature under the Endek banner. But when the Sanacja assumed control of the state, the Church was torn between its traditional policy of supporting the defenders of the status quo against the forces of the Left, and its deep distaste for and fear of the strong anti-clerical sentiments nurtured by certain circles of the regime. The 1935 constitution and its accompanying electoral laws, with their strong authoritarian measures, threatened to split the Church leadership even further along these lines.[12] Those elements who had aligned themselves with the Endeks and the more centrist Christian Democrats criticized the regime as having obvious intents to totalitarianize thoroughly Polish political, social, and economic life. On the other hand, Church leaders who wished to maintain at least the appearance of formal political neutrality saw in the new system a chance to bolster Catholic fortunes while eliminating the perils of direct political involvement.

When Piłsudski's death brought to the fore in the Sanacja those elements favorably disposed to the Church, it appeared that the latter group had been justified in its stand. Now under the control of the uneasy partnership of Marshal Edward Śmigły-Rydz, the Inspector General of the Armed Forces, and President Ignacy Mościcki, the regime in 1936 announced plans to form a new government front to serve as the rallying point for all the community forces supporting the system.[13] Once again, however, Catholic hopes for an improvement in the formal position of the Church in Poland were disappointed. The 'Ideological-Political Declaration' of the new 'Camp of National Unity', officially proclaimed in February, 1937, contained an entire section devoted solely to the Catholic Church. Nonetheless, the extent of its commitment to advancing the Catholic cause in Poland was a bland statement to the effect that the Church should be treated 'with solicitous care'. A period of heightened Church-state tension born of momentary disillusionment followed, after which the two key elements in Poland finally arrived at a mutually acceptable formula to define their formal relationship. The regime, through the public pronouncements of the Camp of National Unity, regularly associated the best interests of the Polish nation with those of the Catholic Church, while the latter reciprocated by endorsing the Sanacja system as being the best one possible given Poland's precarious geopolitical situation.

The division of opinion within the Catholic leadership over the nature and extent of the ideal Church-state relationship did not hinder the pursuit of a vigorous domestic political program in those areas considered important to the Church. While the hierarchy as a rule did not openly pressure Polish governments prior to 1926 to enact or defeat certain measures, the Piłsudski coup apparently convinced them of the need for organized, concerted campaigns in defense of basic Catholic interests. Given its aspiration to mold all Poles into loyal Catholic citizens, it is understandable that the Church was especially interested in exercising direct influence over the country's education system. On the whole, lobbying efforts attained positive results for the Catholic cause. In December, 1926 the Ministry of Cults and Public Education ordered the compulsory participation of all public school pupils, including Jews and atheists, in formal religious observations in addition to their normal religious instructions; supervision of this program was left to local school and church officials. This and related measures were subsequently upheld by the Supreme Court in a 1927 decision denying atheists or agnostics exemption from the rules.[14] The Church protested bitterly when anti-cleric reaction inside the Sanacja and the tendencies toward more open authoritarianism in the regime resulted in some educational moves that hampered Catholic plans in this area. In November, 1927 the government ordered all youth or student organizations, including strictly Catholic groups, placed under the control of school authorities.[15] Another setback occurred in the comprehensive education reform package developed and implemented in 1932 by the two Jędrzejewicz brothers, Janusz and Wacław. Provisions especially irritating to Catholic leaders called for all schools to be coeducational, and be subject to complete state supervision – including those parochial schools maintained by the Church.[16] But in 1936 the altered political conditions inside the Sanacja and the Church's strenuous opposition to the above policies combined to reverse the trend toward exclusive state control of education. In March, the Ministry ordered all public school teachers to familiarize themselves with the program of Roman Catholic religious instruction, so that eventually the religious and secular educational systems could be merged and the two approaches correlated.[17]

Active promotion of government policies favorable to the Church was not limited to education. With its operating costs rising steadily, the

Episcopate became concerned with the financial position of the Church. In 1932 the Sejm yielded to a long-standing Church demand and passed a bill authorizing the imposition of a special 'church surcharge' of 5% on all state revenues received from Catholics. In addition, over the next two years the government exempted Catholic fund-raising activities from the limitations and restrictions imposed on other institutions and organizations.[18] Another Church campaign aimed at securing a monopoly for Catholic cooperatives and associations of the production and sale of religious devotional articles. Hence, Catholic support was instrumental in securing passage of a law prohibiting anyone not of a given faith from producing or distributing religious artifacts of that faith. Since Jewish craftsmen and merchants handled the bulk of this trade, its anti-Semitic overtones pleased the nationalist elements with which the Church was flirting while simultaneously attaining the desired economic results. These were instances in which the Church assumed an active, offensive posture, but there were occasions when the Church was active in a negative, defensive manner as well. Frantic Catholic lobbying, including an organized public opinion campaign, was instrumental in defeating proposed bills which would have given the state complete control over the civil registry of vital statistics and permitted civil marriages and divorces.[19]

There were other, less obvious and formal, ways in which the Church and state interacted in interwar Poland. Their relationship was particularly evident in the area of national religious life. The Catholic hierarchy worked closely with the government apparatus to regain for the Church those properties seized and transferred to the Russian Orthodox Church during the period of Russian rule. Catholic inspiration was also instrumental in convincing the state to launch an organizational drive in the late 1930's to expropriate the Greek Orthodox Churches serving the Ukrainian population in south-eastern Poland on the grounds that they were 'little used'. The fierce resistance with which the well-organized Ukrainians countered this latest attempt at Polonization resulted in an outbreak of armed violence which reached such proportions that regular army troops had to be dispatched to the area to restore peace.[20] Likewise, the Church frequently employed the governmental administrative apparatus to assist in collecting Church taxes (tithes). Perhaps the most revealing connection between Church and state was their financial relationship. Prior to Piłsudski's death, whatever financial connections existed between the secular administration and the leading religious movement in Poland were so carefully concealed that no documentary trace of them exists. But after 1935, the government granted about 20 million *zloty* annually to the Catholic Church as a direct subsidy; these funds were used mainly to pay the salaries of clergy and Catholic administrative personnel.[21] The Church responded to this official generosity by committing its personnel and material resources to the formal, organized struggle against Communism that became an important state activity after 1926. The most visible sign of this aspect of Church-state cooperation was the Catholic participation in the activities of the Institute for the Scientific Study of Communism, organized and directed by the Army General Staff. The Church hierarchy proved especially effective in organizing mass anti-Communist 'educational informative' meetings for both clergy and lay audiences, which were always well attended.[22] Moreover, the Church expanded considerably its propaganda campaign against 'Godless Communism', with a major publication program forming the basis of activities in this direction.[23] Indeed, Catholic participation in this area was so zealous that as early as October 1936 a government official could note with pleasure that the clergy was now a full-fledged partner in the Polish anti-Communist crusade.[24]

The Church also used its numerous theoretically nonpolitical organizations as effective political pressure groups. Such professional organizations as teachers', lawyers', doctors', and writers' associations, labor unions, and youth groups functioning under Catholic auspices served both to implant Catholic viewpoints in those segments of society they served, and to consolidate and project public opinion in a manner that could not escape the attention of the government. Perhaps the most effective non-political Church pressure group was the vast *Catholic Action* movement, which had gained exemption from the strict government control decreed in 1934 for all civic and social organizations in Poland.[25] This particular movement typified the Church's technique of consistently emphasizing its apolitical nature while simultaneously justifying its involvement in politics as a means of preserving and extending Catholic ideals in Poland. Spokesmen declared that "in purely political and economic matters, the *Catholic Action* does not advance any definite views. It only desires that, in these areas of life, *Catholic people be given leaders with Catholic views and convictions.*"[26] Yet in the final years of peace, when the regime sought to draw the *Catholic Action* under its umbrella on the grounds that the Sanacja then fit the above criteria, the movement rebuffed all overtures. Its leaders explained that it could not single out and endorse one party in a nation where Catholics were split in political allegiance, for to do so would "betray the goal of *Catholic Action* – the infusion of all social life in Poland with Catholic principles."[27] Another source of political pressure were the various devotional orders and societies, which were officially concerned with promoting religious practices and zeal through lay involvement at the lowest community levels. While no record exists that these were ever mobilized for political purposes, this possibility remained before the eyes of the Sanacja regime. Leaders of the more militant wing of the Church made certain that government officials were aware of the possibilities for mass pressure campaigns from these organizations. They declared pointedly that, "while not becoming directly involved in political life, the Church hierarchy has the right and the duty, in its best interests, to purify the spirit as well as to fulfill its principal mission: Showing the faithful the proper line of political action in specific instances."[28] No doubt, such threats of this weapon's use contributed to the government's generally conciliatory response to most Catholic demands after 1935.

Despite this impressive scale of Catholic political activity, the net result was not completely successful. The deliberate aloofness of the Church from direct, open involvement in daily political activity prevented it from ever building its own political movement which could participate in the hectic public arena on a par with secular political parties. Moreover, the Church was adamant about retaining its organizational and functional independence from any political alignment, preferring instead to work with individuals or momentary alliances as circumstances dictated. While this general policy did not prevent certain members of the clergy from actively pursuing their own political careers, it did tend to limit the extent to which the Church could commit itself and function effectively in seeking to obtain or prevent the realization of a particular program. Thus, even such officially pro-Catholic parties as the Christian Democrats, which in other European lands enjoyed an intimate formal relationship with the Catholic Church establishment, in Poland were denied the official sanction of the Episcopate. This ambivalence of the hierarchy, no doubt reflecting the divisions over means within its own ranks, was a serious obstacle to the development of both a coherent Catholic program, and a sound, steady Church-state relationship in interwar Poland. For it permitted the government to vacillate and temporize in questions of religious policy, while depriving the Church of a solid framework within which to develop a coherent and consistent approach to this problem.

The single feature of Church-state relations in interwar Poland with the greatest importance for post-1945 developments was the disciplined manner in which the Catholic hierarchy differentiated between its attitude toward the Sanacja regime as a political movement in general, and as the ruling force in the Polish state after 1926. There is little doubt that the Church would have preferred to see the National Democrats, or a Right-Centrist coalition joining them with the Christian Democrats and other conservative parties, establish political power on a lasting basis. When the mortal enemies of the nationalists instead seized control of the state apparatus, it would have been logical for the Church to oppose totally and bitterly the Sanacja regime. Yet, in the resulting situation this course would have cast the Catholic Church as one of the elements in Poland which sought continually to topple the state, to overthrow the existing government and thereby open the way for anarchy and revolution – the very goals of those Leftist, 'radical' elements the Church had fought so staunchly in the past. Ironically, this would have disavowed and reversed the cornerstone of Catholic socio-political strategy since 1918 – the maintenance of the status quo at all costs – and hence was unthinkable to all but the most extreme nationalist followers in the clergy. Accordingly, with the exception of this latter group, who attacked the regime bitterly right up to the outbreak of war in 1939, the Church struck an uneasy *modus vivendi* with the Sanacja. Cardinals, archbishops, and bishops generally supported the regime publicly – but as the current directors of the Polish state, never as a political camp *per se*. When they did oppose the regime, Church leaders never criticized it openly, but instead made their disapproval known implicitly by withholding public support for certain major government programs or gently disavowing them.

This general pattern carried over into the tumultuous years following World War II, when the Polish Communists finally attained and then consolidated political power in Poland. No doubt it surprised many observers that the Roman Catholic Church was not openly fighting the Communists and their Socialist and radical peasant allies – after all, had not the Church singled out these elements as being the gravest threats to the very existence of a free, independent, and Catholic Poland? Of course the Church had, back before 1939–just as many leading Catholic spokesmen had condemned the Sanacja camp prior to 1926 as being a denial of everything true and good in Polish life. But the same pragmatic considerations that had motivated formal Church behavior toward the enemy Sanacja after 1926 functioned in similar fashion after 1945. Once again, the Church was forced to endorse, however coolly, the actions of a political movement it had always hated and feared. As previously, it did this for reasons that were pragmatically political in both the broad and tactical sense. On the one hand, a country run reasonably smoothly by Polish Communists would still remain officially a sovereign Polish state, whereas the failure of the local Communists might well bring total absorption into the U.S.S.R. à la the fate of the Baltic states. Moreover, as the sole organization in the country with an administrative network functioning throughout the land, and a universal positive recognition factor not shared by any political group, the Church could render itself indispensable to the state. This, in turn, would not only insure its continued existence but perhaps also enable it to exert some real influence in the shaping of People's Poland. The Church displayed this 'survival instinct' most noticeably in the regions transferred to Poland from German rule–the so-called 'Western Lands'. As Z. Anthony Kruszewski convincingly demonstrates,[29] in these areas the Church not only did not resist the establishment of Communist control, but instead actively assisted it, in the conviction that the 'Polishness' of the lands should be well-founded before any lesser political questions were taken up. Local and national Communists were smart enough to appreciate the advantage this gave them, and consequently the cooperation between Catholic Church and Communist state became more intense here than elsewhere in Poland – in direct disregard for official Vatican policy of that time. While the failure of the Church to adopt a more militant anti-Communist stance after 1945 may have disappointed many observers, it should have surprised no one familiar with Church-state relations as they evolved in Poland after 1926.

REFERENCES

1 *Konstytucja Rzeczypospolitej Polskiej. Ustawa z dnia 17 marca 1921 r.* Warsaw: Czytelnik, 1921. All references to the 1921 constitution are drawn from this edition.
2 Samples of Catholic response to the constitution are the two press articles by clerical publicists: Rev. Jan Urban, 'Nasza konstytucja a program katolicki', *Przegląd Powszechny* (1921), no. 149/150, pp. 242–43, and Rev. Jan Pawelski, 'Katolicyzm religią państwową w Polsce', *ibid.* (1937), no. 213, pp. 69–70.
3 Adam Vetulani, 'Dążenia powojennej polityki konkordatowej', *Przegląd Powszechny* (1935), no. 207, p. 37.
4 Rev. Jan Urban, 'Jakim winien być konkordat?', *ibid.* (1921), no. 151/152, pp. 360–61.
5 Full text printed as *Konkordat Polski z Stolicą Apostolską*. Lwów: Liga Katolicka dla Archidiecezji Lwowskiej, 1925.
6 For examples of highly favorable Catholic comment on the concordat, see especially Rev. Boleslaw Wilanowski, *Ustepstwa ze strony Kościoła na rzecz Państwa, poczynione w konkordacie z 10 lutego 1925*. Wilno: Księgarnia św. Wojciecha, 1927; *Stosunek Kościoła do Państwa w świetle innych konkordatów*. Wilno: Księgarnia św. Wojciecha, 1930; and Leon Halban, *Konkordat zawarty między Rzecząpospolitą Polską a Stolicą Apostolską*. Warsaw: Księży Jezuitów, 1925.
7 *Miesięcznik Kościelny* (1935), no. 1, p. 5.
8 The more determined anti-Sanacja opposition comments came in such Catholic publications as *Gazeta Kościelna* (1935), no. 18, p. 1, and *Przewodnik Katolicki* (1935), no. 14, pp. 1–3. See also the pastoral letter of the Polish Primate issued in summer 1935 – August Hlond, *Listy pasterskie*. Poznan: Naczelny Instytut Akcji Katolickiej, 1936, pp. 164–65. On the other hand, Catholic sentiments in favor of the document were voiced in such youth-oriented publications as *Młoda Polka* (1935), no. 5, p.1.
9 *Przegląd Społeczny* (1935), no. 8/9, p. 329.
10 *Mały Dziennik*, March 21, 1937.
11 For the Falanga program, see the publication of its leader, Bolesław Piasecki, *Prezelom narodowy. Zarys programu narodoworadykalnego*. Warsaw: Obóz Narodowo-Radylalny *Falanga*, 1937.
12 For a detailed discussion of Church-state relations in Poland after 1935, see the article by Edward D. Wynot, Jr., 'The Catholic Church and the Polish State, 1935–1939', *Journal of Church and State,* 15 (1973), no. 2, pp. 223–40.
13 For developments in this period, see Edward D. Wynot, Jr., *Polish Politics in Transition: The Camp of National Unity and the Struggle for Power, 1935–1939*, Athens: University of Georgia Press, 1974.
14 *Dziennik Ustaw Rzeczypospolitej Polskiej* (hereafter cited as *DURP*) *z 1927 r.*, no. 1, poz. 9, and *Orzecnictwo sadów polskich*, VI, 1927, p. 345, poz. 292.
15 The Church opposed this bitterly as being in violation of the concordat. See Rev. Stanisław Łukomski, *Konkordat zawarty dnia 10 lutego 1925 roku między Stolicą Apostolską a Rzecząpospolitą Polską*. łomża: n.p., 1934, pp. 372–73.
16 *Ibid.*, pp. 351–53, *DURP z 1932 r.*, no. 38, poz. 389. For Catholic reaction, see *Przegląd Powszechny* (1932), no. 193, p. 396.
17 *Dziennik Ustaw Ministerstwa Wyznań Religijnych i Oświecenia Publicznego*, 24/IV, 1936.
18 See the detailed discussion of this state concession to the Church and how it affected Catholic organizations in Rev. Stanisław Sprusiński and Władysław Deptula, *Podręcznik organizacyjny oddziału KSM*, Warsaw: Katolickie Stowarzyszenia Młodzieżowe, 1937, pp. 235–39.

[19] For both public and confidential discussions of the Church's role in killing these bills, see *Gazeta Warszawska* (August 5, 1931) and *Przegląd Powszechny* (1932), no. 193, pp. 118–19, plus the unpublished memoranda written by Franciszek Potocki, a leading official in the Ministry of Cults and Public Education. The two of particular interest and relevance are the undated study *Projekt prawa małżeńskiego*, and his *Notatka z konferencji z dnia 16 listopada 1932 w Ministerstwie Spraw Wewnętrznych w sprawie projektu ustawy zwieniającej niektóre postanowienia o rejestracji stanu cywilnego*; both are deposited in the Archiwum Akt Nowych in Warsaw.

[20] For details on Polish-Ukrainian tensions during this period, see Edward D. Wynot, Jr., 'The Ukrainians and the Polish Regime, 1936–1939', *The Ukrainian Historian* 7, (1970), no. 4, pp. 44–60.

[21] This practice is considered extensively in Henryk Światkowski's *Wyznania religijne w Polsce*, vol. 1, Warsaw: Towarzystwo Naukowe Warszawskie, 1937, p. 90. Budget projects for the Ministry of Cults and Public Education, housed in that ministry's collection in the Archiwum Akt Nowych (file 148, folios VIII, XI) offer the following precise sums of government funds appropriated for this purpose: 20,052,550 *złoty* for both 1935/36 and 1937/38, and 20,407,052 *złoty* for 1939/40. During this period, the approximate value of one *złoty* was U.S. $.20.

[22] For a discussion of Church involvement in the Institute's activities, see Wiesław Mysłek, *Kościół katolickie w Polsce w latach 1918–1939*, Warsaw: Książka i Wiedza, 1966, pp. 558–63. While this book contains much valuable factual material, it is presented with a definite ideological bias.

[23] For samples of the Church's anti-Communist propagandizing, see especially the following contemporary publications: *Bolszewizm. Praca zbiorowa*, Lublin: Drukarnia Narodowa Towarzystwa Wiedzy Chrzescijańskiej, 1938; *Chrystianizm wobec niewiary i ateizmu*, Warsaw: Polskie Towarzystwo Teologiczne, 1935; *List pasterski ks. Adolfa Szelazka, biskupa luckiego, o zwalczaniu niewiary*, Łuck: Drukarnia Kurii Biskupiej, 1935; Mieczysław Skrudlik, *Bezbożnictwo w Polsce*, Katowice: Księgarnia i Drukarnia Katolickie, 1935; Antonio Starodworski, *Katolicyzm a komunizm*, Warsaw: Instytut Naukowy Badania Komunizmu, 1936; and the directives of the militantly nationalist Bishop of Katowice, Stanisław Adamski, *List pasterski o czynnym udziale katolików w walce z bezbożnictwem*, Katowice: Księgarnia i Drukarnia Katolickie, 1937.

[24] As noted in a memorandum prepared by an official in the Polish Ministry of Foreign Affairs dated October 10, 1936 – Archiwum Akt Nowych, Ministerstwo Spraw Zagraniczych, PIW 122, t. 195.

[25] Of the many studies of the *Catholic Action* movement in Poland, see especially those of Bishop Stanisław Adamski, *Podstawy pracy stowarzyszeń Akcji Katolickiej*, Poznan: Naczelny Instytut Akcji Katolickiej, 1937, and Herbert Bednorz, *Udział Akcji Katolickiej w rozwiązaniu kwestii społecznej*, Poznan: Naczelny Instytut Akcji Katolickiej, 1939.

[26] Andrzej Mytkowicz, *Akcja Katolicka u podstaw i w praktyce*, Lwów: Liga Katolicka dla Archidiecezji Lwowskiej, 1929, p. 39. Emphasis in the original.

[27] *Głos Narodu*, May 19, 1937. Mussolini's regime faced a similar problem in dealing with the Italian *Catholic Action* movement. See Giuseppe Dalla Torre, *Azione Catolica e Fascismo*, Rome: A.V.E., 1945, and Daniel A. Binchy, *Church and State in Fascist Italy*, Oxford: At the University Press, 1941.

[28] *Mały Dziennik*, April 27, 1938.

[29] Z. Anthony Kruszewski, *The Oder-Neisse Boundary and Poland's Modernization*, New York: Praeger, 1972, pp. 159–65.

DENNIS J. DUNN

THE CATHOLIC CHURCH AND
THE SOVIET GOVERNMENT IN SOVIET
OCCUPIED EAST EUROPE, 1939–1940

The interplay between the Catholic Church and the Soviet authorities in
Soviet occupied Poland during 1939–1940 offers a unique prism to understand the religious policy and the decision-making process of the Soviet
Government. Before the war the Soviet Government had been quite
hostile to the Catholic Church in the U.S.S.R. and had institutionally
decimated it, leaving by 1939 only a few scattered churches and clerics and
an Apostolic Administrator in Moscow, Leopold Braun, who was tolerated because he was also chaplain to the American embassy.[1] The
Soviets' animosity rested upon a series of reasons. (1) The Communists
believed, as Marxist-Leninists, that religion's extirpation would advance
the socialist revolution.[2] This ideological factor, of course, must always be
balanced by the pragmatic nature of Marxism-Leninism which would
permit tactical changes, including an alliance with religion, if such altera-
tions would serve the interests of the Party. (2) The Bolsheviks inherited
from the tsars a legacy which pegged Catholicism (especially in its Uniate
form) as an historical foe of the Russian people.[3] (3) The Soviets could not
abide Catholicism because it preached a world view irreconcilable with
their own. (4) Catholicism was an international movement competing
with Communist internationalism. (5) It was a religion led by a foreign,
independent authority – the Vatican – over which the Communists had
no influence. (6) It was a source of nationalism for some major, national
minorities in the U.S.S.R., including Poles, Volga Germans, Belorussians,
and Ukrainians (after 1940 one would also include Lithuanians and
Latvians), and thus it blocked not only these peoples' 'Sovietization' but
the totalitarian aspirations of the Soviet Government. Finally, the Church
was identified – dating from the time of the revolution, the civil war, and
the Russo-Polish war – with the internal and external enemies of the
regime.

With the coming of World War II, the Soviet authorities, as they moved
into East Europe, suddenly confronted a strong and vigorous Catholic
Church. Naturally, given the precedent of the 1920s and 1930s in the

De George and Scanlan (eds.), Marxism and Religion in Eastern Europe, 107–118. *All Rights Reserved.*
Copyright © 1976 by D. Reidel Publishing Company, Dordrecht-Holland.

U.S.S.R., the Catholic Church in eastern Poland expected violent persecution. No such persecution took place, however. The following pages outline, primarily on the basis of nuncios' and bishops' reports, the story of the Soviet policy toward the Church in East Europe, and then attempt to offer an explanation for the nature of this policy.

On September 17, 1939, as prearranged in the Molotov-Ribbentrop Pact of August 23, Soviet troops moved in and occupied eastern Poland. Initially the demarcation line separating German and Russian troops ran along the Vistula River; but on September 28 Germany and the U.S.S.R. amended their pact to allow the U.S.S.R. the option of taking Lithuania in exchange for German occupation of all of ethnic Poland. The Soviet Union kept the western White Russian and western Ukrainian parts of Poland, and thus the new demarcation line ran roughly along the famous Curzon line.

All told, the Russian troops controlled, wholly or partly, six Latin dioceses: Lviv, Peremyshl, Lomza, Pinsk, Lutsk, and Vilnius. On October 10 the Soviets allowed the Lithuanians to annex the city of Vilnius and some surrounding land, but they retained control of the greater part of the diocese. The Soviet action undoubtedly was a feeble attempt to convince the Lithuanians and the Balts generally that they had nothing to fear from the Soviet Union, and also to exploit the ill-feeling between the Polish bishop of Vilnius, Mgr. Romuald Jałbrzykowski, and his Lithuanian parishioners.[4] Within the Communist pale there were approximately six and a half million Latin Catholics. In addition to the Latin districts the occupied regions contained the greater part of three Uniate dioceses as well as a number of Uniate enclaves under Latin administration. The Uniate dioceses were Lviv, Stanislav, and Peremyshl and they held approximately 3,200,000 believers.[5]

The first few weeks of the Soviet occupation of the western Ukraine and western White Russia proved to be a capsular glimpse of the attitudes and policies the Soviet Government adopted toward the Catholic Church until the Nazi invasion. In general, in all Latin and Uniate dioceses – and this would apply also to the regions the U.S.S.R. annexed in 1940 – the Soviets implemented, immediately upon occupation, a number of broad policies: Churches and ecclesiastical properties were nationalized and assessed taxes. Schools were taken over by the state and religion was eliminated from the educational curriculum. Monasteries and seminaries, with a few exceptions, were confiscated and used as quarters by the Red Army; the monks and religious who had lived in them were dispersed and forced to find new housing. Atheistic propaganda was spread and supported by the governmental authorities. Communication with the Vatican was disrupted and made exceedingly difficult. Finally, the faithful were deported on an increasing scale to the Soviet Union. One other general characteristic of the Soviet tenure was that the Communists treated the Uniates more harshly than the Latins.

Although such general policies were persecutory, by and large they stood in sharp contrast to the virulence directed against the Russian Catholic Church in the Soviet Union during the 1920's and 1930's. The Soviet Government, to be sure, harassed the Catholic Church in occupied Eastern Europe; but given the reign of Stalin as a continuum, the Soviet Government's anti-Catholic policies between 1939 and 1941 must be classified as temperate. The basis for such an evaluation, as well as for the description of the policies, is predicated mainly, as indicated earlier, upon reports from nuncios and bishops in the occupied dioceses. During 1939 the Vatican obtained official reports on four occupied dioceses and, by 1941, it had received descriptions on the religious situation from all Soviet-controlled dioceses. This material portrayed a picture of anti-religious leniency. In addition, unofficial reports, issued by both Soviet and Papal news media – the latter apparently based partly upon the official commentaries from the dioceses and partly upon other unidentified sources of information – corroborated the rather mild representation of Soviet anti-religious measures delineated in the official accounts.

One of the dioceses which managed to send an exposé on the religious situation in 1939 was the Latin diocese of Peremyshl, one-third of which was under Soviet jurisdiction (the San River separated German and Russian forces in Peremyshl). On November 4, the Latin bishop, Mgr. Francis Barda, who was within the German-held part of Peremyshl, informed Pope Pius XII that the Communists had not interfered with either religious worship in the churches or with the duties of the clergy. The only persecutory note the bishop sounded was that the Soviets, as soon as they moved into Peremyshl, forced the schools to drop religion and to add Communism to their offerings.[6] There was one other anti-religious action the Soviets took, however, which the bishop did not mention but which Moscow Radio, on October 27, announced as general policy throughout the newly occupied territories: the nationalization of ecclesiastical properties, including churches and schools.[7] But on the whole it appears from the sources available that the Soviets treaded more lightly in the Latin diocese of Peremyshl than in other Latin or Uniate dioceses, for they did not, as was customary, close down the Latin seminary.[8] The explanation for the uncommon indulgence must have been tied to the fact that two-thirds of the Latin diocese of Peremyshl was under German control; even though the Germans were persecuting the Catholic Church, the Soviets wanted to keep this vulnerable showcase borderland calm.

The second diocese on which an early report was sent was Pinsk. On November 22, 1939, the chargé d'affaires at Kaunas, Mgr. Joseph Burzio, reported to the Papacy's Secretary of State, Cardinal Luigi Maglione, that thus far religious life in Pinsk was normal, except for the nationalization of ecclesiastical properties and atheistic propaganda, and that no clerics had been arrested.[9] His statement was laconic: the Soviets had not instituted any Nero-type campaign against the Catholic Church.

The diocese of Vilnius was also depicted in Burzio's November 22 report to Cardinal Maglione. Here, the chargé wrote, the Soviets had not arrested or executed any priests and, thus far, had simply demanded that clerics refrain from involving themselves in political affairs.[10] Of course, as in all dioceses, Soviet anti-religious legislation became applicable in Vilnius once eastern Poland was assimilated into the U.S.S.R., and that occurred immediately after occupation. Nonetheless it was obvious in Vilnius as elsewhere in the Soviet-held regions that the Russians did not want to arouse any public resentment over religion.

On December 18, 1939, the Latin archbishop of Vilnius, Mgr. Jałbrzykowski, sent chargé Burzio an up-to-date assessment on Vilnius. He declared that a few priests had been arrested by the Communists, including, most recently, Reverend Antonius Manturzyk, a cathechism scholar and the rector of a church in Podrodzie. Other priests, according to the archbishop, had been obliged to vacate their residences and find new facilities, and Soviet troops had been quartered in the vacated domiciles. Religion, he wrote, had been displaced in all schools by atheistic teachings and there was a surfeit of atheistic propaganda; also, some priests had been restrained from visiting the deceased, the sick, and one another. But, in general, the episcopal leader insisted, religious life continued unobstructed: churches were open, the faithful regularly attended Mass and sacraments, and priests recited their divine office.[11]

The final reports that the Vatican received during 1939 all emanated from and described the situation of the Uniate diocese of Lviv. In this diocese, the stronghold of Uniatism, the Soviets encountered an irreconcilable problem which they did not face in Latin dioceses. On the one hand, the Russians wished to portray themselves to the Ukrainians (and this would be true of the Uniate dioceses of Peremyshl and Stanislav as well) as liberators from Polish cultural suffocation and to exploit the traditional rift between the Ukrainians and Poles.[12] At the same time, however, the Soviets desired to crush the Uniate Church. As logic would have it, they only induced the Uniates into believing, as Archbishop Andrei Sheptyts'kyi, the Uniate leader, commented, that rather than bringing liberation the Russians brought "enslavement". [13]

As for the specific events in the Uniate diocese of Lviv, a fairly detailed picture emerged from the reports issued by the Berlin nuncio, Mgr. Cesare Orsenigo, and by Metropolitan Sheptyts'kyi. On November 23, 1939, Mgr. Orsenigo wrote Cardinal Maglione that Metropolitan Sheptyts'kyi was taxed unreasonably, that monasteries and convents had been confiscated, and that the Soviets were essaying to exploit the cultural cleavage between the Poles and Ukrainians in Lviv.[14] Two days later, the Vatican gave Metropolitan Sheptyts'kyi permission to name Mgr. Josyf Slipyi coadjutor with right of succession to the Lviv diocese and, in a secret ceremony on December 22, Monsignor Slipyi was consecrated.[15] Evidently both the Vatican and the Metropolitan wished to firm up the Uniate Church's ecclesiastical organization in the face of what portended to be a harrowing experience.[16] On December 26, Metropolitan Sheptyts'kyi himself filed a summary of the religious situation in Lviv with Cardinal Domenico Tardini, the Secretary of the Congregation of Extraordinary Affairs. According to Sheptyts'kyi, the Communists confiscated monasteries, secularized schools, propagandized atheism, and in general were intolerant of religion. But, he asserted, religious life in Lviv continued to flourish; members of the Uniate clergy had not been arrested and, although some fled their parishes with the Bolsheviks' arrival, the vast majority were still administering Lviv's 1,267 parishes. The Metropolitan concluded by stating that the faithful, who regularly came to church, protected the priests' personal property and the churches from sequestrations.[17]

In addition to the specific episcopal and ambassadorial information that was given to the Vatican in 1939, there were other descriptions, written after the Soviet retreat, which summarized religious conditions in Lviv and Stanislav from the advent to the exit of the Soviets. These reports, plus chronicles from all other Soviet occupied dioceses in 1940 and in the first half of 1941, emphasized, like the 1939 reviews, that the Soviets had not been frenzied in their anti-religious measures.[18] This conclusion was supported in general summaries on religious conditions issued by Radio Vatican and *L'Osservatore Romano*.[19] It was confirmed, finally, by the fact that Rome's Apostolic Administrator in Moscow, Leopold Braun, experienced no intensification of pressure, although, of course, he was bothered by the constant surveillance of the NKVD.[20] In other words, by the end of 1939, the religious position of the Catholic Church under Soviet control was, relatively speaking (particularly when compared to earlier Soviet policy), quite good.

In 1940 the situation of the Church in East Europe did not significantly change from that of 1939. The Soviets continued to espouse a moderate anti-religious position – increasingly moderate overall, in fact, if juxtaposed to the 1939 performance. Official diocesan reports of 1940 emanated from Lutsk, Lomza, Pinsk, Lviv, and from the newly occupied Baltic States, and all of them – with the exception of Pinsk – reflected a relatively mild degree of Soviet persecution. In addition, unofficial Vatican sources throughout 1940 presented a picture of lenient anti-religious activity in the western Ukraine, western Belorussia and, eventually, in the Baltic States and Bessarabia-Bukovina.

The first official expositions on the status of the Church in Eastern Europe in 1940 came from the Latin diocese of Lutsk. On January 13 Nuncio Orsenigo informed Maglione that conditions in Lutsk were normal.[21] Six days later, Mgr. Petro Verhun, the Apostolic Visitor for Ukrainians in Germany, in a letter to Orsenigo, claimed that the churches in Lutsk were open and that the faithful were not obstructed from attending religious services. Soviet troops, however, according to Mgr. Verhun, were billeted in confiscated monasteries and religious houses.[22]

From the time of Verhun's report until May, the Vatican received no official reports (which have been published) from occupied East Europe.

However, Radio Vatican and *L'Osservatore Romano* as well as Soviet and world news media provided a fragmented commentary on what was generally happening. From the end of January through March, the Papal outlets, in a series of stories, announced that the Communists in Soviet Poland had forged a policy of oblique religious persecution through unfair taxes, the closure of monasteries and seminaries, the abolition of religion in schools, the proliferation of atheistic propaganda, and the jamming of Radio Vatican.[23] On January 22, Radio Moscow confirmed that the Soviets had dispossessed large landowners and appropriated monasteries throughout Soviet Poland.[24] On April 28, *The New York Times* reported that an "Anti-God" organization in Lviv had usurped Metropolitan Sheptyts'kyi's library.[25] Although the latter episode was inconsistent with the waning persecutory stand of Stalin, it was more than balanced in the same month by the fact that the Soviets did not stop Metropolitan Sheptyts'kyi from holding the first Uniate *synod* in Lviv since 1918 – assuming that the secret police knew about it.[26] On May 4, Radio Vatican again broadcast that the Communists still had not openly assaulted the Church, but rather were continuing to ply circuitous methods of persecution.[27]

On May 5, the Latin archbishop of Vilnius, Romuald Jałbrzykowski, sent an up-to-date summary on the diocese of Pinsk to Nuncio Centoz at Kaunas. His recapitulation, in contrast to other official reports received by the Vatican in 1940, revealed an increased anti-religious campaign, but it was only temporary and was probably attributable to the fact that the so-called "phony war" in western Europe had boiled over into a hot war in the Spring of 1940 and, thus, encouraged the Soviets to accelerate the 'Sovietizing' process in their newly annexed lands.[29] For the remainder of May, the only information on events in Soviet Poland came from Radio Vatican broadcasts. On May 13 and 14 the Radio announced that the tax rate for clerical domiciles and for churches under Soviet control was 4.5 rubles per square meter and 8 rubles per square meter respectively.[28]

On June 6 an official report on the Uniates in Lviv was sent by Mgr. Petro Verhun to Nuncio Orsenigo. According to the Ukrainian Apostolic Visitor, religious life in Lviv was thriving. The priest claimed that the churches were crowded and that the clergy operated and performed its functions without many impediments. In the spring of 1940, according to Verhun, Metropolitan Sheptyts'kyi held two diocesan *synods* and also offered theological courses to some thirty seminary students.[30]

In the middle and latter part of June, with France under the guillotine, the Soviet Union moved to gather as quickly as possible the remaining territory allotted to it, as well as some not apportioned, by the revised Nazi-Soviet pact. On June 14–15 Soviet troops occupied the Baltic States, which were allocated to the U.S.S.R. according to the Nazi-Soviet agreement; on June 26 they marched into Bessarabia which the Germans had only recognized as an area in which the Soviets had an "interest", and into northern Bukovina, which was not even mentioned in the accord with Germany. Stalin wanted the Baltic States to improve his defenses in the West and he desired Bessarabia and Bukovina not only to protect the U.S.S.R.'s underbelly but also to remove two exploitable sources of Ukrainian irredentism.

Once the Russians occupied these new regions, the anti-religious measures which had been instituted in Soviet Poland were introduced. The spatial limitations of this essay do not permit a detailed examination of the nuncios' and bishops' reports from Soviet occupied dioceses during the latter half of 1940 and the first half of 1941, but, in general, these ecclesiastical summaries reiterated the theme of Soviet toleration depicted in the 1939–1940 reports.[31]

Why did Moscow display a relatively lenient policy *vis-à-vis* the Catholic Church during its first occupation of Eastern Europe? Four reasons suggest themselves and, in the process, hopefully offer some insight into the mind and concerns of the Soviet Government during the initial years of World War II.

(1) The Church was, relatively speaking, a low priority. The Soviet Government was preoccupied with integrating the newly occupied territories of Eastern Europe into the Soviet system as quickly as possible. The scheme of assimilation was not dissimilar from that followed in the Soviet Union, where during the first years of Soviet power the churches were left alone while the Communists consolidated their position over political affairs. In Eastern Europe, the Soviet regime undoubtedly planned to use violence eventually against the Church, but initially it was overwhelmed with the immediate needs of establishing its political control. And, of course, the Germans pushed the Soviets out of East Europe in 1941, precluding such a violent anti-religious campaign from developing later.

(2) Moscow was tolerant of the Catholic Church because it did not want to sacrifice western public opinion (any more than it already had by the Molotov-Ribbentrop Pact) by immediately launching a vicious onslaught against the Catholic Church. The Kremlin was certainly aware of the fact that all of the major powers had diplomatic ties with the Vatican and that the Church had millions of adherents in Europe and the Americas.

(3) The Soviet Government was awakening to the utility of organized religion as a tool to enhance its policies. The twin fillips for this renaissance were probably Soviet awareness that an 'areligious' or at least a diminished anti-religious policy would rob the Nazis of an anti-Soviet propaganda weapon and at the same time sit well with the West, and, secondly and more importantly, Soviet recognition of Orthodoxy's usefulness as a tool to assimilate and thus help 'Sovietize' the Uniates in the western Ukraine. Cognizance of religion's utility, although initially and principally concerned with the Russian Orthodox Church, was general knowledge which Moscow could easily apply to the Catholic Church and the Vatican. Certainly Moscow realized that an aroused and vehement Vatican, with concrete proof of violent persecution of Catholics in Soviet-controlled East Europe, could do damage to the international interests of the Soviet Union whereas a low profile on religion might tend to neutralize the Vatican. The joker in this deck, however, was that the Kremlin hoped to use Orthodoxy to absorb the Uniate *Catholic* Church and, thus, compromised any hope of impressing the Vatican with its toleration. But it is logical to believe that the Communists did not want to antagonize the Catholic Church, in the early and critical stages of World War II, any more than they felt necessary.

Finally, and most importantly during the first occupation, the Kremlin treated the Catholic Church cautiously because of its fear of Nazi Germany. The Soviets knew that Hitler was an anti-Communist and that he controlled a powerful military machine. As of the end of September, 1939, and until April, 1940, the Germans and the western states were not directly engaged in war; and once they did clash the Reich annihilated France and forced England off the continent by the middle of June. At no time, except for a few months in the spring of 1940, did the pulverizing western war which Moscow had banked upon when it signed the Nazi-Soviet Pact develop or seem to be on the verge of burgeoning. Thus it was of the utmost import to the Soviets to remove and/or forestall any complications in Soviet-German relations, for without the exigency of a Western-German front, there was a real possibility of Hitler's tearing up the Molotov-Ribbentrop agreement and moving against the U.S.S.R. Moscow no doubt felt that a bloody persecution of the Catholic Church in Eastern Europe would place it at a disadvantage *vis-à-vis* Hitler. The Communists certainly realized there would be a popular reaction to open assaults on religion in the newly occupied territories and that such resistance would complicate and possibly weaken Soviet control. The latter potentiality, in turn, might tempt Hitler to take advantage of the Soviets' difficulties and invade; but even if it did not lead to that extremity, it certainly would lower Hitler's opinion of Soviet strength, causing him to disregard Soviet interests and eventually inducing him to believe that the Soviet Union would be an easy mark. To present Hitler with such possibilities was politically asinine and Moscow was not about to commit such an error. An all-out persecution in Eastern Europe might, in addition, rekindle Hitler's apparently latent anti-Communism. Anti-religious attacks were a well-known Communist policy and, if the Soviets launched an anti-Catholic pogrom, Hitler might lose his illusion, which Ribbentrop had assiduously fashioned, of Stalin as a non-Communistic, Russian national. Finally, the vast majority of the people in Soviet-annexed East Europe were Catholic – either Latins or Uniates – and the Kremlin had to be aware of the fact that Hitler had diplomatic relations with the Vatican. Such knowledge, despite the fact that the Nazis themselves persecuted the Church, had to be perplexing: why would the most powerful country in Europe maintain formal ties with a man who had "no divisions"? The Soviets could not but conclude that the Catholic Church was important to Hitler, at least as a tool of expediency, and that an attack upon it might provoke him.

REFERENCES

[1] On the position of the Catholic Church in the Soviet Union before the war, see James Zatko, *Descent into Darkness* (Notre Dame: The University of Notre Dame Press, 1965); Walter Kolarz, *Religion in the Soviet Union* (New York: St. Martin's Press, 1962); and this author's 'Pre-World War II Relations Between Stalin and the Catholic Church', *Journal of Church and State*, vol. 15 (1973), no. 2 (1973), pp. 193–204.
[2] For Marx's and Engels' writings on religion, see *On Religion*, intro. Reinhold Niebuhr (New York: Schocken Books, 1964). For the best available collection of Lenin's views on religion, see *V. I. Lenin ob ateizme, religii i cerkvi* (Moscow: Mysl', 1969). For the

best Soviet study of Lenin's religious positions, see M. I. Šaxnovič, *Lenin i problemy ateizma* (Moscow: Izd. Akademii Nauk SSSR, 1961). For an excellent western analysis of the problem, see Bohdan R. Bociurkiw, 'Lenin and Religion', in Leonard Schapiro and Peter Reddaway, eds., *Lenin: The Man, the Theorist, the Leader. A Reappraisal* (New York: Praeger, 1967), pp. 107–34.

[3] On Soviet policy toward the Uniates see Bohdan R. Bociurkiw, 'The Uniate Church in the Soviet Ukraine: A Case Study in Soviet Church Policy', *Canadian Slavonic Papers*, vol. III (1965), pp. 89–113; and this author's 'The Disappearance of the Ukrainian Uniate Church: How and Why?' *Ukrains'kyi Istoryk*, 1–2 (33–34) (1972), pp. 57–65.

[4] Pierre Blet *et al.*, *Actes et documents du Saint Siège relatifs à la seconde guerre mondiale*, 7 vols. to date (Citta del Vaticano: Libreria Editrice Vatican, 1967–1973), vol. III: *Le Saint Siège et la situation religieuse en Pologne et dans les Pays Baltes (1939–1945)*, 2 parts, part 1, nos. 41, 43, 44.

[5] *Ibid.*, pp. 3–4, 24; Radio Vatican, *Monitoring Service*: British Broadcasting Corporation (BBC), February 28, 1940, 3C, ii.

[6] *Actes et documents*, III, part 1, nos. 40, 54.

[7] Radio Moscow, BBC, October 27, 1939, 4B, ii.

[8] This was also the case in the Latin diocese of Lviv. See *Actes et documents*, III, part 1, nr. 297.

[9] *Ibid.*, no. 48.

[10] *Ibid.*

[11] *Ibid.*, no. 73.

[12] *Ibid.*, nos. 50, 105.

[13] *Ibid.*, no. 297.

[14] *Ibid.*, no. 50.

[15] *Ibid.*, no. 52 and note 3, p. 135. Bishop Slipyi thanked Pius XII on August 5, 1941. See *ibid.*, part 2, no. 288.

[16] Metropolitan Sheptyts'kyi also named, during 1940–41, four exarchs for both Latin and Uniate dioceses under Soviet control.

[17] *Actes et documents*, III, part 1, no. 79.

[18] *Ibid.*, nos. 153, 159, 160, 165, 166, 167, 170, 174, 177, 179, 187, 191, 199, 208, 214, 219, 265, 270, 288, 289, 297, 307, 310, 316; part 2, nos. 355, 400, 425, 482, 529; and pp. 257 and 565, note 1.

[19] Radio Vatican, BBC, January 3, 2C, i; January 4, 2C, i, February 28, 3C, ii, 1940; *L'Osservatore Romano*, January 3, 25, 1940.

[20] Leopold Braun, *Memoirs* (my title) (Unpublished manuscript, 1961, located in Assumptionist Provincial House, New York City), pp. 50, 130, 254. Braun was in Moscow from 1934 to 1946 and the manuscript represents the story of his experiences. Also see 'Leopold Braun au Père Gervais Quenard, A. A.', Moscou, 4 mars 1946, *Documents divers 1946–1949*, Archivio, Padri Assunzionisti, Roma, 2ET, N. 74.

[21] *Actes et documents*, III, part 1, no. 94.

[22] *Ibid.*, no. 105.

[23] Radio Vatican, BBC, January 22, 2C, i; January 24, 2C, i, 1940; January 25, 2C, i; February 4, 2C, ii; February 13, 2C, i; February 28, 3C, ii; March 4, 3C, i; March 11, 3C, ii; March 12, 3C, i; March 18, 3C, ii, 1940; *L'Osservatore Romano*, January 25, 1940.

[24] Radio Moscow, BBC, January 22, 1940, 4B, i.

[25] *New York Times*, April 28, 1940.

[26] *Actes et documents*, III, part 1, no. 144.
[27] Radio Vatican, III, part 1, no. 134.
[28] *Actes et documents*, III, part 1, no. 134.
[29] Radio Vatican, BBC, May 13, 3C, i; May 14, 3C, i, 1940.
[30] *Actes et documents*, III, part 1, no. 144.
[31] See note 18, above.

VASYL MARKUS

THE SUPPRESSED CHURCH:
UKRAINIAN CATHOLICS IN THE SOVIET UNION

The dialectics of Soviet religious policy repudiate any uniform and universally held theoretical premises valid under all conditions and historical
circumstances. Identical treatment or consistent rules have not been
applied to the "opiate of the people" everywhere in the U.S.S.R. or in all
periods of Soviet rule. Religion, like nationality and democracy, is viewed
not abstractly but specifically, as a concrete phenomenon or situation in a
given setting of events and interacting forces. Seen in some settings as
useful, in others it may be viewed as a nuisance or an outright social-
political peril. Expediency, prompted by opportunism, defines the criteria
which determine the course to be followed towards a certain ecclesiastical
community. Contradictory policies may even be pursued simultaneously
in one and the same case, depending on the particular context of the
episode and the objectives set by the policy-makers. Thus any course of
action may be chosen – alliance, toleration, deliberate exploitation,
hostility, or suppression – *vis-à-vis* a religious community. Any course but
passivity, disinterest, or benevolent neutrality, which would dispute the
very nature of the Soviet system and ideology.

The case of the Ukrainian Catholics under Soviet control fits this
scheme well. Specifically, it occupies a unique position within the Soviet
religious spectrum. The existing religious and ecclesiastical communities
in the U.S.S.R. can be grouped into four categories, depending on the
regime's treatment:

(1) Controlled but, compared with other religions, treated preferentially
and assigned a broad social role (the official Russian Orthodox Church,
hereafter R.O.C.).

(2) Controlled and tolerated but comparatively restricted in the scope of
its activities, with only limited functions assigned (Russian Old Believers,
the Armenian Apostolic and Georgian Orthodox Churches, Moslem and
Buddhist communities, the Lutheran Church, and the official Evangelical-
Baptist community).

(3) Controlled with excessive restrictions; covertly persecuted or

De George and Scanlan (eds.), Marxism and Religion in Eastern Europe, 119–132. All Rights Reserved.
Copyright © 1976 by D. Reidel Publishing Company, Dordrecht-Holland.

allowed only minimal functions (Roman Catholics, Jews,[1] and marginal Christians not integrated into official Protestant bodies, such as the Baptist splinter group called '*Iniciativniky*' as well as unintegrated, Russian Orthodox groups).

(4) Prohibited and openly persecuted; outlawed as inherently noxious elements (Jehovah's Witnesses, Adventists, Pentecostals, Ukrainian Catholic-Uniates).

The Ukrainian Catholic (formerly called the Greek-Catholic) Church, the largest in the last category of treatment[2], has since 1945 experienced unique treatment at the hands of the Kremlin rulers. In March 1946, the Metropolitan province of Halyč-Lviv, which constituted the core of that Church, was formally dissolved and "reunited with the Russian Orthodox Church". In August, 1949, another Ukrainian Eastern Catholic eparchy (Mukačevo) was brought into union with Russian Orthodoxy. The latter act abrogated the Union of Užhorod (1646) while the Lviv Synod of 1946 suppressed the Union of Brest (1596). These unions were major historic events by which segments of the Ukrainian (Ruthenian) Church were united with Rome, preserving their rite and a degree of self-government.

The scenario of this process did not follow any particular precedent in Soviet religious policies, except for a remote analogy with the dissolution of the Ukrainian Autocephalous Orthodox Church in the years 1928–1930. However, there are other precedents resembling this religious-political episode: the dissolution of the same Uniate Church in Byelorussia and the Ukraine in 1839 and 1875 by the Russian tsarist regime, and the pattern of synchronized sovietization of Eastern Europe, *mutatis mutandis*, show an analogy with the religious scene in the Western Ukraine.

As in the suppression of the once flourishing Eastern Catholic community on the territory of the Polish Commonwealth to which the Russian Empire succeeded at the end of the eighteenth century, the Soviets applied well-proven methods, such as administrative and political control of the hierarchy, restriction of its contacts with Rome, appointment of loyal bishops, preliminary measures of 'Orthodoxization', utilization of Uniates as key figures in the conversion drive (Bishops Semashka in 1839 and Popel in 1875 in the Kholm region, Rev. Dr. H. Kostelnyk in 1945–46), exertion of governmental pressures, and, finally, the legitimization of the 'reunion' by quasi-legal (canonical) procedures.[3] The chief points of similarity between the present case and the forced liquidation of the Eastern Catholic eparchy in Kholm in 1875 were the high degree of violence applied and the martyrdom that the 'recalcitrant' Uniates suffered. In the present case the Soviets, who otherwise disclaimed any continuation of tsarist policies, used the experience of the tsarist regime. It was also used, with greater legitimacy, by the Russian Orthodox Church herself.

The strategy and the tactics of the sovietization of Eastern Europe find their counterpart in the 'Orthodoxization' of the Ukrainian Catholics which occurred about the same time. While the former policy aimed at the closer integration of Eastern Europe as the 'external security zone' of the U.S.S.R., the latter was supposed to integrate the West Ukrainians into the Soviet Russian body politic by restraining their separatism and pro-Western orientation. It was also meant to strengthen a highly sensitive area in the 'internal security zone'[4] of the Russian core, and to weaken the devisive factor there, Ukrainian nationalism.

Though the effort of the East European people's democracies to set up regime-sponsored Catholic Churches independent of Rome has little resemblance to the policy vis-à-vis Ukrainian Uniates (except in its basic objectives), a number of tactical analogies between the latter and the processes of political Sovietization can be singled out .The in-groups were entrusted with carrying out the policies while the external power served as an instrument of pressure and created a subdued climate of terror. Leading opponents were eliminated as a result of charges of collaboration with pro-Nazi regimes and/or foreign-based interests. Mass terror, primarily in the form of deportations, served as a deterrent to potential challengers. Mock trials became legitimizing devices. The subjects were manipulated into 'progressive' and 'reactionary' roles, and the population as a whole became atomized, so as to prevent an organized mass reaction.

In this process a new political leadership, amenable and submissive, was formed within the East European political systems, whereas the Western Ukraine's newly formed Orthodox Church was provided with a leadership that was only nominal and could not be trusted. The process of consolidation in both cases was continuous and marked by crises and stresses. It has resulted in a precarious normality on the East European political scene and in the unresolved open problem of the Uniates in the Ukraine.

Notwithstanding the public claims on the part of the Soviet regime and the claim made by spokesmen of the Russian Orthodox Church that "the Union [with Rome] has been once and forever struck from the pages of Ukrainian Church history",[5] the problem is still there. It remains painful to many, troublesome to others, and cryptic to most observers.

The fact is that the Ukrainian Catholic communities persist in the Soviet Union almost thirty years after the official abolition of their Church organization. Numerous references in Soviet sources attest to this. Other proofs, including evidence coming from Catholic sources in the Ukraine, demonstrate conclusively that the Russian Orthodox Church has not, to this day, been fully accepted in western Ukrainian regions. The most telling proof of this is that the Soviet propaganda apparatus and the representatives of the Orthodox Church continue to wage a vigorous campaign against the Uniate Church. Pamphlets are published by the dozens and distributed in hundreds of thousands of copies. In the same vein pseudo-documentary films are shown, lectures delivered, and special programs broadcast to the West Ukrainian audience. Moreover, severe reprisals continue to be applied against those who, in one way or another, publicly profess their outlawed religion.

Actually, the seriousness of the situation in the Western Ukraine for the R.O.C. is illustrated by a speech made to the clerics of the Odessa seminary by the Metropolitan Sergei on December 12, 1973, admonishing them to be concerned with Uniatism in their future pastoral work:

Of course, it is not easy to root out within several decades that which had been implanted for three and a half centuries. The remnants of the Uniate and 'Autocephalous' clergy and laymen living out their life among Ukrainian émigrés... have lately stepped up their hostile activities against the Russian Orthodox Church and our Motherland.[6]

Diverse degrees of intensity in the expression of Catholic consciousness among Ukrainians as well as several levels of its practical manifestation are observable.

First, there are those among the clergy and the laity who have acquiesced in their fate. They have become Orthodox, have accepted the existing Church system, and are trying to accommodate optimally the cherished values of their past to their new ecclesiastical status, especially with respect to retaining the national characteristics of Orthodoxy in the Ukraine. They can be considered full-fledged Orthodox faithful who, in all probability, would for the most part remain Orthodox even if given genuine freedom of religious choice.

The second group consists of the clergy and the faithful who, though still feeling themselves to be Catholics, formally adhere to the existing Orthodox Church out of practical necessity. There they practice their religion in accordance with the old rituals and customs, and – what is most essential – they have as their priests former Uniates who have been officially converted to Orthodoxy. They maintain that the official R.O.C. in the Western Ukraine is the continuation of the Ukrainian Greek Catholic Church. To this group the Orthodox Church in formerly Uniate regions is, according to one observer, like a "branch of the Catholic Church, forcefully separated from the Vatican and subjected to the régime".[7]

The bulk of the faithful and a significant number of clergy are in this category. They are the staunchest defenders of the existing Church and of religion in general against administrative chicanery. Under conditions of any relative religious freedom they would join the restored Ukrainian Catholic Church which, with its aura of martyrdom, becomes even more enticing. Many of them view the 'underground' Church with sympathy. But realistically they prefer, along with the masses of people, to avoid the reprisals and harassments inflicted on this proscribed minority.

The third segment of the Ukrainian Catholics are those who have been most influenced by dogma, being products of a western-type pre-Conciliar Catholic psychological orientation. They consider the Orthodox Church schismatic, doctrinally untrue, and ethically wrong because of its subservience to the atheistic regime. Wherever possible they join Catholic communities of the Latin Rite and attend their services. Only in cities, of course, is this possible, because in the countryside Latin parishes are dwindling in number and they lack priests.[8] What the number or proportion of Ukrainians is in the present Roman Catholic communities cannot be assessed even approximately. It is well known that Ukrainian city dwellers and believers from among the intelligentsia – mostly retired people – do attend Roman Catholic services wherever they can.[9]

The last category is constituted of hard-liners, those who tend even now to remain Ukrainian Catholics of the Eastern Rite, members of the illegal, suppressed Church. They form the so-called 'underground' Church, the 'Church in the catacombs'. The hard-core of this group asserts that conversion to Orthodoxy was heresy from a religious point of view and equivalent to national treason politically. In many ways they are militants, religious zealots, overt or secret members of the opposition to the regime.

Organizationally, they have only an embryonic structure, intra-personal ties, and informal channels of communication among nuclear groups of believers. A priest or a nun (sometimes a small community of nuns), or an aged person constitutes the organizational center. Often women are the visible activists, the agents of communication. Their adherents meet together for religious services, mostly in private homes or in the woods. They assist a few 'illegal' priests in carrying out pastoral work (distribution of the Sacraments, help in organizing baptisms or religious weddings, instruction in catechism, etc.) There is also dedicated humanitarian and charitable activity conducted by the group, mainly among their own kind.

The priests of the illegal Church are those who did not sign the conversion to Orthodoxy in 1945–49 and remained Catholics, formally giving up the public exercise of clerical duties. A large group of them were arrested and deported, including their ten bishops, who secretly carried on religious functions and pastoral work among the exiles. Upon the completion of their sentence or upon amnesty granted to some of them by Khrushchev's regime in 1955–56, they have continued the same activity in their homeland. This group of priests has been slightly augmented by new, secret ordinations both in exile and even more in the western Ukraine since the 1950's.[10] The Soviet press reported on two secretly conducted theological 'seminaries' in the 1960's in connection with the arrests of their organizers. This has been confirmed by Ukrainian *Samvydav*.

A vague assessment of the fate of the Ukrainian Catholic clergy in the late 1940's may be summed up in the following estimate: 40% joined the R.O.C., 25–30% were arrested and deported, 20–25% officially "left the priesthood" (were laicized), and 10% emigrated (including those who found themselves in the Polish People's Republic). As for the present, there are about 700–800 Orthodox priests in the four West Ukrainian, formerly Catholic dioceses (70% of them former Catholics); and some 350–400 Ukrainian priests not united with the R.O.C. live in the same area.[11] According to R.O.C. sources, 32 priests joined the official Church in the Ternopil region in 1953-1960, after the main wave of conversions.[12] A certain number of Ukrainian Catholic priests live outside the Western Ukraine, as deportees to or free settlers in Siberia, Kazakhstan, Lithuania, and the East Ukrainian regions. Already in the 1940's and 1950's Uniate priests were conducting pastoral work in the new 'missionary' territories among resettled Ukrainians and other Christians.[13]

Members of religious communities and monastic orders in particular have maintained close contacts with each other and most have remained faithful to their vows. In a few cases they have even preserved nuclei of communal living. Secular priests have also tried to establish channels of communication among themselves. Because of their exile, bishops have exercised only a minimal jurisdiction, but they have continued to enjoy recognition and loyalty among their followers. Some of them have written pastoral letters from their detention, and the letters have been copied and clandestinely distributed. Metropolitan Josyf Slipyj was repeatedly convicted for such activities. According to a number of sources, new bishops have been consecrated. One case became internationally known: Vasyl Velychkovskyj was arrested in 1969 as a secretly consecrated bishop.[14]

There are in the Ukraine, and perhaps also outside the Ukraine, still other secretly consecrated bishops. Their number may be four or five[15] but their identity, with the exception of the late Bishop Velychkovskyj and the Carpatho-Ukrainian priest, Alexander Khira, has not been revealed.[16]

A tradition of secret episcopal consecrations is familiar to the Ukrainian Church. The late Metropolitan Andrej Sheptytskyj, while in Russian tsarist exile in 1916, appointed and consecrated two Ukrainians and one Russian as Catholic Uniate bishops. In order to exercise such exceptional prerogatives, he had special authorization from Pope Pius X. In December 1939, the present Head of the Ukrainian Church, Josyf Slipyj, was secretly consecrated in the Soviet-occupied city of Lviv. His nomination, however, came from the Vatican. Since 1946 new nominations have been made by the existing hierarchy, based on the precedent of the extraordinary powers granted to the head of the Ukrainian Church during World War I, and also in view of the extreme circumstance of an abandoned and persecuted flock being left without a normally functioning Church leadership. Rome, however, remains silent on this issue and has not publicly endorsed these procedures, if for no other reason than that of not compromising its dialogue with Moscow.

The activities of the underground Church can be detected from the Soviet sources to which we have already referred. Not all of these publications are accessible in the West; most are only distributed locally in the Western Ukraine. Another important source of information is Ukrainian *Samvydav*.

Some of the illegal religious activities carried out by the priests and faithful are the conducting of religious services, the education of children in the Catholic faith, baptisms, nuptial rites, confessions and anointment of the sick (particularly in hospitals), burials by 'illegal' priests, and listening to and taping the religious programs broadcast by Vatican Radio. Other incriminating activities are the copying (by photostating and otherwise) of religious materials such as prayerbooks, icons, and Christmas cards, the preservation and circulation of religious books and other sacred objects, and alleged contacts with Western tourists and through them with the émigré Church circles.[17]

Soviet sources themselves reveal numerous instances of such actions by "unmasking the activities of Churchmen". A recent example is the case of Rev. Ivan Kryvyj, who was arrested in 1973 for organizing the illegal printing of an Ukrainian Catholic prayerbook in three consecutive editions (1969, 1971, and 1972), totalling 3500 copies. The printing was done by two employees of the Lviv state printing shops. Another person was involved in distribution of the materials. The priest himself worked on binding the books. The reprint was made from a prayerbook published in Canada in 1954. "Around the cathedral in Lviv appeared some unknown women who offered to the faithful a prayerbook for 10–12 rubles", wrote a Soviet paper.[19] Two Ukrainian (presently Orthodox) priests in Ivano-Frankivsk ordered 500 copies of the prayerbook, 150 copies of a book of *Carols and Church Songs*, and 150 copies of the special 'Missal' for priests.

In recent years, the faithful have resorted to an active defense against the closing of churches. *Kolkhoz* strikes have been initiated in retaliation against administrative measures. For instance there was a strike in the village of Yaremče, where local authorities intended to convert the church into an atheistic museum. In Rus'ka Mokra, villagers defended their church for three days against a force of police and specially dispatched armed units. In light of these incidents there appears to be no truth in the statement by the Kiev Metropolitan Filaret that during his eight years in the Kievan See there was not one case of the confiscation of a church building or any persecution of believers.[18]

Those most active among the laity try to use legal means to defend their rights by sending delegations to higher authorities protesting the measures of local agents, collecting signatures of believers, and defending priests who have been harassed or arrested by the authorities. Similar methods are used by those who openly profess their Catholic religion. As early as

1956–57 there were cases where believers tried to legalize their Ukrainian Catholic communities according to Soviet law. This was attempted by petitioning the proper authorities to grant a permit to their parish congregation. A number of such petitions were sent in the late 1960's, mainly under the influence of the liberalizing events in Czechoslovakia. Every petition was turned down. According to M. P. Mčedlov, the Uniate clergy "inspired letters to various Soviet organs, demanded the registration of Uniate communities, and urged the reestablishment in the Ukraine of the Greek-Catholic Church".[20] Most recently an Ukrainian Catholic priest, Volodymyr Prokopiv, was arrested and placed in a psychiatric institution in Kiev for having accompanied a delegation of Ukrainians to Moscow with a petition signed by 1200 believers asking for the legalization of their Church in the Lviv region.[21]

Academician A. Sakharov, in his appeal to Brezhnev and Nixon urging the two leaders to work for the release of dissenters in the U.S.S.R., mentioned, among others, two Ukrainian priests, Vasyl Romaniuk and Zalyvayko.[22]

The most radical group of Ukrainian Catholics resorts to extreme methods of religious resistance. In the 1960's they mounted a clandestine movement known as *Pokutnyky* (Repentants), led by a priest, Ivan Šoltys. The group acted as a militant sect, rejecting the official Orthodox Church and criticizing the passive 'underground Church' as not sufficiently militant. The *Pokutnyky* assembled secretly for religious observances, organized mass pilgrimages (in defiance of the authorities) to the place of the 'apparition' of the Blessed Mother in the village of Serednya, boycotted civic functions, and so on. They refused to work in state enterprises and collective farms and they objected to carrying passports issued by an 'atheist government'. They also advocated militancy against the public authorities, called for repentance for the sins of the Ukrainian people, and preached a messianic faith in the 'resurrection of the Ukraine'. A Soviet source thus characterized this movement:

The most strikingly anti-social and anti-Soviet form of the intertwining of religion and nationalism is the "Neo-Uniate faith," the so-called *Pokutnyky* movement which has found a certain number of followers in the Western regions of the Ukraine... Although the *Pokutnyky* are not widespread, this nonetheless means that, under particular conditions, there is a possiblility of close interaction between religion and nationalism.[23]

The active Uniate resistance in the Western Ukraine and the fact of the

overt or underground existence of that Church has considerably compli-
cated the Vatican's attempts in the last ten years to normalize relations
with the Soviet government and the R.O.C. Although based on different
premises, both sides have a vital interest in the rapprochement. The Soviet
government is interested in weakening the anti-Communist stand of
Roman Catholicism and in getting the Vatican to cooperate in certain
areas of foreign policy. The R.O.C. is pressing the Vatican to acquiesce in
the fact of the abolition of the Uniate Church and accept it as a *fait
accompli*. The Holy See, in its turn, expects the Communist government
to make concessions in the treatment of Roman Catholicism in Eastern
Europe and in the U.S.S.R. The status of a sizable Latin Rite Catholic
community in Lithuania as well as Catholic minorities in Latvia, Western
Byelorussia, and the Ukraine are the particular focus of the Vatican's
interest.

The existence of the Uniate Church in the Ukraine is an obstacle to this
normalization, as well as being a pawn in the Soviet-Vatican negotiations.
Eventually, with the Vatican's recognition of the *status quo* of the political
and ecclesiastical situation in the U.S.S.R., the Soviet and Orthodox
parties should be willing to make certain concessions in favor of Roman
Catholicism. On the other hand, acceptance of such a *quid pro quo* would
certainly compromise the moral position of the Holy See. The latter
would have to abandon its previous stand in defense of the persecuted
Uniates. The Vatican's ecumenical and political tightrope diplomacy up
to now has produced only minor and questionable practical results while
incurring serious moral losses. As to the concessions made by the Vatican
to its partners, the following have already been made at the expense of the
Ukrainian Catholics:

(a) The Holy See's previous critical stand against the Soviet and the
R.O.C. actions *vis-à-vis* Ukrainian Catholics (*cf.* the encyclical *Orientales
Omnes* of Pius XII) has vanished.

(b) The Vatican tends to accept tacitly the liquidation of the Uniate
Church. Thus the confirmation of the Lviv Synod of 1946 at the Zagorsk
Local Synod of the R.O.C. in 1971, in the presence of Cardinal Wille-
brands, was not publicly questioned by the Holy See.

(c) Consequently, Vatican spokesmen do not have as an objective in
their contacts with the Soviets the issue of restoring the Ukrainian
Catholic Church in the U.S.S.R.

(d) In the face of a hostile Russian attitude, the Vatican deemphasizes the status of the Ukrainian Uniate communities in Poland and Czechoslovakia.

(e) The Vatican also restricts the claims and aspirations of Ukrainian Catholics abroad to forge a particular national self-governing church as a continuation of the Uniate Church in the Ukraine as well as a guarantee of her revival in the future.

(f) The position and authority of the exiled Head of this Church, Major Archbishop Josyf Cardinal Slipyj, who symbolizes the suppressed Church in the Ukraine, have been diminished by the Vatican (through non-recognition of the Ukrainian Synod, refusal to grant patriarchal status to this church, strict control of its units in the free world, etc.).

In terms of ecumenical relations between the R.O.C. and Roman Catholicism, Ukrainian Catholics are viewed by the Orthodox party as an impediment. It appears that the Vatican is sensitive to the following statement by the Metropolitan Filaret of Kiev, made at the twenty-fifth anniversary of the Lviv Synod which 'reunited' Uniates with the R.O.C.:

The suppression of the Union [of Brest] became one of the prerequisites that made possible the development of relations between the Orthodox and Roman Catholic Church. The ecumenical dialogue is conducted on equal footing, primarily in practical cooperation in the service of contemporary mankind and the cause of peace among nations.[24]

A similar tone was echoed in the interview with the Lviv Metropolitan Nikolai given to the New York-based Communist paper *Ukrainiski Visti*, which, in addition, strongly criticized Cardinal Slipyj's activity abroad.[25]

In conclusion, the present status of the Ukrainian Catholic Church in the U.S.S.R. can be summed up in the following observations:

Thirty years after the persecution began, the Church continues to exist in the precarious state of an alien body within the official Church or as an intransigent group of hard-liners forming an illegal community. Those Ukrainian Catholics who have had to join the Russian Orthodox Church have strengthened that Church in the U.S.S.R. and, at the same time, contributed to the Ukrainization of the R.O.C. in Ukraine. Likewise, the nationality-religion symbiosis in the Ukraine continues through the suppressed Uniate Church, counterweighing the Russianizing ('universalist') tendency of the R.O.C.

The continuity of the Ukrainian Catholic religion in the U.S.S.R. proves that the feudal maxim *cuius regio, eius religio* practiced in a twentieth-century secular state is doomed. Moreover, the Soviet pretense to the separation of Church and State and the development of a secularized model of society is repudiated by the State's strong involvement in atheist propaganda, and particularly by the State-sponsored struggle against Ukrainian Catholics.

As for the R.O.C., which is the *beata possedens* in the Western Ukraine, her reward for having played an instrumental role in the actualization of the Soviet nationalities policy in the Ukraine was to receive millions of forced converts. Consequently, among the socially conscious public this church lacks popularity. Contrariwise, the representatives of the Ukrainian intelligentsia active in the national dissent movement give their moral support to religious resistance and to the cause of the Ukrainian Catholic Church in the name of democracy, human rights, and the defense of the national heritage, as is seen in the activities and statements of the present-day Ukrainian dissenters Valentyn Moroz and Ihor Kalynec.[26]

REFERENCES

Bibliographic note: The Uniate Church in the Ukraine has been treated in most of the general works devoted to the problems of religion in the U.S.S.R. by such authors as M. Bourdeaux, R. Conquest, A. Galter, W. Kolarz, and N. Struve. A number of monographs and articles dealing specifically with the Uniate Church have also been published, primarily by Ukrainian authors, with a view to documenting the fate of the persecuted Church. Most of these writings present a historical account; some of them also possess broader analytical value. The following are the principal English-language publications: *First Victims of Communism: White Book on the Religious Persecution in the Ukraine* (Rome: Analecta OSBM, 1953); W. Dushnyk, *Martyrdom in Ukraine* (New York: UCCA, n.d.); I. Hrynioch, 'The Destruction of the Ukrainian Catholic Church in the Soviet Union', *Prologue* (New York), vol. 4 (1960), pp. 5–51; L. Mydlowsky, *Bolshevik Persecution of Religion and Church in the Ukraine: 1917–1957* (London: Ukrainian Publishers, 1962); B. Bociurkiw, 'The Uniate Church in the Soviet Union: A Case Study in Soviet Church Policy', *Canadian Slavonic Papers* (Toronto), vol. 7 (1965), pp. 98–113, and 'The Orthodox Church and the Soviet Regime in the Ukraine, 1953–1971', *loc. cit.*, vol. 14 (1972), no. 2, pp. 191–212; *The Tragedy of the Greek Catholic Church in Czechoslovakia* (New York: Carpathian Alliance, 1971). The present author has written two papers on the subject: 'Religion and Nationality; The Uniates of the Ukraine', published in a volume edited by B. Bociurkiw and J. Strong, *Religion and Atheism in the U.S.S.R. and Eastern Europe* (London: Macmillan, 1975, pp. 101–122), and 'Religion in Soviet Ukraine, a Political Problem of a Modernizing Society', to be published in I. Kamenetsky (ed.), *Nationalism and Human Rights: Processes of Modernization in the U.S.S.R. and Eastern Europe*). Among the sources published in the U.S.S.R. are the following: *Diyannia Soboru Hreko-Katolyc'koji Cerkvy u L'vovi, 8-10, III, 1946* (Lviv, 1946), and the periodicals *Žurnal Moskovskoj Patriarxii* (Moscow) and *Eparxial'nyj* (later: *Pravoslavnyj*) *Visnyk* (L'viv, later Kiev). A wealth of materials can be found in the Soviet press, especially in regional periodicals and anti-religious publications.

¹ Their role may evolve depending on various foreign-policy implications, e.g., the progress in Soviet-Vatican dialogue, the policy of rapprochement with the West.

² In 1944, the Ukrainian Greek-Catholic Church on Ukrainian ethnic territory comprised one Archeparchy and four eparchies of which one (Priašiv) remained in Czechoslovakia and one (Peremyšl') partially in Poland; of three Apostolic Administrations, one remained in Poland and one partly in Rumania. The Church had 3,500 priests, over 1,000 nuns, and 500 seminarians; the total number of the faithful approached five million, of whom four and a half million were incorporated in the Soviet Union as a result of new Soviet territorial acquisitions. Cf. *First Victims of Communism, Annuario Pontificio*, and other sources.

³ For a detailed account of the events of the 1830s see W. Lencyk, *The Eastern Catholic Church and Czar Nicholas I* (Rome: Centro di Studi Universitari Ucraini, 1966). (The dioceses mentioned in this paper were known in Polish or Hungarian at that time as follows: Halyč-Lviv=Lwów; Mukačevo=Munkácz; Kholm=Chełm; Ternopil= Tarnopol. *Ed.*)

⁴ This author has developed an approach to the interpretation of Russian foreign policy in terms of moving 'zones of security' in his unpublished monograph, *The Western Republics of the U.S.S.R.*

⁵ *Pravoslavnyi Visnyk* (Kiev) (1971), no. 6, p. 27.

⁶ *The Journal of the Moscow Patriarchate* (Moscow) (1974), no. 2, p. 24.

⁷ *Nova Zoria (The New Star)*, Chicago, (August 18, 1974), no. 31.

⁸ In 1961, there were 132 Latin Rite Catholic parishes in the Ukraine. See *Ukrains'ka Radians'ka Encyklopediya* (Kiev), vol. 6, p. 253.

⁹ There are indications that Soviet public authorities and the Orthodox leaders would prefer to have the Ukrainian Catholics join the Latin Rite rather than remain Uniates.

¹⁰ *Ukrains'kyi Visnyk* gives the name of one priest with the notation that he was ordained after 1946; see the Paris-Baltimore edition, 1971, vol. I, p. 61. The same source mentions ordinations of two young priests by Bishop Velychkovskyj of the 'underground Church'.

¹¹ A visitor to the Ukraine reported that in 1970 in a typical West Ukrainian *rayon* city of about 10,000 there lived three Ukrainian priests: the pastor of the open Orthodox church (a former Catholic priest) and two priests who did not join the R.O.C.; all three were actively performing their priestly functions. Russian dissident Anatoly Levitin estimates that in the city of L'viv and its vicinity alone reside 80 Ukrainian Catholic priests. See 'Soviet Writer Appeals to U.N. Against Persecution in Ukraine', *The New World* (Chicago), 22.11.1974

¹² *Pravoslavnyi Visnyk* (1968), no. 8, p. 20.

¹³ In one of his sermons Archbishop Major Josyf Slipyj recalled that in his Siberian exile he extended pastoral care also to the Orthodox Christians who asked for it. Bishop Velychkovskyj also related his missionary work while in captivity; see V. Markus, 'Vladyka Vasyl Velychkovskyj – Ispovidnyk Viry', *Cerkovnyi Kalendar-Almanach na 1974 rik* (Chicago, 1974), pp. 158–159. Testimony on the life and work of imprisoned Ukrainian Catholic priests and nuns can be found in the memoirs of

W. Ciszek, *With God in Russia* (New York: McGraw-Hill, 1965), A. Shifrin, *Chetvertyi Vymir* (Munich: Sučasnist', 1973), Radiguin, Klainer, and others.

[14] Bishop Velychkovskyj was sentenced to three years of imprisonment for the second time (he was first sentenced in 1946), was released in 1972 and expelled from the country. He lived in Rome and in Canada, where he died June 30, 1973. See V. Markus, 'Vladyka V. Velychkovskyj...', *op. cit.*, pp. 153–164.

[15] Archbishop Major J. Slipyj, at the papal audience of the Ukrainian Catholic hierarchy in November, 1973, spoke "on behalf of thirty bishops". The exact count of all Ukrainian (Ruthenian) bishops outside the U.S.S.R., including four Ruthenian bishops of the Byzantine rite in the U.S.A., comes to only 25 prelates. It appears that the remaining five are those in the Ukraine. According to A. Levitin (see above), three Uniate bishops in the Ukraine function illegally. "As soon as one dies or is arrested, another is immediately consecrated", adds Levitin.

[16] There were notices in the émigré press on the episcopal status of the Užhorod canon Alexander Khira in 1968–1969, when he was evicted from the Transcarpathian region and lived as a priest among Lithuanian Catholics.

[16] A revealing document about the recent reprisals against the Ukrainian Catholics is the article 'A Few Remarks about Freedom of Conscience' in the *Ukrains'kyi Visnyk* (Paris-Baltimore: Smoloskyp, 1971), vol. I, pp. 56–63. Other issues of the *Visnyk*, as well as of the Russian *Khronika*, contain occasional references to the situation of Ukrainian Catholics.

[18] *Zovten'* (L'viv), (1974), no. 4, pp. 92–95.

[19] *Visti z Ukrainy* (Kiev), 21 March, 1974; this newspaper along with an English counterpart, *News from the Ukraine*, is distributed among the Ukrainians abroad.

[20] M. P. Mčedlov, *Katolicizm* (Moscow: Politizdat, 1970), p. 244.

[21] *Chronicle of the Lithuanian Catholic Church* (1974), no. 8.

[22] *New York Times*, June 25, 1974.

[23] V. L. Bodnar, 'Osobennosti razvitija ateizma v processe kul'turnoj revoljucii v nacional'noj respublike', in *Ateizm i socialističeskaja kul'tura* (Moscow, 1971) pp. 37–52.

[24] *Pravoslavnyi Visnyk* (1971), no. 7, p. 11.

[25] *Ukrainis'ki Visti* (New York), (30 March 1972).

[26] Cf. materials in the Samvydav *Ukrains'kyi Visnyk*. A particularly sympathetic treatment of the Uniate Church is given by V. Moroz in his essay 'Chronicle of Resistance', in *Report from the Beria Reserve*, by Valentyn Moroz (Chicago: Cataract Press, 1974). The religiously inspired poems of I. Kalynec have been published abroad: *Poeziyi z Ukrainy* (Bruxelles: Lettres et Art, 1970), and *Pidsumovujučy Movčannia* (Munich: Sučasnist', 1971).

ALEXANDRE A. BENNIGSEN AND S. ENDERS WIMBUSH

MUSLIM RELIGIOUS DISSENT IN THE U.S.S.R.

The term 'Muslim' as it is now used by Soviet authorities applies to the
various peoples, mostly turkic, who before 1917 belonged to the Islamic
faith. In its present usage, however, the term does not apply only to those
Muslims who still practice their religion. Soviet authorities continue to
use this designation to express the confusion in Islam between religion and
nationality, a confusion which would be impossible between 'Russian' and
'Orthodox', for example. In the Soviet Union one can find in use the
expression *neverujuščie Musul'mane*, the "non-believing Muslims". Islam
is more than a religion: it is a way of life, a culture, a transcendent identity.
There are forty to forty-five million Muslims in the Soviet Union today
and their number is rapidly increasing: an increase of more than 50%
occurred between 1959 and 1970, as against the very modest growth (13%)
of the Russian population.

The problem of Muslim religious dissent is a complex one. Whenever it
occurs, it differs radically from expressions by other dissenting religious
groups – Catholics, Baptists, Adventists, or even the more independent-
minded members of the Russian Orthodox Church. Our sources of
information are scarce. They include:

(1) Some rare documents emanating from the Official Muslim Administration (the four muftiats in Ufa, Tashkent, Baku, and Makhach-Qal'a),
fetwas, sermons, and declarations by religious leaders. These sources
indicate that Islam is becoming more traditional and more conservative
than it appears to have been in the first decade of the twentieth century
and certainly more so than in 1917 – that is, from the point at which the
Revolution arrested Muslim intellectual life. Nevertheless, we do discover
in these sources demands for the personal interpretation of the Koran and
the rediscovery of the pure, frugal, and ascetic Islam of the Medina
Califat. These demands are not dissimilar from those of other dissenting
intellectuals in other parts of the Soviet Union, such as Solzhenitsyn, who
have become disgusted with the primitivism and stupidity of the official
ideology.

De George and Scanlan (eds.), Marxism and Religion in Eastern Europe, 133–146. All Rights Reserved.
Copyright © 1976 by D. Reidel Publishing Company, Dordrecht-Holland.

Soviet Muslim officials are never attacked in official propaganda. They are loyal to the regime and the same kind of non-political role to Islam as the Moscow Patriarchate ascribes to Orthodoxy. Their religious activity generally is confined to administering some 500 'working' mosques, less than 1000 'register' clerics, and 2 medressehs, the latter serving possibly 60 to 80 students.

(2) More revealing still are *samizdat* publications, although the bulk of this material is limited to reporting the tribulations of two deported Muslim groups: the Crimean Tatars and the Meskhetian Turks. Both of these groups present exclusively political demands, particularly the right to repatriation in their traditional homelands. Religious questions are seldom if ever discussed. In fact, religious demands – freedom of worship, the re-opening of closed mosques, the right to circumcision – are seldom advanced in *samizdat* by Muslim nationalities in Central Asia, the Caucasus, or the Central Volga; there is nothing which could be construed as an answer to the extremely boring but massive quantities of anti-Islamic propaganda. Even more striking, perhaps, is the almost total absence of those popular political demands which typify dissent in the non-Muslim areas of the Soviet Union: adherence to Soviet legality, a return to true Leninism, evolution toward liberal-democratic socialism, or strong denunciations of Stalin's atrocities and the present regime's inclination to re-Stalinize. Instead, the few glimpses of Muslim attitudes which *samizdat* does provide suggest that the primary concerns of these groups are national. Indeed, recent *samizdat* materials from these areas are notable for the frequent appearance of slogans such as "Russians go home" or "Uzbekistan for the Uzbeks, Russia for the Russians".

(3) The most revealing source, and in many respects the most interesting, is the enormous periodical and non-periodical anti-religious literature which includes books and articles in all pertinent languages. In some semi-literary languages, such as the various Daghestani dialects, anti-religious literature makes up the greater part of all published titles.

To appreciate the significance of the Soviet anti-religious campaign we must consider it in its proper historical context. Following the revolution of 1917, the Soviet Government – ruling a Federation of "state nations" of which one, the Great Russian, assumed for various reasons the status of leader – repeatedly was forced to manoeuvre between two perils: the nationalism of the non-Russians and their own great-power chauvinism.

From Lenin through Brezhnev the regime has sought (but never found) the ideal "middle way", that is a compromise which, while acknowledging and guaranteeing the supremacy of the Russian "Elder Brother", would avoid offending the sensibilities of their "junior partners" and permit them to satisfy their own aspirations. The evolution of Soviet nationalities policy and the non-Russian nationalities' reactions to it is a most fascinating subject which has yet to undergo a thorough examination. The present study aims at investigating but one aspect of this larger project: the struggle against "survivals of the past" (*perežitki*) in the conscience and customs of the Soviet Muslims.

From the onset, the Soviet government considered the anti-religious campaign as exceptionally important, relenting only during the war years. The present-day campaign is as intense as it was under Khrushchev, Stalin, and Lenin. It finds expression in publications in all the languages of the Soviet Union, in the organization of atheistic museums, in permanent and traveling exhibitions, in anti-religious schools, and even in universities, official conferences and talks, and films. According to an editorial in *Uzbekistan Kommunisti*[1] entitled 'We Must Intensify Anti-Religious Propaganda – An Important Sector of Ideological Work', 42,000 conferences on scientific atheism had been organized during the years 1969–1970 in Uzbekistan alone, despite the fact that the Muslim population of that republic numbered less than ten million. The anti-religious agitation and propaganda network in Uzbekistan included 20 anti-religious universities and 218 special schools with 3,000 students who were being trained to fill high staff positions in the organization. Some twenty years earlier in 1951, the number of conferences devoted to atheism in that republic was 10,000, according to *Kizil Uzbekistan*.[2] It would appear, therefore, that in spite of the political rapprochement between the U.S.S.R. and the Arab world, the anti-Islamic effort, far from relaxing, has intensified.

The essential direction of anti-religious activity is entrusted to the Society for the Diffusion of Political and Scientific Knowledge, which replaced the Association of Godless Militants after the war. All Soviet political and social organizations must cooperate. As organizations such as the Communist Party, the Komsomol, the Pioneers, Profsoyuz, the Union of Writers, and schools of all types – from the primary schools through the universities – are affected, this effort aims at mobilizing a high percentage of the politically active population of the U.S.S.R. A recent article in the anti-religious magazine, *Nauka i Religija*, notes, for example, that in an Uzbek kolkhoz of relatively minor importance in the Samarkand region, the anti-religious *agitkollektiv* consists of "over one hundred agitators" working full- or part-time.[3] With the assistance of professors from Samarkand University, this *kollektiv* organizes "three or four" seminars per year whose purpose is to train anti-religious agitators. These agitators in turn organize "several thousand conferences on different scientific subjects, one-third of which are devoted to anti-religious topics". If we can assume that "several thousand" means at least a minimum of three thousand, then we can conclude that the anti-religious conferences per year for this small kolkhoz number at least one thousand, to be spread over a total population excluding infants and invalids – which doubtless numbers less than one thousand individuals. This absurdly high figure surely must include 'private talks' with believers and non-believers in the *Chay-Khanehs*, the cultural parks, at home during the evening meal, or on rest days.

The central themes of anti-religious propaganda, which have remained unchanged since the 1930's, are well known: extensive explanations here are unnecessary. For the purpose of exposition they can be divided into two categories:

(1) General arguments used indiscriminately against all religions. Religion in general is denounced as a relic of the capitalist era and a barrier to progress, as the opium which inhibits active participation in the construction of socialism, or as phantasmagoric schemes which, in any event, will disappear automatically as socialism takes hold. Scientific agitation and propaganda, and if need be coercion, are viewed as means of hastening this inevitable denouement.

(2) Specific arguments used against certain "cosmopolitan" religions (Lutheranism and protestant sects, Catholicism, Judaism, Islam) whose spiritual centers lie outside the U.S.S.R. and therefore escape direct Soviet involvement. These "foreign" religions can be contrasted with the "national" religions; that is, those whose spiritual centers lie within Soviet borders (Russian Orthodoxy, the Armeno-Gregorian Church, the Orthodox Church of Georgia, Russian Old Believers, etc.). "Cosmopolitan" religions are subjected to sustained and bitter attacks. This is especially true in the case of Judaism, but neither Catholicism nor Islam is spared in spite of various political rapprochements. The arguments used

against Islam can be categorized as follows:

(1) The "anti-scientific" and/or "primitive" character of Islam.

(2) Its "anti-social" features, in particular its anti-feminism.

(3) Its inherent "fanatical xenophobia" – meaning its inherent anti-Russian character.

(4) The extreme conservatism of Shari'yat, the Koranic law.

(5) Islam's foreign roots, and particularly the idea that this religion was forced upon the peoples of the Caucasus and Central Asia by Turkish, Arabic, and Persian invaders.

(6) The "cosmopolitan", "anti-national" character of Islam, which, because Islam is a supra-national religion, tends to erase national differences and thereby prevents the formation of "modern nations".

It seems likely that Soviets who are actively engaged in anti-Islamic work are well versed in the very rich anti-Islamic literature of the nineteenth and early twentieth centuries composed by semi-private organizations such as the Organization of the Missionaries of Kazan or the Fraternity of St. Gurii of Kazan, which specialized in anti-Muslim polemics. Many of the arguments found in today's anti-religious articles and books, in fact, are poor albeit slightly modified reiterations of these older works. It is significant that Soviet sources themselves widely condemn the current anti-religious campaign as insufficient and its literature as boring and inadequate.

Inasmuch as the ecclesiastical hierarchies, Christian as well as Muslim, display a sincere loyalty toward the State, one must question the motives behind this extremely costly effort. On the surface, the new theories advanced by the few religious thinkers stress the compatibility of religion and Marxism; that is, that by 'modernizing' the former it can be made into a positive contribution to Communist development. In the case of Islam, members of the official Muslim hierarchy in recent years appear to be leaning toward the following ideological positions:

(1) "As opposed to Judaism, Christianity, and other religions, Islam is endowed with a flexibility which allows it to adjust itself better to the conditions of the modern world. Within the framework of the Communist way of life, Islam survives in a new modernized form; all redundant encumbrances which burdened it in the Middle Ages, now outdated, must and can be weeded out".[4]

(2) "Islam fights for Peace against Imperialism".[5]

(3) "The genius of our Prophet has foreseen the principles of Socialism... I am happy to note that the numerous achievements of Socialism justify the ideas of Mohammed."[6]

(4) "Communist society cannot exist without the Muslim religion".[7]

These expressions of fidelity to the regime by Muslim chiefs could be quoted endlessly. It is clear that the regime has much less to fear from the various ecclesiastical hierarchies than from political dissenters: liberals, anarchists or radicals, representatives of the Soviet intelligentsia within the Communist Party itself or in the ranks of its youth organizations such as the Komsomol. Moreover, behind the facade of an organized religion – represented by the religious administrations of the four Muftiats with their associated clerics, which are maintained largely for the benefit of foreign tourists – little remains to threaten the regime, as noted before: two medressehs with about 60 students, fewer than 500 working mosques, and perhaps 1000 mullahs to serve some 40–45 million Muslims.

Soviet Muslim intellectual life has suffered accordingly. The bold and modern character of the Islam of the Tatars and the Azeris at the beginning of the twentieth century, far in advance of the Islam of the Arabs, Turks, and Iranians, is no longer apparent. Rather, Muslim intellectual life seems to have stagnated at precisely the point where the October Revolution stopped its progress. Such at least is the impression left by the *fetwas* and sermons of Muslim religious chiefs, sources which are quoted abundantly in the articles of N. Aširov. In many ways, in fact, Islam is less advanced in the U.S.S.R. than in other Muslim countries. We find, for example, that in 1970 the Mufti of Ufa, leader of one of the most 'progressive' regions of Soviet Islam (Tatarstan, Bashkiria, and the Tatar colonies of the larger Russian towns) thought it necessary to proclaim in a special *fetwa* that the playing of musical instruments was now permissible, as was attending theatres and cinemas.[9]

In Central Asia and the northern Caucasus, the situation is reminiscent of the ultra-conservative Islam which existed in these areas prior to the Revolution. Daghestani women are still forbidden to enter mosques during Friday prayers. Central Asian women and north Caucasian women may not participate in funeral ceremonies.

In summation, we find that the Muslim hierarchy resembles all other Soviet ecclesiastical hierarchies: spiritual life is strictly limited to public worship; intellectual life is staunchly conservative and without a hint of the bold reformist tendencies so much in evidence in the two decades immediately preceding the Revolution; and, perhaps even less than in other religious hierarchies in the Soviet Union, there is little open dissent directed at the regime.

Given the inclination of the official Islamic hierarchy to avoid direct confrontations with the regime, one must wonder why the anti-religious campaign proceeds unabated. The answer can be found, perhaps, in the general anti-religious bias of Soviet officialdom which has developed proportionately to the ongoing internalization and routinization of Soviet political culture; in an overly faithful pursuit of "the Leninist policy", which was drafted at a time when churches represented overtly conservative forces – often pro-monarchist and always anti-revolutionary; and in the prevalent belief that a 'New Soviet Man', a *homo sovieticus*, his pysche purged of fantasies from the past, could be created. This latter hope now has been abandoned, at least inasmuch as it pertains to Soviet Muslims.

However, another dimension exists apart from the political and legal relationship of the church hierarchy to the Soviet state. This dimension, the complex interaction between religion and national consciousness, requires our full attention. To appreciate fully this intricate conjunction between Islam and national consciousness one must bear in mind that Islam, like Judaism, is a religion without a clergy; that is, without any interposition of an ecclesiastical hierarchy between the believer and the Creator. It should be noted that the four spiritual Muslim administrations in the U.S.S.R. are actually legal in character and can be by-passed by the devout Muslim – who can do very well without mosques and clerics – in the exercise of his religious duties. The "official" Islam, which these administrations purport to represent, thus fails to satisfy that important proportion of the Muslim population which still adheres to Islam, whether from a whole-hearted acceptance of its religious teachings or from a reluctance to break completely with the cultural values of their ancestors which are embodied in Islam. It should not be surprising, therefore, that a "non-official" Islam has arisen to challenge the "official" hierarchy. Nor is it incomprehensible why the former is so difficult to control, as it has its own clandestine organizations which, although no longer possessing the sanctity of Islam, are nevertheless highly influential among the masses.

"Non-official" or popular Islam in many respects may be compared to the numerous, often highly differentiated sects whose original ties were with the Russian Orthodox Church. Like these sects, "non-official" Islam draws upon old cults and practices: the pre-Islamic rites and practices of Zoroastrianism, Manicheism, Buddhism, Nestorianism, or even Paganism (worship of the *pir*, pilgrimages to *mazars* and the local holy places, etc.), deviations which orthodox Islam views with suspicion. In its extreme forms, this tendency to seek religious satisfaction among alternatives from the past often leads to a confusion between Islam and primitive Shamanism. In the latter form Muslim clerics assume witch doctor-like functions.

Unlike official Islam, popular Islam displays an astonishing vigour. It has its own prayer houses which are officially forbidden but tolerated in practice by local authorities. In Azerbaidzhan alone, with its sixteen official mosques, there were in 1967 three hundred holy places of pilgrimage.[9] A network of clandestine Koranic schools is also in existence, a fundamental requisite for maintaining an elementary proficiency in Arabic, the language of worship, among the faithful. The unregistered Mullahs who direct these activities, while certainly deficient in theological training, appear to be sufficient in number to perform the essential rites of marriage, circumcision, and death; to organize occasional collective prayers;[10] and to preach actively among the population, despite official prohibition. In such fashion is the dull *Agitprop* campaign counteracted.

Most of the unregistered Mullahs manage to evade control by the official hierarchy of the four Muftiats. Usually they are members of various Soufi fraternities (*tarika*). In some cases these fraternities were created after the second World War, but most are remnants of the ancient *Naqshbandiyeh tarika* which from the eighteenth century has represented the hard core of Muslim resistance to Russian conquest. This strong tradition includes Imam Mansur, the three great imams of the Caucasian Muridizm of the nineteenth century (Ghazi Mohammed, Hamzat beg, and Shamil), Madali Ishan (the organizer of the Andjan revolt in 1897), and Uzun Hadji (the *Naqshbandiyeh* murshid, leader of the last great insurrection in Daghestan in 1920–22). In stark contrast to the quiescent registered clergy, members of the *tarika* are openly hostile to the Soviet establishment, leading one Soviet Central Asian newspaper to declare unequivocally that popular Islam "had developed a plan to destroy the social order".[11]

Due largely to this semi-clandestine popular Islam, powerful religious feelings still survive among the Muslim rural masses (comprising approximately 70% of the total Muslim population). The effects are extremely interesting. As soon as adults reach what Soviet authorities call the "critical age" (between 45 and 55 for men and 35 to 45 for women), these "former atheists" proclaim anew their faith in God: not so much from religious conviction but because any expression of non-belief would have the effect of excluding the non-believer from the national community. "I am a believer, because as a non-believer I would be a public laughing stock"; "I believe because my parents were believers"; and "I am a believer because I am a Muslim", are some of the replies collected by an anti-religious interviewer in a native quarter of Tashkent.[12] Still another study discovered that, "I am a Muslim because I am a Kirghiz", or "because I have been circumcised".[13]

The espousal of religious beliefs of any kind does not necessarily mean open and active hostility toward the regime. For a large number of Muslims and Christians all authority comes from "above" and therefore must be obeyed. It should be noted that at the present time – and this may be contrasted with the situation in the 1920s – it is possible to be both a Soviet citizen and a practicing believer, especially if one belongs to one of the great, officially recognized churches.

In one important aspect Soviet Islam differs markedly from Soviet Christendom. The heterodox Christian sects are violently hostile toward the regime *and* the "compromised" official Orthodox Church. In Islam, on the other hand, no such rift is evident. Both the "official" and the "popular" Islam are perceived as being from the same root and therefore of the same realm. The official Muftiats ignore the existence of a parallel Islam; advocates of the latter refrain from criticizing the official hierarchy.

To Soviet authorities, the overt hostility of the clandestine clergy is but symptomatic of a larger problem: the persistence of strong religious sentiments among the masses and some members of the intelligentsia. These sentiments permit social customs of the past (*perežitki*) to survive. In both practical and theoretical terms, these *perežitki* constitute an insuperable barrier to the process of national rapprochement (*sbliženie*) and to its final stage, the "merging" of Russians and other Soviet ethnic groups (*slijanie*). The pursuit of these ends constitutes the main thrust of Soviet nationalities policy.

Perežitki impede the realization of Soviet nationalities policy on a number of levels. According to Soviet theory the rapprochement of nations can take place successfully only between those nations which have attained equivalent levels of Stalin's four criteria for nation status: territorial unity, linguistic unity, cultural unity, and economic unity. Without these pre-conditions no rapprochement can take place; rather, the weaker cultures will be assimilated by the stronger. In the pre-1924 period, of all the "Muslim nations" in the Soviet Union only the Volga Tatars and the Azerbaidzhani's could meet Stalin's terms. Thus, a tremendous effort was required to raise the other Muslim peoples (Uzbeks, Kazakhs, Turkmen, Tadzhiks, and so forth) from their tribal state to the level of modern nations. Obstacles to this effort, *perežitki*, can be put in two main categories: "sub-national" or social survivals and "supra-national" survivals, for example pan-Turkism or pan-Islamism.

We are concerned here only with the "subnational" survivals, as they serve to differentiate clearly Muslim society from Russian (or Western) society. These social survivals originate with the Muslim family, the formative cell of that culture. In some respects, the Muslim family does represent the Russian family, insofar as both are, with few exceptions, restricted families; that is, they are comprised of parents and unmarried children. Beyond this, however, the Muslim family preserves a number of customs and traditions which are inherited from the formerly patriarchal (undivided) Muslim family and from the large joint family. The patriarchal family – parents, their married sons, grandchildren, unmarried daughters, and occasionally the father's brothers with their families (in some cases up to thirty persons) – still exists as an economic unit in certain rural districts side by side with restricted families.[14] Even where it has disap-peared it leaves a legacy of vital traditions and customs which, in turn, create a moral climate distinct from that of the Soviet Russian family.

Two *perežitki* of the patriarchal family, in particular, hamper Russian efforts to smooth over relations between the dominating power and the dominated minorities:

(1) The authority of the elders remains undisputable. This *aksakalizm*– exaggerated respect for the "white beards" – slows the gravitation of younger generations toward a class or Party loyalty. If the father is a believer, such a shift of loyalties is highly unlikely. The observation of one Soviet anthropologist in 1957, that Muslim youth "can fight against tradition only within the framework of tradition", is accurate still today.[15]

(2) In all facets of Muslim life women remain inferior. Young girls of eleven to fifteen years of age are still married off by their father; polygamy is still practiced; women are secluded and excluded from participation in political, economic, and social affairs.

Contrary to claims in Soviet publications, these customs are sanctioned not by *Shari'yat* (Koranic) law, but by the pre-Islamic unwritten *Adat*, or customary law. Some of these customs (marriage of under-age girls, polygamy), in fact, are criminal offenses by Soviet law. Nevertheless, natives including Soviet intelligentsia, members of the Communist Party, and Komsomolites rather easily circumvent these restrictions. Thus, it is not unusual to find a divorced man living in the same household with his new wife and the one whom he has divorced. To this practice and others local authorities turn a blind eye.

Segregation of sexes and the inferior status which Muslim women endure surely deters Russian (or "Western") girls from marrying Muslim men. Such marriages, however, are permitted by the Koran as long as the prospective bride belongs to the "People of the Book" (*Ahl al-Kitab*). When a Russian woman becomes part of a Muslim family and they reside in a Muslim territory, she is quickly assimilated and the children adopt the father's nationality. If the couple chooses to live in a predominantly Russian territory the opposite usually occurs: the husband abandons his own nationality and is Russified. The marriage of Muslim women with non-Muslim men is practically unknown, as it is forbidden by *Shari'yat* law. To what extent these traditional anti-feminist customs are endangered by the dramatic demographic expansion of Muslim nationalities over the last few decades has yet to be determined.

The large joint family, similar to the Yugoslav *zadruga*, is made up of the offspring of a common ancestor – perhaps four or five generations totaling as many as two or three hundred persons – who consider themselves kinsmen. This unit no longer fulfills an economic function, a purpose which disintegrated even before the Revolution. Rather, it constitutes a strong spiritual-psychological community and is the source of some of the most tenacious *perezitki*. These survivals cannot be regarded as products of Islam in the religious sense of the word. Instead, they are sanctioned by an unwritten law. In any event, they are continuing barriers to any rapprochement between Muslims and non-Muslims, to the development of modern nations, to the formation of class consciousness, and, hence, to the realization of the *Družba Narodov*. These obstacles include:

(1) *Kalym*, or the purchase price of a bride. According to Soviet sources this payment is still rendered, often in the form of a present to the bride's father. Those who are unable to meet the payment find other ways to satisfy the requirement.

(2) *Kaitarma*, or the young husband's obligation to work for a specified period of time for the bride's family.

(3) *Kudalyk*, or the contract for marriage between young children.

(4) *Karsha*, or the arranged marriage between two families each having a son and a daughter.

(5) *Amengerstvo*, or sororate and levirate.

(6) Elopement arranged by the parents, or with the bride's but not the parents' consent, or even by force.

At another level, in the remote rural regions of Central Asia the clan, or rather its subdivision, the *elat* – a community of from twenty to forty families descending from the same eponymous ancestor – still survives as both a spiritual and functional unit. With an elected elder as president and a traditional council of elders, the *elat* bears a strong resemblance to the kolkhoz.[16] Where the *elat* has disappeared it is survived by endogamic and exogamic taboos (*rodovye perežitki*). The first, which is sanctified by *Adat* law, effectively opposes assimilation of small ethnic groups by larger nationalities, thus retarding national consolidation. Having belonged to nomadic tribes before 1928, the Muslims of the U.S.S.R. are well aware of their appurtenance to a clan. This fact tends to limit the focus of Muslim loyalty to kinship groups, while depriving larger political and social causes of their whole-hearted support.

The tribe has ceased everywhere to fulfill a political function, although members continue to acknowledge one another as kinsmen. This is true even if the tribe is scattered over many thousand kilometers and among a half dozen modern nationalities speaking different languages (Bashkirs, Nogays, Karakalpaks, Kazakhs, Uzbeks, and Kirghiz). Such is the case, for example, of the former Turkish tribes of Mongolian origin: Nayman, Ktay, and Mangyt. The most characteristic tribal survival is *mestničestvo*, the practice of reserving high positions at one's place of employment, including the Communist Party hierarchy, for members of one's own tribe.

In light of the social *perežitki* discussed above, Soviet anti-religious propaganda efforts, while inept, are at least understandable. They have three salient objectives:

(1) The destruction of 'dangerous social customs' inherited from the past which are inconsistent with the building of socialism and with cultural and biological symbiosis.

(2) The destruction of 'superstitions' (*sueverija*), an expression which encompasses not only religiosity but also different manifestations of popular religion.

(3) 'Materialistic scientific education', which seldom directly confronts officially recognized churches but which endeavours to demonstrate the unscientific character of all religion and its incompatibility with Communism. Concomitantly, the right to worship to which all Soviet citizens are entitled and the necessity of respecting the faith of believers are stressed. On the other hand, Soviet anti-religious propaganda violently attacks political movements such as pan-Islamism, which are based upon religious ideology.

In the 1920's the Soviet Government attacked the churches from all angles: their hierarchies, their legal structures, their economic foundations, their scholarly establishments, and even the church buildings themselves. This struggle, like the present one, was carried on by aggressive propagandizing but even more by unsubtle coercion. It was a mismatch, although Soviet leaders foresaw an early victory. Today, fifty years later, the regime confronts a popular religion which is elusive and hostile and a set of customs and social practices which refuse to go away. These *perežitki* spring not from religion, as Soviet authorities insist, but from the innermost Muslim desire to preserve their traditional culture; a culture which is intimately and intricately bound up with national consciousness. Caught in the paradox of their own propaganda, Soviet authorities since Stalin have complained unceasingly of the lack of cooperation, indifference, and reluctance on the part of local officials to take sides against their own national religion. Therefore, the inevitability of the following incident should surprise no one: in 1968 local officials in Tadzhikistan refused to permit a showing of an anti-Muslim film on the ground that it would affront the *national* sensibilities of the Tadzhik people.

REFERENCES

1 *Tashkent* (1971), no. 6.
2 *Tashkent* 18 March 1952.
3 No. 3 (1971).
4 Declaration by the Mufti of Azerbaidzhan at the Tashkent conference of Muslim religious chiefs in October, 1970, in N. Aširov, 'Changes in the Social Position of Islam', *Nauka i Religija* (1971), no. 4, p. 41.
5 Declaration by Ahmedjan Mustafin, Imam of the Moscow Mosque, in *ibid.*, p. 39.
6 Declaration of Ahmed Agaev, in *ibid.*, p. 40.
7 *Idem*, p. 41.
8 *Nauka i Religija* (1971), no. 6, p. 41.
9 N. P. Andrianov and V. V. Pavljuk, 'Kulturnaja Revolucija v Nacional'nyx Respublikax: Razvitie Ateizma Mass', *Voprosy Naučnogo Ateizma* (1967), no. 4.
10 *Sosialistik Tatarstan* (Kazan), 7 July 1972.
11 *Sovet Tadzhikistan* (Dushambe), 16 September 1970.
12 I. Irbutov, 'V Makhalle Yangi Hayat', *Nauka i Religija* (1965), no. 9.
13 S. Dordženov, 'Musul'manin li Ja?', *Nauka i Religija* (1967), no. 4.
14 M. I. Bikžanov, *Family Life on Collective Farms in Modern Uzbekistan* (Moscow, 1960); in English.
15 S. M. Abramzon, 'Kirghizakaja Semja v Epoxu Socializma', *Sovetskija Etnografija* (1957), no. 5.
16 G. P. Snesarev, 'O Nekotoryx Pričinax Soxranenija Religiozno-Bytovylx Perežitkov u Uzbekov Xorezma', *Sovetskija Etnografija* (1957), no. 2.

BOHDAN R. BOCIURKIW

RELIGIOUS DISSENT IN THE U.S.S.R.:
LITHUANIAN CATHOLICS

Lithuania – the only Soviet Republic with a Roman Catholic majority –
has been the scene of the latest and the most powerful surge of religious
dissent in the Soviet Union. Like the earlier waves of religious protest –
most notably, the *iniciativniki* movement among the Evangelical Christians and Baptists[1] and the ferment within the Russian Orthodox Church[2]
– the Lithuanian Catholic dissidents have overtly repudiated the existing
pattern of church-state relations, challenging the legitimacy of the norms
and structures governing these relations.[3] But in contrast to these earlier
protest currents, the Lithuanian dissent was not primarily generated by
Khrushchev's anti-religious campaign of 1959–64, a campaign which had
largely spared the local Catholic Church.[4] The latter had experienced
much more severe persecution during the years 1945–53 at the very time
when the Russian Church, the Evangelical Christians and Baptists, and
some other 'loyal' denominations were enjoying the full benefits of Stalin's
'religious NEP'. During that period all but one of the Lithuanian bishops
were imprisoned or deported and one of the imprisoned bishops was
executed.[5] Perhaps as many as one third of the clergy – 350 in all – were
arrested or shipped away to Soviet Asia; all monasteries and convents
were suppressed or driven underground, while of the four theological
seminaries only one, the Kaunas seminary, was allowed to subsist, its
enrollment reduced from 350 to 75 by 1949. Over 300 chapels and some
ten per cent of churches were closed during these years.[6]

Like its attack against the Uniates in the Western Ukraine, the regime's
assault on the Lithuanian Catholic Church appeared to be motivated
much less by anti-religious zeal than by political hostility to these two
branches of the Catholic Church, on account of their links with the Vatican
and their close identification with the anti-Russian nationalism of their
flock. However, unlike in the Ukraine, the authorities in Lithuania stopped
short of a complete suppression of the Church.[7]

Following Stalin's death, the Lithuanian Church experienced several
years of a 'thaw'. Some 130 priests – less than half of the numbers exiled

De George and Scanlan (eds.), Marxism and Religion in Eastern Europe, 147–175. *All Rights Reserved.*
Copyright © *1976 by D. Reidel Publishing Company, Dordrecht-Holland.*

after the war – were then allowed to return home, together with two surving bishops.[8] Meanwhile, in 1955, the government consented to the consecration of two new bishops – Julijus Steponavicius and Petras Mazelis[9] – and permitted a few 'loyal' priests to pursue their advanced studies in Rome. A Catholic prayerbook was published in a small edition at that time.

By 1958, the regime resumed the harassment of the Church. Bishop Vincentas Sladkevicius, recently ordained (evidently without the government's consent), was barred from his see and confined to a remote village; in 1961, the same fate befell Bishop Steponavicius.[10] The enrollment in the Kaunas seminary was further reduced to 25 students. Some churches, especially in urban centres, were closed and a major church in Klaipeda – one of the two built by believers in Lithuania since 1945 – was confiscated and turned into a concert hall. Chapels and crosses in the principal pilgrimage centres were destroyed by the authorities. While a massive anti-religious propaganda drive was launched in the Republic, new restrictions were imposed upon the performance of certain religious rites, and more severe sanctions were applied against the clergy for religious instruction of children and for allowing active participation of the youth in religious ceremonies.[11]

In the wake of Khrushchev's fall came some abatement in anti-religious pressures. The authorities permitted the ordination of two new bishops – Juozas Matulaitis-Labukas, in 1965, and Juozapas Pletkus, in 1968.[12] The enrollment in the Kaunas seminary was raised to 30 students. The Church was able to publish, in a miniscule edition, a volume containing decisions of the Second Vatican Council. Nevertheless, the anti-religious propaganda – though less abusive than during the early sixties – has not lost much of its intensity[13], with the authorities resorting to administrative and judicial weapons to minimize the clergy's influence upon children.

Despite nearly 25 years of legal and administrative restrictions and a steady barrage of atheist propaganda, the Roman Catholic Church in Lithuania remained at the end of the 1960's still a potent force in Lithuanian society. Perhaps as many as two-thirds of the Lithuanians have retained links with the Church. The latter's basic organizational structure has largely remained intact: six dioceses[14], 54 deaneries, and over 600 parishes (compared with 717 in 1940). More serious was the situation with the clergy: where there were once ten bishops, only two active bishops remained by 1968[15], with approximately 800 active priests (a reduction by about 40% since 1940), not counting some 176 retired or 'unregistered' clergy. Though over three hundred priests have been ordained since 1945, only a handful had left the Church by 1967.[16] A few clergymen were reportedly recruited as police informers and some have become apologists for the regime's policies.[17] But the majority, while overtly professing their loyalty to the Soviet state, have been conscientiously carrying under difficult conditions a heavy burden of pastoral work, abstaining from any political involvement for or against the regime. By the end of the 1960's there had also emerged an increasingly vocal group of activist clergy and young lay intellectuals who were prepared to risk their personal careers in order to break the seal of silence imposed upon the Church by more than two decades of intimidation.

I. THE RISE OF THE CATHOLIC DISSENT MOVEMENT

The first manifestations of organized Catholic dissent in Lithuania date from 1968. Proclaimed by the United Nations as the Year of Human Rights, 1968 was something of a turning point for the human rights movement in the U.S.S.R.: it opened with the Trial of the Four in Moscow which triggered the greatest wave of petitions ever to emerge from the Soviet intellectual community in defense of the rule of law and against the portends of re-Stalinization.[18] This year witnessed the rise and suppression of the 'socialism with a human face' experiment in Czechoslovakia and the parallel surges of hope and despair within the incipient 'democratic movement'; it saw the marked politicization and radicalization of dissent epitomized by the appearance of the *Chronicle of Current Events* and the symbolic demonstration in Red Square against the invasion of Czechoslovakia; it was during 1968 that yesterday's 'Jews of silence' joined the Crimean Tatars and other dissident currents in speaking out in word and deed in defence of their national rights; and it was the year characterized by a significant escalation in the severity of the régime's reprisals against its critics.

In Lithuania, 63 priests of the Telsiai diocese protested to Premier Kosygin on January 8, 1968, against the arbitrary government restrictions on the training of the clergy. On August 7 of the same year, Rev. V. Sliavas of the Adakava parish addressed a similar petition to Premier Kosygin, "on behalf of all clergymen and believers".[19] These were the first protests in the series of collective and individual petitions which marked the crystallization of a dissent movement within the Lithuanian Church, its rise undoubtedly stimulated by other manifestations of protest in the U.S.S.R. It was from the 'older' dissent currents that the Lithuanian movement adopted the epistolary weapon of protest: to seek the redress of grievances by publicizing at home and abroad, in the form of open letters to the authorities, the regime's violations of its own laws and of constitutional and international guarantees of religious freedom. Underlying this quite legal tactic[20] was the expectation that such publicity would, on the one hand, help to mobilize domestic and foreign support for the Catholic demands and, on the other hand, sufficiently embarrass the Soviet authorities to bring about at least partial restoration of the Church's legitimate rights. Essential to the success of such an epistolary campaign was some kind of clandestine organization to gather and verify the facts, to document the claims, and to collect signatures under petitions; such organization was also necessary for the purpose of circulating the Lithuanian protests via *samizdat* and through foreign publicity media, which in turn may have called for links with the dissident circles in Moscow and some access to the capital's foreign colony.

Between 1968 and mid-1972 at least fifteen more protest documents were addressed to the Soviet authorities by the Lithuanian Catholic clergy.[21] Considering the vulnerability of the 'servants of cult' to administrative reprisals, the support they gave to this action was unprecedented in any religious group in the U.S.S.R.: in five dioceses, 362 or nearly 47% of all the 770 priests signed at least one of the petitions, and in the dioceses of Panevezys and Vilkaviskis the share of protesters reached 83 and almost 56% respectively.[22]

Since August 1971, the clergy petitions have been overshadowed by a succession of protest documents signed by large numbers of believers, ranging from several hundred to more than 17,000 (petition to Brezhnev of Dec. 1972/Jan. 1973).[23] Twelve such documents which appeared during the two years since the summer of 1971 carried a total of 59,769 signatures from all over Lithuania[24]; only the Crimean Tartar dissidents have been able to mobilize larger numbers to support their demands. Undoubtedly, such an extensive involvement of the Lithuanian clergy and believers could only be explained by their acute anxiety about the prospects of the Church's institutional and spiritual survival in a hostile political environment and about the progressively contracting scope for the open practice and propagation of the faith; no doubt, also, their protests were motivated – like those of the Baptist and Orthodox dissenters before them – by the realization that the established channels for the articulation of the Church's interests – via the official church leaders and the government's Council for Religious Affairs – could not anymore be relied upon, owing either to a combination of arbitrariness and bias on the part of the atheist CRA officials or to the timidity of the episcopate.

The grievances of the clergy and believers centered around several critical issues affecting the fate of the Lithuanian Catholic Church. The first and foremost target of the clergy's protests was the existing systems of pervasive, restrictive, and discriminatory regulations impeding the normal functioning of the Church even within the narrow framework provided by the Soviet Constitution and the legislation on religious cults. In particular, the protesters complained about the continuing arbitrary banishment of Bishops Steponavicius and Sladkevicius at the time when some dioceses remained for years without episcopal leadership[25]; about restrictions on the exercise of some canonic functions by bishops, including the conferring of the sacrament of confirmation[26]; about the deliberately low *numerus clausus* imposed by the authorities on the sole Kaunas seminary with only 5–6 new priests allowed to be consecrated annually at the time when 12 to 22 priests die each year[27]; about the illegal interference of the CRA officials with the work of the Seminary, as well as the official measures to prevent potential students from entering it or to recruit informers among the seminarians.[28] The protest documents criticized numerous administrative obstacles – some of which arbitrarily 'reinterpreted' the published legislation on religion, while others clearly violated this legislation – obstacles designed to further restrict the activities of the clergy to the performance of religious rites within the assigned houses of worship and to prevent them from assisting each other at the time of special local celebrations or at the traditional pilgrimage sites.[29] Other complaints were directed against the virtual prohibition of the construction of new churches and the difficulties encountered in repairing the older shrines, as well as against discriminatory taxation and utility rates levied on churches by the authorities.[30] Some petitions demanded the return of churches confiscated during the previous two decades.[31] The ridiculously low printings of the few religious books allowed to be published by the authorities, the shortage of prayerbooks, and the absence of certain kinds of religious literature and of the Catholic press were also listed among the grievances of the Church.[32]

The second category of complaints related to the arbitrary rulings by the authorities which placed the traditional examination of the children's religious knowledge by priests prior to their First Communion under the Criminal Code prohibition of any systematic religious instruction of minors; and which extended the prohibition of the individual membership of minors in religious associations to their active participation in religious processions, church choirs, and orchestras and to assisting the priest at the Mass.[33] This was a common theme of the believers' petitions, which protested against the harsh court sentences and administrative penalties imposed upon the clergy and laymen for these alleged violations of the "laws on cults".[34] Closely associated with these grievances were the parents' protests against the compulsory anti-religious indoctrination of their children in schools; the use of harassment, ridicule, and discrimination directed against religious pupils; intimidating interrogations and questionnaires employed in schools to reveal the parents' and clergy's involvement in the religious upbringing of children; and the abuse of teachers' and administrative authority to bar school pupils from attending religious services with their parents and, in general, to undermine the parents' influence over their own children.[35]

Like the Baptist and Orthodox dissidents before them, the Lithuanian protest movement supported its demands with references to Lenin's programmatic writings and appeals to the Soviet Constitution and legislation on religion, the Universal Declaration of Human Rights, the International Convention against Discrimination in Education, and the UN Covenants on Human Rights. Significantly, several protest documents contrasted the plight of the Lithuanian Catholics with the much more tolerant treatment of the Roman Catholic Church in Poland and other "people's democracies".[36] Progressively, the scope of Lithuanian protests extended to include other violations of "socialist legality" in the Republic[37]; to express concern about the official treatment of the national heritage, history, culture, and language both in Lithuania and with regard to the Lithuanian diaspora elsewhere in the U.S.S.R.[38]; to plead for the restoration of the Ukrainian Greek Catholic (Uniate) Church[39]; and to voice the growing dissatisfaction of at least some clergy and faithful with what they regarded as appeasement of Moscow by the Vatican at the expense of the Lithuanian Catholic Church.[40]

II. THE CONFRONTATIONS

At the time when the first clergy declarations concerning restrictions on religion in Lithuania were addressed to the Soviet Government [noted, early in 1974, the *samizdat* organ of the Lithuanian dissidents], the priests and faithful in all the dioceses approved the thought [that] one ought to fight for the faith. Many regretted that they had waited much too long and had not done anything in this direction.[41]

The clergy's declarations soon brought their authors and supporters into an escalating series of direct confrontations with the Soviet authorities who were determined to break the protest movement at its inception by singling out and punishing the suspected leaders of this movement. As a rule, the priests' petitions remained unanswered by the authorities to which they were addressed (despite their legal duty to do so within a month)[42]; the latter usually passed them on to the republican representative of the Council for Religious Affairs (the very official whose abuses of authority have motivated many of the clergy's complaints) – a practice which seemed to be designed to impress the clergy with the utter futility of their protests.[43] The common response of the CRA representative was to summon the petition writers, to reprimand and threaten them, and often have them transferred to other parishes.[44]

Before long, the police and the courts were employed to isolate the most vocal spokesmen of the movement. The pretext seized upon by the authorities was the alleged "violation of the laws on cults", specifically, "the organization and systematic conduct of religious instruction of minors" prohibited under Article 143 of the Lithuanian Criminal Code.[45] This prohibition was conveniently extended, by an unpublished government instruction, to cover also the examination of the children's religious knowledge by the priests prior to the First Communion, whenever more than one child was examined at a time or when other children were present at such an examination[46] – *caveats* which many Lithuanian priests found physically impossible to observe.

In July, 1970, the police arrested a Jesuit priest, Antanas Seskevicius

(*1914) of Dubingiai parish, charging him with the illegal religious instruction of minors. Fr. Seskevicius had been previously exiled from Lithuania for some twenty years, fourteen of which he had spent in Siberian concentration camps.[47] Accused of violating Article 143, in the Moletai court in September, 1970, he eloquently defended his actions as legitimate under the Constitution and international human rights conventions, and he attacked the arbitrary secret instructions which have been used by the CRA officials to bar the youth from the Church. Seskevicius' sentence to one year in prison evoked a series of protests signed by a total of 283 priests from four dioceses.[48] In the summer of 1971, two more priest activists were arrested on the same charges – Juozas Zdebskis (*1929) of Prienai and Prosperas Bubnys of Girkalnis; they were sentenced, in separate trials in November, to a one-year term each.[49]

The case of Fr. Zdebskis was of major significance in the final crystallization of the Catholic dissent movement in Lithuania. Considered by the KGB as a principal leader of the movement[50], Zdebskis was reportedly brutally beaten during the pre-trial investigation. In violation of the established procedures, his trial was transferred to Kaunas and was actually held *in camera*.[51] At the trial, Zdebskis accused the authorities of systematic discrimination against believers, persecution of the Church, and its internal subversion through some submissive ecclesiastical leaders.[52] During the Zdebskis trial came the first major physical confrontation – between some 500–600 Catholics who were barred from the court proceedings, and the police, who used force to disperse the crowd; some twenty people, including two priests, were arrested in the ensuing disorders.[53]

The arrest and trial of Fr. Zdebskis marked the beginning of an increasing involvement of laymen in the Catholic protest movement. Within three days of the priest's arrest, a petition demanding his release was signed by about 350 of his parishioners and personally delivered to the Procurator-General's Office in Moscow; representatives of believers also made personal representations to the Republican Procurator and the CRA representative, Rugienis. In September 1971, 2,000 Prienai believers (some 25% of all the parishioners) addressed to the Party and Government leaders in Moscow a petition demanding the release of Fr. Zdebskis and the lifting of discriminatory restrictions on religion. They were soon joined by 1,190 members of the Santaika parish. A similar letter of protest was sent to the government in December by 1,344 believers calling for the release of Fr. Bubnys.[54]

In December, 1971, and January, 1972, 17,059 signatures were collected throughout Lithuania under a "Memorandum of the Roman Catholics of Lithuania" addressed to Brezhnev; along with the imprisonment of Zdebskis and Bubnys, this document enumerated the main grievances of the believers.

We therefore ask the Soviet Government [concluded the Memorandum] to grant us freedom of conscience, which has been guaranteed by the Constitution of the U.S.S.R. but which has not been put into practice heretofore. What we want is not pretty words in the press and on the radio but serious governmental efforts that would help us, Catholics, to feel like citizens of the Soviet Union with equal rights.[55]

An addendum to the Memorandum signed "Representatives of Lithuanian Catholics", noted that only "an insignificant portion of religious believers in Lithuania", were able to sign the memorandum "since the organs of the Militia and the KGB have used all kinds of means to interrupt the collection of signatures", including arrests of those collecting them.[56]

This massive protest document was sent the following month to the Secretary General of the United Nations for transmission to Brezhnev. In their appeal to Kurt Waldheim "Representatives of Lithuania's Catholics" justified this course by the fact that none of the earlier protests[57] had elicited any official reply but only "increased repressions"; they also pointed to the fact "that religious believers in [Lithuania] cannot enjoy the right set out in Article 18 of the Universal Declaration of Human Rights".[58]

Even before *samizdat* and foreign communication media gave publicity to this latest initiative of the Lithuanian dissidents, the Soviet police – already busy with the round-up of dissident Ukrainian, Russian, and Jewish intellectuals[59] – intervened to stop further collection of signatures under the December protest petition in Lithuania and launched searches and interrogations to uncover "anti-Soviet priests" suspected of having organized this action. In April, the authorities compelled the administrator of the Vilnius Archdiocese, Msgr. Krivaitis to offer an interview for foreign consumption in which he declared that there is "freedom of religion in Lithuania".[60] On April 11, the functioning Lithuanian bishops and administrators of dioceses were summoned to Kaunas by the CRA representatives from Vilnius and Moscow, and told to sign a "pastoral letter" to be read in all churches on April 30. The "letter" condemned the "irresponsible individuals" who "gather signatures" under pretext of "fraud", and warned the flock that

the signing of irresponsible documents affects relations between the church and the state and gives rise to misunderstandings. These kinds of things can bring no good to the Church...[61]

Despite the pressure exerted on the clergy by their canonical superiors and the civil authorities, "very few priests" reportedly read the bishops' condemnation on the appointed date. A clandestine appeal circulated among the clergy in April exposed the "pastoral letter" as a "slanderous" and "compromising" declaration which was "forced" upon the episcopate against their will.[62] The sequence of events in Lithuania culminated, on May 14, in the self-immolation of Romas Kalantas in protest against the suppression of freedom in the country. Though not directly motivated by religious oppression, Kalantas' tragic end triggered on the day of his funeral a mass demonstration demanding national and religious freedom and ended in clashes between the demonstrators and the militia and security troops.[63]

III. THE CHRONICLE OF THE CATHOLIC CHURCH IN LITHUANIA

On March 19, 1972, appeared the first issue of the clandestine *Chronicle of the Catholic Church in Lithuania*. Modelled, obviously, on the older *samizdat* newsletters – the *Chronicle of Current Events* and the *Ukrainian Herald*, soon to be suppressed in the KGB dragnet of dissidents – the Lithuanian *Chronicle* signalled a new stage in the consolidation of the Catholic dissent movement. The emergence of a more regular communication medium was an important step towards the integration of the clerical and lay dissidents in a "quasi-organization" – a loose network of the editors, informants, producers, and distributors of the *Chronicle*.

In the subsequent issues of the *Chronicle*, its editors enlarged on the reasons for its appearance: it was to bring out true facts about "the situation of the Catholic Church, the nation's present, the arbitrary actions, repressions, and other discriminatory means of the government organs..." The newsletter "will stop appearing only when the Government will grant to the Church and the believers at least as much freedom as is guaranteed by the Constitution of the U.S.S.R."[64]

Significantly, the *Chronicle* was conceived by its editors as a vehicle for articulating authentic interests of "the persecuted Church" not only to the Soviet authorities, but also to the Holy See, which, the journal noted, "while defending victims of discrimination all over the world, barely recalls the 'Church of Silence and Suffering', does not bring up and does not condemn covert and overt persecution of the faithful in the Soviet Union".[65] Such actions of the Vatican, noted the *Chronicle*, as the conferring of ecclesiastical distinctions on "certain priests 'loyal' to the Soviet system"[66] the nomination as bishops of "the hand-picked candidates of the government", and the Vatican's "dialogue with the Soviet government", have created among the Lithuanian Catholics, the feeling that "the Vatican is being deceived", or that they have been "betrayed" and abandoned by the Roman Curia.[67]

At such a difficult time, the only recourse left to Catholics of Lithuania is to trust in Divine Providence and to seek ways by which the true message might reach the Vatican and the rest of the world, that the most deadly thing for the Catholic Church in Lithuania is not persecution, but the noose being tied by some of our own people.[68]

The Church in Lithuania will not be destroyed by repressions, declared the *Chronicle*, but it "will lose the people if it loses credibility by bootlicking the Soviet regime. This is what happened to the Orthodox Church in Russia."[69]

In the tradition of the Moscow *Chronicle*, the Lithuanian dissident newsletter insisted on acurate, verified information:

The *Chronicle of the Catholic Church in Lithuania* has no use for inconcrete information and inaccurate facts ... [the information] must be thoroughly checked, [made] clear and accurate. Numbers, dates, last names, names of places and other data must be especially intelligible, correctly recorded and authenticated.[70]

The informants were requested to "specify which names are to be withheld".[71]

The readers of the *Chronicle of the Lithuanian Catholic Church* were asked to "protect the *Chronicle of the L.C.C.* from the KGB organs" and to pass it from "hand to hand".[72]

The first issues of the *Chronicle*, which has been appearing since March 1972 on a roughly quarterly basis[73], have been largely devoted to the documentation of the Soviet violations of religious freedom, including complaints and declarations of the clergy and laymen; reports of arrests, interrogations, and trials of the alleged violators of the "laws on cults"[74]; administrative harassment of the clergy and believers, especially for their work with minors; anti-religious indoctrination in schools and discrimination against religious pupils and students; protests of religious parents, etc. Since its December 1972 issue (No. 4), the publication has begun to carry lengthy unsigned articles outlining the objectives and attitudes of the movement, evaluating Soviet church policy and anti-religious activities, polemicizing with the atheist writers, and criticizing the "appeasement" of the Communist regime by the official Lithuanian Church leaders and the Vatican. These evidently editorial articles speaking for the "Representatives of Lithuanian Catholics" offer an important insight into the ideological orientation and political strategy of the Lithuanian dissidents.[75]

With the May, 1973 issue (No. 6) the *Chronicle* began to dedicate more and more space to other, not strictly religious, manifestations of dissent, to Soviet persecution of Lithuanian intellectuals and students suspected of "bourgeois nationalism", violations of civil rights, denationalization policies in education and culture, and occasionally, to other religious groups, most notably the Ukrainian Catholics.[76] Along with an increasing politicization of the publication and its more open identification with Lithuanian nationalism, the *Chronicle's* style has lost some of its early naive, provincial flavour, has become more sophisticated and precise, with occasional touches of irony and sarcasm.

IV. SOCIAL BASE AND IDEOLOGICAL ORIENTATION OF LITHUANIAN CATHOLIC DISSENT

From a careful reading of the Lithuanian *samizdat*, it appears that the core of the Catholic dissent movement has consisted of a tightly-knit group of provincial priests, including a few survivors of Stalin's concentration camps, some younger clergy educated and ordained since World War II, and individual clerics who, for political reasons, have been barred by the authorities from legally performing their pastoral duties.[77] Their loyalties have not been with the officially sanctioned bishops and diocesan administrators[78], but with the two exiled hierarchs – Steponavicius and Sladkevicius.

The leaders of the movement were probably able to rely on strong support from the "illegal fringe" of the Church – underground monastic communities (especially nuns working in a variety of secular jobs), un-official candidates for priesthood, and lay producers of "illegal" religious literature and articles of worship. From the very beginning, it seems, the movement has also attracted some lay Catholics – urban intellectuals, students and workers – the so-called "clerical elements" who have shown "lively interest in the church life and its future".[79] While the underground convents and individual monastics have been carrying much of the burden of the religious education of children and the work with youth,

it is no secret [wrote the *Chronicle* early in 1974] that almost all prayerbooks, catecheti-cal books and other religious literature were published in exceptionally difficult and dangerous conditions precisely by those "clerical elements".[80]

Judging by the numbers of priests who signed protest petitions during the years 1968–72, almost one half of the Lithuanian clergy at one time or another has expressed its solidarity with the objectives of the dissent movement, and in two dioceses – Panevezys and Vilkaviskis – the majority of the local priests joined in the movement's epistolary campaign.

Compared to the Baptist and Orthodox dissent currents, the Catholic protest movement has been able to draw upon a much larger social base. In numerical (but not necessarily qualitative) terms, most of its support has evidently come from outside the major metropolitan centres, from the provincial town and village parishes which are or have been served by the dissident priests, with church attendants and, particularly, women playing the most active part in the 'grass-roots' protest activities. In a number of cases, the parish executive committees have been working closely with the activist pastors. (Few Roman Catholic priests have been reduced in fact to the status of hired "servants of cult".) Undoubtedly, too, the dissidents could draw strength from the eschatological undercurrents among the believers which manifested themselves in certain pilgrimages, penitent movements such as the "carrying of crosses", chain "letters from heaven", and similar activities.

Like the catacomb Uniate Church in the Western Ukraine, the Lithuan-ian Catholic dissidents have appealed also to the national sentiments of the flock, to the widely shared belief in the interdependence and insep-arability of the traditional faith and nationality. But in contrast to the Uniates whose parishes and churches have been forcibly incorporated into the Russian Orthodox Church, the Lithuanian Catholic dissenters

have had the immense advantages of working within a relatively autonomous ecclesiastical organization, little infiltrated by the police; of legally
operating churches with their physical facilities, financial base, institutional lines of communication; of open contacts with other priests and
believers; and of opportunities, however limited, for socialization of the
believers in the religious and national 'subcultures'.

Eventually, as the episcopate was compelled by the authorities to
condemn the protest activities and as the police intensified their reprisals
against the suspected dissident leaders, their base of support among the
clergy was bound to contract somewhat, though simultaneously the movement's reputation must have been attracting larger numbers of lay
supporters.

"Representatives of Lithuanian Catholics" – as the movement's leaders
have come to call themselves – have neither formulated nor attempted to
develop a systematic political ideology. One can assume that they have
included individuals of differing ideological inclinations, as well as people
concerned only about certain specific, practical goals. Nevertheless,
scattered throughout the Lithuanian Catholic *samizdat* – and particularly
evident in some petitions and defense statements of such prominent dissidents as the priests Seskevicius and Zdebskis, as well as in the *Chronicle's*
editorials – are values, behavioural norms, implied models of alternative
social order, of the 'proper' kind of church-state relations, of the 'natural'
and 'just' rights of the Lithuanian nation. Some of the ideas dispersed
throughout the Lithuanian dissident literature are unmistakenly products
of pre-Soviet political-cultural socialization and of traditionalist Catholic
education, definitely *ante* Vatican II: like most of the Roman Catholic
Church in other Communist states, Lithuanian dissidents have considered
'modernization' and 'liberalization' of the Church, and, especially its
"dialogue" with the Communists as either a dangerous luxury, a definite
mistake, or something close to capitulation – in *their own* conditions of a
total siege of the Church by the much more powerful atheist state.[81]

The uncompromising "one must hearken to God rather than to man"
has been perhaps the dominant note in the dissident literature.[82] The
Church cannot be destroyed from without, even if it should be deprived
of legal conditions of existence: it can only be destroyed from within,
through the compromise of its leaders and pastors with atheism, through
abdicating some of its intrinsic spiritual duties, in particular that of teach-

ing the young and old. One must, therefore, fight, whatever the risks, for the rights of the Church. Initially, the dissidents were restricting their demands to the actual realization of the rights specifically provided for believers in the Soviet constitituon and international conventions; later the *Chronicle* has carried appeals demanding the extension to believers of the general democratic rights under Article 125 of the Constitution, including access to all mass communication media, the publication of religious books and newspapers, and the establishment of religious organizations.[83]

The dissidents' notion of 'proper' church-state relations has largely centered around the unfulfilled Bolshevik promise of a 'complete' separation of church from state, i.e., the classical liberal formula which presupposes the state's indifference to various religious creeds and its impartiality in the treatment of believers and non-believers; and which also demands that religious organizations be left free to manage their own internal affairs without the state's interference. On the other hand, the dissidents have stressed on many occasions the historical and cultural interdependence, indeed a symbiotic relationship between Roman Catholicism and Lithuanian nationality, as well as the ultimate dependence of private and public morality on absolutist, religious ethical norms.

The nationalist orientation has in time become more pronounced in the Lithuanian Catholic protest movement, as can be seen in the more recent issues of the *Chronicle* referring to the "occupiers of Lithuania"[84], approving patriotic manifestations among the youth such as the marking of Lithuania's Independence Day, and condemning official profanation of national monuments, neglect or distortion of the Lithuanian past, discrimination against the Lithuanian culture, and, in general, denationalization policies of the regime. One is left with little doubt that the emancipation of Lithuania from Soviet Russian control – at least to the extent enjoyed by neighbouring Poland – has been viewed by the Lithuanian Catholic dissenters as the political guarantee of the nation's survival.

IV. LITHUANIAN CATHOLICS AND OTHER DISSENT MOVEMENTS

Catholic dissenters in Lithuania have shared many of their demands and objectives with other protest currents in the U.S.S.R., above all their joint aspirations to a rule of law ('socialist legality') and 'publicity' – free flow of information, the abolition of preliminary censorship and of secrecy about the actual treatment of Soviet citizens by the authorities. Closer to the Baptist *iniciativniki* than the Orthodox dissenters in their uncompromising stand over the right to instruct children and youth in religion, the Lithuanian *Chronicle* has criticized church-state relations in the U.S.S.R. in almost the same terms as these two earlier dissent currents.[85] It is highly unlikely that the leaders of the Catholic protest movement were unfamiliar with the religious *samizdat* emanating from other dissent currents in the U.S.S.R. From them, too, they must have adopted their tactical weapons, including the use of Soviet and international law against the arbitrary officials and the police; the mass petitions and delegations; and the *samizdat* techniques, including the *Chronicle*.

One can assume that personal links were developed between some leading spokesmen of the Lithuanian movement and representatives of other protest currents at the time they shared a common fate as political prisoners and deportees (this was especially true of the Lithuanian-Ukrainian contacts), and that these links were later extended through exchange of visits, information, advice, documents, and publications.

The growing contacts between the Lithuanian dissenters and the civil rights movement are reflected in the increasing space which the *Chronicle of Current Events* has been devoting, since its December, 1970 (No. 17) issue, to events in Lithuania, beginning with the reports of Frs. Seskevicius' and Zdebskis' trials and the protests of the Catholic clergy. It was significant that when, upon his release from prison, Seskevicius was refused at first a government permit to continue his pastoral duties, he turned for help to Sakharov's Human Rights Committee in Moscow.[86] On another occasion, Valery Chalidze appealed on behalf of the same Committee to the Presidium of the Lithuanian Supreme Soviet and to the Director-General of UNESCO, in protest against Zdebskis' arrest which, he claimed, violated both Soviet laws and the International Convention on the Struggle against Discrimination in Education.[87] On its part, when the regime's campaign against Solzhenitsyn reached its peak, the Lithuanian *Chronicle* "saluted" Solzhenitsyn as "an example of how one must love one's Fatherland and not bow to brutal force..."[88]

Perhaps the closest bonds of sympathy and solidarity are those uniting the dissident Lithuanian clergy with the 'illegal' Ukrainian Catholic priests with whom they came to share years of imprisonment and exile during the wave of anti-Catholic persecution in the late 1940's and early 1950's. At the time of the suppression of the Ukrainian Greek Catholic Church, a few Uniate priests found shelter with the Lithuanian clergy; it was rumoured that for a while an underground Ukrainian Uniate bishop had his 'base' in Lithuania. Some other Uniate clergymen, when they were released from exile along with deported Lithuanian priests, chose to accompany the latter to Lithuania where they offered their pastoral services to Lithuanian believers as 'illegal' 'worker-priests'. Among them were those who continued to serve their Ukrainian flock from afar, such as priest Volodymyr Prokopiv of Vilnius, whose arrest in late 1973 was reported by the *Chronicle*, after he personally accompanied to Moscow representatives of the 12,000 Ukrainian believers who signed a petition asking for the restoration of the Uniate Church.[89]

Earlier, in December, 1971, a petition of 47 Vilnius diocese clergy[90] requested Soviet leaders, among other things, to permit "all priests living in our country (including the Ukrainians) freely and publicly to do their work as priests".[91] Months later, when one of the organizers of this petition, priest B. Laurinavicius, was summoned by the CRA representative J. Rugienis and accused of "insolence and anti-Soviet activity", he responded with a lengthy written explanation of the priests' action. He justified reference to the Uniate clergy in the following words:

Our colleagues, the Ukrainian priests... are dear to us... We requested that the Ukrainian priests be allowed to go back to work, because the faithful of the Ukraine give us no peace, asking us to work among them. We asked that their priests be put back to work, since they have never been sentenced by the court.[92]

Among the issues that united the Lithuanian dissidents and the banned Ukrainian Uniates has been their opposition to the Vatican's *Ostpolitik*, its 'dialogue' with the Kremlin. Commenting on Gromyko's visit with the Pope, a recent issue of the *Chronicle* observed that

dialogue, it seems, is useful to [the Communist regime] only in order to [have] the Vatican maintain silence about the persecution of Catholics in the Soviet Union...[93]

V. THE SOVIET RESPONSE

In trying to cope with the growing unrest among the Lithuanian clergy and faithful, the Soviet authorities typically combined 'carrot and stick' measures to isolate the 'hard core' dissidents from their following and to strengthen the hand of the 'loyal' church leaders, Together with direct repression – administrative fines, police interrogations and threats, and eventually arrests and trials of the suspected animators of the protest movement – the government applied against them indirect sanctions, through their canonical superiors, who were compelled to restrict the activities or to order transfers of the 'troublesome' priests; those clerics who refused to submit to such orders as uncanonical[94] were threatened or actually punished with suspension; on occasions the authorities stepped in to help enforce these ecclesiastical sanctions.[95] While such use of the episcopate by the government – including the issuance of the April 1972 'pastoral letter' slandering the organizers of protest petitions – did help to 'pacify' those strata of the clergy who offered a passive or lukewarm support to the dissenters, it only deepened the alienation of the dissident priests from their submissive ordinaries and contributed to the further radicalization of the dissent movement.

Some concessions were offered to the Church. In December, 1969, two new bishops were consecrated with prior governmental approval: the once persecuted Klaipeda pastor, Liudas Povilonis[96], and the former Chancellor of the Kaunas Archdiocese, youthful Romualdo Kriksciunas.[97] In the wake of the 'protest explosion' during the winter and spring of 1972 came a short-lived relaxation of anti-religious pressures and even some self-criticism in the Soviet press. In August the Vilnius daily *Sovetskaja Litva* warned that

irreparable damage could be inflicted by administrative attacks [on the Church], by any insult to the sentiments of believers. Wrong methods of combatting religion not only fail to undermine the basis for its dissemination, but, on the contrary, they lead to the intensification of religious fanaticism, hidden forms of service and rites, cause discontent and distrust among the believers and aggravate them.[98]

Towards the end of 1972, the government allowed publication of 10,000 copies of the *New Testament*.[99] In February 1973, Justas Rugienis, a former security officer who was repeatedly criticized by dissenters for his highhandedness and ruthlessness, was recalled from the post of the Republican representative of the Council for Religious Affairs. His successor, a Party propaganda specialist, Kazimieras Tumenas, proceeded to reassure the Lithuanian hierarchy about the good will of the government and promised to allow publication of a catechism, but at the same time called for intensified action against the 'anti-Soviet' clergymen associated with the publication of the underground *Chronicle* and the organization of protest petitions.[100]

Meanwhile, the Party and Government leaders took time to carefully assess the situation in Lithuania. Along with the police and its informers among the clergy and faithful, scholars, teachers, reporters, and local *activists* were put to work to collect information about the actual strength and composition of the Catholic dissent movement, its base of support, the extent of its influence, its methods, communication network, and facilities for producing *samizdat*. In particular, the authorities attempted to discover the movement's links with other dissidents and with foreign organizations and communication media which have been publicizing the dissident protests abroad and – through broadcasts beamed to the U.S.S.R. – among the Soviet population as well. A special conference on 'Catholicism in the U.S.S.R.' was organized in Siauliai by the Lithuanian Academy of Sciences in December, 1969.[101] 'Concrete sociological investigations' of religion in Lithuania were supplemented with crudely administered interviews and surveys of religiosity among school children and parents.[102] Local authorities were requested by a classified government instruction to gather precise information 'for scientific purposes' on various aspects of the Church's activities:

Preaching activities and other forms of pastoral work, the role of the active church elements in the community of believers, and in the activities of ministers of cult; the material base of religious propaganda (churches, articles of worship, choirs, etc.) and modernization of cult should be watched.[103]

Early in 1973, the government authorities ordered all institutions, including parishes, to send in samples of typing from all typewriters in their possession, as well as samples of their typing paper.[104]

At the same time, the regime escalated its propaganda attacks against the Lithuanian dissidents. To counter unfavourable publicity abroad, declarations from "loyal" bishops and prelates about "freedom of religion in Lithuania" were publicized by the Soviet news media, and at least one Lithuanian cleric was sent abroad with a group of "representatives of Soviet nationalities" to help repudiate foreign criticism of the regime's nationality policies. For the domestic public, the official spokesmen presented the Catholic dissidents as a numerically insignificant band of reactionary and subversive "extremists", agents of "international clericalism", including some churchmen of the older generation who had close links with the exploiting classes of bourgeois Lithuania; individuals who collaborated with the bourgeois-nationalist underground during the period of the post-war class struggle; as well as part of the fanatically-disposed former members of monastic orders. Linking up sometimes with this very small group are some representatives of the younger Catholic clergy.... Religious propaganda of the extremist churchmen ... is pervaded by a masked hostility to all things Soviet. Playing upon the national sentiments of believers, they attempt to present [their] cause in such terms as if Catholicism were the most important attribute of the "Lithuanian national spirit", as if the Catholic Church were the "centre of national culture".[105]

By the winter of 1973–74, Soviet propaganda media admitted that "there are still not a few clerics who actively fight for the preservation of the Church's influence upon people".[106] They singled out for special attack those "servants of cult" who "interfere with public life, inculcate people with bourgeois nationalist ideas... evoke distrust of the Soviet system, spread all possible fabrications".

The disloyal priests have intensified their activities here and there. They exert negative influence on loyal clergy, activate clerical elements, illegal monasteries, instigate people to write complaints and declarations, demand change in the laws on religious cults, struggle for so-called "complete freedom". Reactionary priests attempt to raise a ballyhoo about the allegedly disastrous situation of the Church, undermine normal relations of the Church with the Government.[107]

The police intensified, during 1973, their anti-dissident drive, detaining and interrogating collectors of signatures under protest petitions, searching their homes, confiscating petitions with lists of signatures, harassing and threatening those who signed the complaints in an attempt to 'prove' 'fraud' on the part of protest organizers.[108] According to the dissident sources, on November 14, 1973, the KGB reached a decision to launch mass searches of churches, offices, and private homes in order to suppress the Lithuanian *Chronicle*, liquidate underground printing facilities, and destroy the religious literature they had produced.[109]

Since that time a massive KGB dragnet has uncovered a home-made printing press and printing matrices in Vilnius and Kaunas, together with large numbers of clandestine religious publications. Several laymen were arrested in this connection, including Parturbavicius, who was charged with the "multiplication" of the *Chronicle*. Nearly 30 laymen were searched and "crudely interrogated" by the KGB. One of the investigating officers was quoted by the *Chronicle* as rationalizing the repressions in the following terms:

If we were to grant the freedom of the press, you would demand that priests [be allowed to] teach religion in schools, and then to establish a Christian party...[110]

A wave of searches and interrogations descended on the priests suspected of playing a leading role in the dissent movement, including Fr. Zdebskis. Large quantities of religious literature, manuscripts, documents, and other materials, as well as typewriters and typing supplies were confiscated from the clergy, with several of them reportedly detained on charges of "anti-Soviet activity".[111]

So far, however, these measures have failed to stop the appearance of the *Chronicle*, whose tenth issue reached the West in the summer of 1974.[112] While it is quite possible that the police may succeed in silencing this mouthpiece of the Lithuanian Catholic dissent through further arrests and confiscations, by no means will this campaign help to remove the causes which have generated and continue to inspire the movement of religious and national protest in Lithuania.

VI. SOME GENERALIZATIONS

Our examination of the developments in Lithuania may help us to identify the several roles which religious dissent has performed within the Soviet system of church-state relations and society in general. In particular, it has functioned as an autonomous vehicle for the articulation of the Church's real interests, compensating for the failure of the established channels of communication between the official church leaders and the government to impress the latter with the legitimacy, importance, and urgency of believers' demands and to change its religious policy accordingly. To press their demands on the system more effectively, religious dissenters had to develop, at least in an embryonic form, some kind of organization, free from government controls, especially for the purpose of collecting, verifying, and documenting facts supporting demands of the dissenters, as well as for communicating these facts to those making and executing official church policy. Short of political resources, dissenters sought to mobilize support for their demands from several sources: from other members of the Church, from vocal and influential individuals and groups in society at large, and from abroad – foreign churches, opinion-makers, governments, and public opinion at large. Foreign radio stations – especially those broadcasting to the U.S.S.R. in the languages of its

peoples – have performed an invaluable service for the dissenters in helping them to overcome the physical, technological, and political communication barriers in reaching their target audiences.

Inevitably, too, in claiming to speak for the Church and the faith, the
dissidents have, as a rule, challenged the legitimacy and credibility of the
official, 'recognized' Church leaders or at least their capacity to perform
this role. Whether or not they intended it, the dissidents' function has been
that of a 'revivalist' or 'purifying' counter-elite seeking to displace the
ecclesiastical 'establishment' – which has turned passive, intimidated,
opportunistic, or corrupt.[113] The repudiation by dissenters of the governmental and self-imposed restrictions on religious thought, on polemics
with official atheism and the ruling ideology, on philosophical confrontation with urgent social and political questions – could not but make
religion intellectually more 'respectable' as an alternative to the ossified
dogmas and canons of the established political faith. In this sense – by
helping to extend the Church's spiritual and intellectual horizon beyond
narrow ritualistic concerns, by reasserting within the Church, through
their personal example, the values of intellectual and moral integrity – the
dissenters have been instrumental in bridging the gap between religion
and intellectuals, and have contributed to the revival of the intelligentsia's
interest in religion.[114] This process has in turn strengthened the dissidents'
constitutency within the Church, supplying them with new cadres,
refining their own philosophical and political frame of reference and, in
particular, solidifying their links with other currents of dissent – the civil
rights and nationality rights movements. Just as religious dissenters soon
realized that real freedom of conscience could not be secured in the
U.S.S.R. without the realization of the rule of law and of other democratic
freedoms, the democratic movement discovered the importance of religious (as well as national) dissent as a potential bridge from the intellectuals to the masses.[115]

In Lithuania, as in the Western Ukraine and some other borderlands
where religion and nationality have historically been intertwined, local
dissent currents have from the very beginning combined religious and
national aspirations and enjoyed a significant measure of popular support.
Though representatives of the national intelligentsia have been involved
in these movements from their inception, their relative weight and influence have progressively increased within the dissident leadership.[116] This

relative "laicization" of religious protest movements was also reflective of a process that is particularly disturbing to the Soviet leaders who must be well aware of the role which religious dissent has played in history as a vehicle of social, national, and political unrest. In a way, in Soviet conditions, where religion has remained the only, however combatted, legally existing alternative to the official *Weltanschauung*, and the church the only, however restricted and watched, relatively autonomous institution outside the Party's regular ideological, institutional, and personnel controls – in these conditions religious dissent may provide an ideological and organizational framework for the articulation and mobilization of those non-religious interests and social forces that, lacking channels and means in the existing system for their expression and self-realization, have accumulated a massive revolutionary potential.

REFERENCES

[1] On the genesis of the movement, see M. Bourdeaux, *Religious Ferment in Russia: Protestant Opposition to Soviet Religious Policy* (London, 1968).

[2] See M. Bourdeaux, *Patriarch and Prophets: Persecution of the Russian Orthodox Church Today* (New York, 1970); and D. Konstantinov, *Zarnicy duxovnogo vozroždenija* (London, Ontario, 1973).

[3] For an analysis of the origins, evolution, and patterns of religious dissent in the U.S.S.R., see this writer's 'Religious Dissent and the Soviet State' in B. R. Bociurkiw and J. W. Strong (eds.), *Religion and Atheism in the Soviet Union and Eastern Europe* (London & Toronto, 1975), pp. 58–90.

[4] Cf. Gerhard Simon, 'Die Unruhe in der katholischen Kirche Litauens', *Berichte des Bundesinstituts für ostwissenchaftliche und internationale Studien* (Cologne), No. 19/1972, p. 5; and 'Recent Events among Lithuanian Catholics', *Radio Liberty Research* (Feb. 15, 1973), no. 46/73, p. 2.

[5] Bishop V. Borisevicius of Telsiai was arrested in 1946, condemned to death, and executed in January, 1947. His auxiliary bishop P. Ramanauskas and bishop T. Matulionis of Kaisiadorys were imprisoned in 1946 and released only in 1956; the former died in 1959, Matulionis in 1962. The Apostolic Administrator of Vilnius, Archbishop M. Reinys, was arrested in 1947 and died in the Vladimir prison in 1953. After 1947 only Bishop Kazimieras Paltarokas of Panevezys (†1958), was allowed to remain in his see. He alone of the bishops submitted to the government pressure in calling upon nationalist guerillas to lay down their arms. See V. Stanley Vardys, 'Catholicism in Lithuania', in Richard H. Marshall, Jr. (ed.), *Aspects of Religion in the Soviet Union, 1917–1967* (Chicago, 1971), p. 384; V. Brizgys, *Religious Conditions in Lithuania under Soviet Russian Occupation* (Chicago, 1968), pp. 12–14; V. Vignieri, 'Soviet Policy Toward Religion in Lithuania: The Case of Roman Catholicism', in V. Stanley Vardys (ed.), *Lithuania under the Soviets: Portrait of a Nation, 1940–65* (New York, 1965), p. 221; and J. Savasis [pseud.], *The War against God in Lithuania* (New York, 1966), pp. 26–27.

⁶ R. Krasauskas and K. Gulbinas, 'Die Lage der Katholischen Kirche in Litauen', in Institutum Balticum, *Acta Baltica*, vol. 12 (1972), (Koenigstein i. T., 1973), p. 33. Of some 1450 diocesan and regular clergy in Lithuania in 1940, 257 emigrated to the West during the war and 176 left for Poland. Another writer speaks of 100 imprisoned and 180 deported priests – V. Maculis, 'Das religiöse und kirchliche Leben in Litauen', *ibid.*, vol. 8 (1968) (publ. in 1969), p. 27. Vardys (*loc. cit.*, p. 385) lists only 180 priests banished from Lithuania after the war. According to the Lithuanian Chronicle (*CCCL* (Feb., 1974), no. 9, pp. 7–8), during 1944–62, 44 priests of the Kaisiadorys diocese, the smallest in Lithuania, were sentenced to prison, most of them to 10 years (including the present bishop Matulaitis-Labukas, in 1945), and some even to 25 years.
⁷ On the liquidation of the Ukrainian Catholic Church, see this writer's 'The Uniate Church in the Soviet Ukraine: A Case Study in Soviet Church Policy', *Canadian Slavonic Papers*, vol. 7 (1965), pp. 89–113. There were many analogies between the campaigns in the Western Ukraine and Lithuania: in both cases, bishops were requested to assist the authorities in overcoming the nationalist resistance to Soviet occupation; virtually all priests in both areas were summoned for police interrogation sessions, compelled to sign loyalty declarations, pressured to become police informers, urged to break away from Rome; however, in Lithuania, the plan for a 'national' Catholic Church was soon dropped, whereas in the Western Ukraine, the refusal to leave the Uniate Church and join the Russian Orthodox Church was punished with lengthy imprisonment or deportation sentences. Cf. Vardys, *loc. cit.*, p. 385; and Maculis, *loc. cit.*, p. 27.
⁸ Bishops Ramanauskas and Matulionis were released in 1956. Ramanauskas, who returned to Lithuania as an invalid, was not allowed to resume his archpastoral duties and died in 1959 in a village to which he was confined by the authorities. Matulionis apparently was able to perform at least some episcopal functions and in December, 1957 he consecrated, with papal approval, Vincentas Sladkevicius (*1920) as auxiliary bishop for Kaisiadorys diocese. But in 1958, both Sladkevicius and Matulionis were banished to remote villages. Matulionis (made Archbishop by the Pope) died in 1963. Vardys, *loc. cit.*, p. 387; Brizgys, *op. cit.*, p. 14; *Annuario Pontificio 1968* (Rome, 1968).
⁹ They were consecrated by Bishop Paltarokas in September, 1955, Mazelis (†1966) as bishop of Telsiai, and Steponavicius (*1911) as Apostolic Administrator for Vilnius and Panevezys.
¹⁰ Bishop Steponavicius was banished from Vilnius to the remote town of Zagare, in January, 1961, reportedly for assuming without the government's permission K. Paltarokas' see after his death in January, 1958. *ACEN News* (Nov.–Dec., 1970), no. 148, p. 25.
¹¹ Rev. J. Stankevicius, Administrator of the dioceses of Kaunas and Vilkaviskis, instructed the clergy on May 31, 1961: "According to the directive of the Deputy for Religious Cults, Rugienis, [only those] young men and women may participate publicly in liturgical services, who have attained eighteen years of age. Younger children may not serve [at the] Mass, may not sing in the choir, may not carry banners, or scatter flowers in procession. Children are to take part in liturgical-religious events only in the company of their parents"; cited in *Chronicle of the Catholic Church in Lithuania* [hereafter *CCCL*]. no. 4 (1972) (publ. by the Lithuanian Roman Catholic Priests' League of America, Maspeth, N.Y. [1973?]), p. 8. On other restrictions, see Vardys, *loc. cit.*, pp. 390–93; Krasauskas & Gulbinas, *loc. cit.*, pp. 35–41; and Savasis, *op. cit.*
¹² Matulaitis-Labukas (*1894) was consecrated in December, 1965, as Apostolic Administrator for Kaunas and Vilkaviskis, and Pletkus (*1895) was consecrated in

February, 1968 as Apostolic Administrator for Telsiai diocese and the Prelatura of Klaipeda.

[13] See a survey of anti-religious activities in Lithuania by the head of the CPL Central Committee Department of Propaganda and Agitation, P. Misutis, 'Na naučnoj osnove', *Nauka i religija* (March 1972), no. 3, pp. 27–34, as well as other reports from Lithuania in that issue of the principal Soviet atheist periodical.

[14] Including Archdioceses of Kaunas and Vilnius; Dioceses of Kaisiadorys, Panevezys, Telsiai and Vilkaviskis; and Prelatura of Klaipeda. In 1972 they contained 622 operating Catholic churches in Lithuania (a loss of 95 since 1940), 61 of them without a priest (Krasauskas & Gulbinas, *loc. cit.*, pp. 32–33).

[15] Bishops Matulaitis-Labukas (Kaunas and Vilkaviskis) and Pletkus (Telsiai and Klaipeda).

[16] From 1940 to 1971, 658 priests died in Lithuania (592 by 1967); of the 440 new priests ordained from 1940 to 1968, only 17 have left the priesthood (13 from 1945 to 1967). There were reportedly 834 priests in Lithuania in 1968. In 1972, the total was said to be 804, including 62 completely disabled, 105 pensioned and only partly capable of performing pastoral duties. Of the remaining 649 priests, 566 serve as parish priests and 83 as their vicars. Ten Lithuanian priests work outside the Republic, two in Latvia, one each in Moscow, the Ukraine, and Poland, three in Siberia. Some are imprisoned. Krasauskas & Gulbinas, *loc. cit.*, pp. 33–34; Maculis, *loc. cit.*, p. 24. *Annuario Pontificio* 1972 lists a total of 884 clergymen in Lithuania. According to Rev. A. J. Contons ('Religious Persecution in Lithuania – Soviet Style', *Litaunus* (1972), p. 56), 97 priests are forbidden to perform pastoral duties. It was calculated that, in 1971, the median age of Lithuanian priests was 55 (Lithuanian American Community, *The Violations of Human Rights in Soviet Occupied Lithuania. A Report for 1971*, Delran, N. J., 1972, p. 36).

[17] Cf. *CCL* (1972), no. 4, pp. 7–10.

[18] See Pavel Litvinov, comp., *The Trial of the Four: The Case of Galanskov, Ginsburg, Dobrovolsky, and Lashkova*, ed. by P. Reddaway (New York, 1972).

[19] The January 1968 petition is listed under AS1247 in Radio Liberty, *Arkhiv Samizdata*; cf. reference to the Telsiai clergy protest in the Jan. 1, 1969 petition signed by over 30 priests of the Vilkaviskis diocese (Krasauskas & Gulbinas, *loc. cit.*, p. 47). Rev. Sliavas' petition is reproduced in full in *CCCL*, No. 9, 1974, pp. 47–48. The *Chronicle* almost certainly refers to the latter petition in dating the beginning of the Catholic dissent movements from 'Summer 1968' (*CCCL*, no. 4, p. 1).

[20] This tactic may have even been encouraged by the publication, in April, 1968, of a Supreme Soviet Presidium decree which set down what appeared then to be a firm procedure for the prompt consideration of citizens' petitions by the government authorities. See also below, fn. 42.

[21] For an incomplete list, see 'A Bibliography of Lithuanian Samizdat Documents', *Radio Liberty Research Bulletin*, no. 8 (2691), Feb. 21, 1973, no. 47/73, pp. 8–12.

[22] Calculations for individual dioceses (except for Kaunas and Prelatura of Klaipeda) were made on the basis of diocesan statistics supplied in the Vatican yearbooks, *Annuario Pontificio*, 1968–72, and the maximum number of signatories under any single clergy petition from each of the five dioceses.

[23] An incomplete list appears in 'A Bibliography of Lithuanian Samizdat Documents', *loc. cit.* It has been supplemented with data from the ten issues of *CCCL*.

[24] Reproduced in full with appendices in *CCCL* (1972), no. 2, pp. 2–7. It is rumoured that the speed with which it reached the West was due to the services provided by Lithuanian Jews emigrating from the Soviet Union.

[25] Of all the clergy petitions, the most complete catalogue of grievances appears in the August 1969 'Declaration by the Priests of the Catholic Church in Lithuania' addressed to the Chairman of the Lithuanian Council of Ministers and the Catholic Church leaders in Lithuania by 40 priests of the Vilnius Archdiocese (reproduced in *Litaunus*, vol. 19, (1973), no. 3, pp. 46–53 (*AS* 766). More extensive examination of the plight of the Lithuanian Church appears in the *CCCL* editorial articles: 'The True State of the Catholic Church in Lithuania' (no. 4 (1972), pp. 1–12); and 'Freedom to Die' (no. 9, (1974), pp. 1–13).

[26] Thus, e.g., between 1961 and 1969, the sacrament of Confirmation was conferred only once in the Panevezys diocese, according to the 'Declaration by the Priests...', *loc. cit.*, p. 49.

[27] Bishop Labukas secured permission in 1966 to raise the enrollment in the Kaunas Seminary from 25 to 30. Since 1968, admissions have been restricted to 6 per year (one for each diocese, apparently). Thus during 1968–72, only 30 seminarians were admitted while a total of 83 priests died during these years (*CCCL* (1973), no. 6, pp. 34–35). In 1973, the Seminary was allowed to admit 10 new students, with its total enrollment increasing to 48 (*CCCL* (1973), No. 8, p. 26).

[28] See the Jan. 8, 1969 petition to Kosygin, Kuroedov (Chairman of the governmental Council for Religious Affairs [hereafter CRA]), and the Lithuanian Church leaders, signed by Priests Petras Dumbliauskas and Juozas Zdebskis (cited in 'The Voice of Lithuanian Catholics', *Religion in Communist Lands*, vol. 1 (July–Oct. 1973), nos. 4–5, pp. 50–51).

[29] See *CCCL* editorials: 'The True State...', *loc. cit.*, and 'Freedom to Die', *loc. cit.*

[30] For local examples, see 'Events in Klaipeda', *CCCL*, No. 2, 1972, pp. 10–15; 'Statement of the Catholics of Ceikiniai Parish' of Sept. 5, 1972, addressed to the Soviet and Church authorities by 1709 parishioners of Ceikiniai (*CCCL* (1973), no. 5, pp. 29–41); and the Aug. 7, 1968 petition from Rev. Sliavas (*CCCL* (1974), no. 9, pp. 47–48) which pointed out that while collective farms pay only 1 kopeck per KW electricity, the churches are charged 25 kopecks.

[31] See 'Appeal' to Brezhnev from 3,023 believers of Klaipeda of March 19, 1972 (*CCCL* (1972), no. 2, pp. 14–15).

[32] Note in particular 'A Statement of the Believers of Lithuania' addressed in March, 1973 to the Lithuanian CRA Representative, K. Tumenas, by 16,498 believers (*CCCL* (1973), no. 6, pp. 10–11); and 'A Statement of a Group of Believers' sent in August, 1973 by 540 laymen to the Presidium of the Lithuanian Supreme Soviet (*CCCL* (1973), no. 7, pp. 11–14).

[33] See note 11, above.

[34] Cf. a statement submitted to the CRA representative Rugienis in July, 1972 by Rev. B. Laurinavicius of Adutiskis, elaborating on the Dec. 24, 1971 Memorandum of the Vilnius diocese clergy (*CCCL*, No. 4, 1972, pp. 13–25).

[35] This has been the prime complaint of the massive laymen's petitions – 'Memorandum' to Brezhnev of Dec. 1971–Jan. 1972 (signed by 17,054) (*CCCL*, no. 2, 1972, pp. 1–7); and a 'Declaration' of 14,284 parents and school children addressed to the Lithuanian Ministry of Education in March, 1973 (*CCCL* (1973), no. 6, pp. 7–9). See also 'Letter to the Teacher' in *CCCL* (1973), no. 7, pp. 1–5.

[36] See, e.g., the defense speech of Rev. A. Seskevicius at his trial in September, 1970; and the August, 1973 'Statement of a Group of Believers' (*loc. cit.*).

[37] Thus the *Chronicle* reported on the KGB interrogations in Vilnius of 23 Lithuanian ethnologists and the arrest, in Kaunas, of five suspected members of an 'anti-Soviet

group' (no. 6 (1973), pp. 23–28, 35); repressions against 'nationalistic' Vilnius students (no. 7 (1973), pp. 18–19); and interrogations and arrests of alleged Lithuanian 'nationists' (nos. 9 and 10, 1974).

[38] Especially the Lithuanian minority in Belorussia, as well as Lithuanians who were banished to the Urals and Siberia.

[39] *CCCL* (1972), no. 1, p. 53; (1972), no. 4, p. 16; and (1974), no. 9, pp. 34–35.

[40] See, in particular, 'The True State of the Catholic Church in Lithuania', *loc. cit.*, pp. 3–4, 10; and 'Gromyko Received by the Roman Pope', *CCCL* (1974), no. 9, pp. 16–17.

[41] *CCCL* (1974), no. 9, p. 49.

[42] Art. 9 of the Decree of the Presidium of the Supreme Soviet of the U.S.S.R. of Apr. 12, 1968 'On the Procedure for Consideration of Citizens' Proposals, Declarations and Complaints', reproduced in *Vidomosti Verxovnoi Rady SRSR* (1968), no. 17, p. 144ff.

[43] Art. 5 of the 1968 Decree states: "It is prohibited to send citizens' complaints for decision to those officials whose actions are being compained about."

[44] *CCCL* offers a number of specific examples of such response both from Rugienis and from Tumenas who replaced the former as the republican CRA representative in Feb. 1973.

[45] Most sentences of the Lithuanian clergy since 1955 have been for teaching religion to children.

[46] See Rev. Zdebskis' final statement at his trial in November, 1971, *CCCL* (1972), no. 1, pp. 18–31.

[47] 'The Case of the Rev. Antanas Seskevicius, S.J.', *loc. cit.*, p. 41; Simon, *loc. cit.*, p. 13: *Chronicle of Current Events* [hereafter *CCE*], no. 17, p. 39.

[48] See 'The Case of the Rev. Antanas Seskevicius, S. J.', in American Lithuanian Community, *op. cit.*, pp. 36–44; *AS*882, *AS*653, *AS*654, *AS*655, *AS*656; and the Dec. 1971–Jan. 1972 'Memorandum' of 17,059 to Brezhnev.

[49] *CCCL* (1972), no. 1, pp. 1–40; *CCE*, no. 21, p. 17.

[50] *CCCL* (1974), no. 9, p. 24.

[51] *CCCL* (1972), no. 1, pp. 8–10; Dean Mills in *Baltimore Sun*, Nov. 27, 1971.

[52] *CCCL* (1972), no. 1, pp. 18–31.

[53] *Ibid.*, pp. 8–10.

[54] *Ibid.*, pp. 3–8; cf. *The New York Times*, Nov. 27, 1971.

[55] *CCCL* (1972), no. 2, p. 4.

[56] *Ibid.*, pp. 4–5.

[57] *Ibid.*, p. 6. The appeal to Waldheim also pointedly noted that "Lithuania does not have its own representative at the United Nations."

[58] *Ibid.*

[59] See *CCE* (1972), nos. 24–27.

[60] *CCCL* (1972), no. 4, pp. 3–4.

[61] *CCCL* (1972), no. 2, p. 7.

[62] *Ibid.*, pp. 8–9, cf. *CCE* (1972), no. 25, pp. 27–28.

[63] See 'Self-Immolation as National Protest', in Lithuanian American Community, Inc., *The Violations of Human Rights in Soviet Occupied Lithuania. A Report for 1972* (Delran, N. J., 1973), pp. 17–24; *CCE* (1972), no. 26, pp. 22–25, and (1972), no. 27, pp. 17–20.

[64] *CCCL* (1973), no. 7, p. 56; (1974), no. 9, p. 53.

[65] *CCCL* (1972), no. 4, p. 10.

[66] *Ibid.*, p. 4.

[67] *Ibid.*, p. 4.
[68] *Ibid.*
[69] *Ibid.*, p. 10.
[70] *CCCL* (1974), no. 9, p. 53.
[71] *CCCL* (1973), no. 6, p. 51.
[72] *CCCL* (1972), no. 2, p. 47.
[73] So far, the *CCCL* has appeared in Feb.–March, May–July, Sept. and Dec.
[74] Especially those violating the prohibition of religious instruction to minors under Art. 143 of the Lithuanian Criminal Code.
[75] These include: 'The True State of the Lithuanian Church' (no. 4, Dec. 1972, pp. 1–12); 'The General Situation' (no. 5, Feb. or March, 1973, pp. 1–29); 'The Freedom to Die' (no. 9, March 1974, pp. 1–13).
[76] See note 39.
[77] There were reportedly 97 priests in this category in 1971 (Contons, *loc. cit.*, p. 56).
[78] The only acting hierarch who has not been criticized in the *CCCL* appears to be Bishop Povilonis, present Coadjutor of Kaunas; he was sentenced to eight years in 1961 for the allegedly 'illegal construction' of the church in Klaipeda, but was released before the completion of his sentence. See *CCCL* (1972), no. 2, pp. 12–13; and Simon, *loc. cit.* p. 11.
[79] *CCCL* (1974), no. 9, p. 4.
[80] *Ibid.*
[81] *CCCL* (1972), no. 4, p. 10; (1974), no. 9, pp. 16–17.
[82] Cf. defense speeches of Seskevicius and Zdebskis and their trials in 1970 and 1971, respectively.
[83] See July, 1973 appeal of 540 believers to the Presidium of the Lithuanian Supreme Soviet, *CCCL* (1973), no. 7, pp. 11–14.
[84] *Ibid.*, p. 11.
[85] Cf. this writer's 'Religious Dissent and the Soviet State,' *loc. cit.*
[86] *CCCL* (1972), no. 1, pp. 44–45.
[87] *CCE* (1971), no. 22, pp. 15–16.
[88] *CCCL* (1974), no. 9, p. 15.
[89] *Ibid.*, pp. 34–35. Cf. *CCE* (June 17, 1974), no. 32, p. 37.
[90] Several Ukrainian-sounding names appear among the signatories of this petition.
[91] *CCCL* (1972), no. 1, p. 53.
[92] *CCCL* (1972), no. 4, p. 16.
[93] *CCCL* (1974), no. 9, p. 17.
[94] *CCCL*, no. 4, pp. 3–7. "Under direct or indirect pressure, Bishop Labukas on November 19, 1970, obtained from the Holy See a dispensation from canons regulating the assignment of priests... [which] in the opinion of the priests, subjected the bishop still more to Rugienis' manipulations" (*ibid.*, pp. 5–6).
[95] See, e.g., the cases of priests V. Pesliakas (*CCCL* (1973), no. 5, pp. 44–46) and J. Zdebskis (*CCCL* (1973), no. 6, p. 47).
[96] See fn. 78, above. Born in 1910 and ordained in 1934, Povilonis was consecrated in December, 1969 as Apostolic Administrator of Telsiai diocese; in July, 1973, he was transferred to the Kaunas see as Coadjutor with the right of succession.
[97] Kriksciunas, born in Kaunas in 1930, was ordained in 1954. Reportedly he spent four years in Rome studying canon law. Having served as Chancellor of the Kaunas Archdiocese, he was consecrated in December 1969, as Auxiliary Bishop for Kaunas and Vilkaviskis dioceses. In July, 1973, he was appointed Apostolic Administrator of

the Panevezys diocese. He has been occasionally criticized in the Lithuanian Catholic *samizdat* for making propaganda statements on behalf of the regime concerning 'freedom of religion' in Lithuania.

[98] K. Rimaitis, 'Cerkovniki prisposablivajutsia', *Sovetskaja Litva*, Aug. 12, 1972.

[99] *CCCL* (1973), no. 6, p. 10.

[100] *Ibid.*, p. 24; (1973), no. 7, p. 17.

[101] See Akademija nauk Litovskoj SSR. Otdel filosofii, prava i sociologii pri Institute istorii. *Katolicizm v SSSR i sovremennost'* (*Materialy naučnoj konferencii, sostojavšejsja v g. Siauliai, 17–18 dekabrja 1969 g.*), Vilnius, 1971, 245 p.

[102] *CCCL* (1973), no. 6, pp. 43–45.

[103] *Ibid.*, pp. 17–20.

[104] *Ibid.*, pp. 21–22.

[105] I. Anichas, 'Evoljutsija social'no-političeskoj orientacii katoličeskoj cerkvi v Litve v uslovijax socialističeskogo stroja', in *Katolicizm v SSSR i sovremennost'*, pp. 81–82.

[106] Articles of P. Misutis, 'Sovetskij zakon i religija ' and 'Cerkov i religioznost' v naši dni', which were published in the Soviet Lithuanian press in December, 1973 and January, 1974, cited in *CCCL* (1974), no. 9, p. 3.

[107] *Ibid.*

[108] *CCCL* (1973), no. 7, pp. 5–8.

[109] *CCCL*, no. 8, 1973, cited in *ELTA* Information Service bulletin, no. 3 (182), May–June 1974, p. 1.

[110] *Ibid.*

[111] *Ibid.*, pp. 1–2; *CCCL* (1974), no. 9, pp. 18–24.

[112] For description of contents of *CCCL*, no. 10, see *ELTA*, no. 4 (183), July–Aug. 1974.

[113] Cf. *CCCL* (1972), no. 4, pp. 1–12.

[114] In religious doctrine, ethics, philosophy, history, and art, rather than in the institutional Church and its ritual. This 'religious revival' has even brought into the Orthodox and Catholic churches some Jewish intellectuals and students.

[115] Compare this process with the Populist and even Bolshevik treatment of religious sectarianism in Russia prior to 1905, as a 'bridge' to the peasantry.

[116] Michael Parks reported recently from Moscow to the *Baltimore Sun* (Feb. 2, 1974) that "during the period of confrontation... laymen increasingly took over the Catholic leadership. They circulated the petitions, organized demonstrations and met with Soviet officials to work out compromises. Priests, according to accounts here [in Moscow], played a relatively smaller role than before..."

INDEX

180 INDEX

SOVIETICA

Publications and Monographs of the Institute of East-European Studies
at the University of Fribourg/Switzerland
and the Center for East Europe, Russia and Asia
at Boston College and the Seminar for Political Theory and Philosophy
at the University of Munich

1. BOCHEŃSKI, J. M. and BLAKELEY, TH. J. (eds.): *Bibliographie der sowjetischen Philosophie*. I: *Die 'Voprosy filosofii' 1947–1956*. 1959, VIII+75 pp.
2. BOCHEŃSKI, J. M. and BLAKELEY, TH. J. (eds.): *Bibliographie der sowjetischen Philosophie*. II: *Bücher 1947–1956; Bücher und Aufsätze 1957–1958; Namenverzeichnis 1947–1958*. 1959, VIII+109 pp.
3. BOCHEŃSKI, J. M.: *Die dogmatischen Grundlagen der sowjetischen Philosophie (Stand 1958)*. *Zusammenfassung der 'Osnovy Marksistskoj Filosofii' mit Register*. 1959, XII+84 pp.
4. LOBKOWICZ, NICOLAS (ed,): *Das Widerspruchsprinzip in der neueren sowjetischen Philosophie*. 1960, VI+89 pp.
5. MÜLLER-MARKUS, SIEGFRIED: *Einstein und die Sowjetphilosophie. Krisis einer Lehre*. I: *Die Grundlagen. Die spezielle Relativitätstheorie*. 1960. (Out of print.)
6. BLAKELEY, TH. J.: *Soviet Scholasticism*. 1961, XIII+176 pp.
7. BOCHEŃSKI, J. M. and BLAKELEY, TH. J. (eds.): *Studies in Soviet Thought*, I. 1961, IX+141 pp.
8. LOBKOWICZ, NICOLAS: *Marxismus-Leninismus in der ČSR. Die tschechoslowakische Philosophie seit 1945*. 1962, XVI+268 pp.
9. BOCHEŃSKI, J. M. and BLAKELEY, TH. J. (eds.): *Bibliographie der sowjetischen Philosophie*. III: *Bücher und Aufsätze 1959–1960*. 1962, X+73 pp.
10. BOCHEŃSKI, J. M. and BLAKELEY, TH. J. (eds.): *Bibliographie der sowjetischen Philosophie*. IV: *Ergänzungen 1947–1960*. 1963, XII+158 pp.
11. FLEISCHER, HELMUT: *Kleines Textbuch der kommunistischen Ideologie. Auszüge aus dem Lehrbuch 'Osnovy marksizma-leninizma', mit Register*. 1963, XIII+116 pp.
12. JORDAN, ZBIGNIEW A.: *Philosophy and Ideology. The Development of Philosophy and Marxism-Leninism in Poland since the Second World War*. 1963, XII+600 pp.
13. VRTAČIČ, LUDVIK: *Einführung in den jugoslawischen Marxismus-Leninismus. Organisation. Bibliographie*. 1963, X+208 pp.
14. BOCHEŃSKI, J. M.: *The Dogmatic Principles of Soviet Philosophy (as of 1958). Synopsis of the 'Osnovy Marksistskoj Filosofii' with complete index*. 1963, XII+78 pp.
15. BIRKUJOV, B. V.: *Two Soviet Studies on Frege*. Translated from the Russian and edited by Ignacio Angelelli. 1964, XXII+101 pp.
16. BLAKELEY, TH. J.: *Soviet Theory of Knowledge*. 1964, VII+203 pp.
17. BOCHEŃSKI, J. M. and BLAKELEY, TH. J. (eds.): *Bibliographie der sowjetischen Philosophie*. V: *Register 1947–1960*. 1964, VI+143 pp.
18. BLAKELEY, THOMAS J.: *Soviet Philosophy. A General Introduction to Contemporary Soviet Thought*. 1964, VI+81 pp.

19. BALLESTREM, KARL G.: *Russian Philosophical Terminology* (in Russian, English, German, and French). 1964, VIII+116 pp.
20. FLEISCHER, HELMUT: *Short Handbook of Communist Ideology. Synopsis of the 'Osnovy marksizma-leninizma' with complete index.* 1965, XIII+97 pp.
21. PLANTY-BONJOUR, G.: *Les catégories du matérialisme dialectique. L'ontologie soviétique contemporaine.* 1965, VI+206 pp.
22. MÜLLER-MARKUS, SIEGFRIED: *Einstein und die Sowjetphilosophie. Krisis einer Lehre. II: Die allgemeine Relativitätstheorie.* 1966, X+509 pp.
23. LASZLO, ERVIN: *The Communist Ideology in Hungary. Handbook for Basic Research.* 1966, VIII+351 pp.
24. PLANTY-BONJOUR, G.: *The Categories of Dialectical Materialism. Contemporary Soviet Ontology.* 1967, VI+182 pp.
25. LASZLO, ERVIN: *Philosophy in the Soviet Union. A Survey of the Mid-Sixties.* 1967, VIII+208 pp.
26. RAPP, FRIEDRICH: *Gesetz und Determination in der Sowjetphilosophie. Zur Gesetzeskonzeption des dialektischen Materialismus unter besonderer Berücksichtigung der Diskussion über dynamische und statische Gesetzmässigkeit in der zeitgenössischen Sowjetphilosophie.* 1968, XI+474 pp.
27. BALLESTREM, KARL G.: *Die sowjetische Erkenntnismetaphysik und ihr Verhältnis zu Hegel.* 1968, IX+189 pp.
28. BOCHEŃSKI, J. M. and BLAKELEY, TH. J. (eds.): *Bibliographie der sowjetischen Philosophie. VI: Bücher und Aufsätze 1961–1963.* 1968, XI+195 pp.
29. BOCHEŃSKI, J. M. and BLAKELEY, TH. J. (eds.): *Bibliographie der sowjetischen Philosophie. VII: Bücher und Aufsätze 1964–1966. Register.* 1968, X+311 pp.
30. PAYNE, T. R.: *S. L. Rubinštejn and the Philosophical Foundations of Soviet Psychology.* 1968, X+184 pp.
31. KIRSCHENMANN, PETER PAUL: *Information and Reflection. On Some Problems of Cybernetics and How Contemporary Dialectical Materialism Copes with Them.* 1970, XV+225 pp.
32. O'ROURKE, JAMES J.: *The Problem of Freedom in Marxist Thought.* 1974, XII+231 pp.
33. SARLEMIJN, ANDRIES: *Hegel's Dialectic.* 1975, XIII+189 pp.
34. DAHM, HELMUT: *Vladimir Solovyev and Max Scheler: Attempt at a Comparative Interpretation. A Contribution to the History of Phenomenology.* 1975, XI+324 pp.
35. BOESELAGER, WOLFHARD F.: *The Soviet Critique of Neopositivism. The History and Structure of the Critique of Logical Positivism and Related Doctrines by Soviet Philosophers in the Years 1947–1967.* 1975, VII+157 pp.

DATE DUE